MW00592235

Virus of FEAR

by W. Horace Carter
Pulitzer Prize-winning Author

Dedication

This book is dedicated to my late wife Lucile, who suffered from fear as much or more than I did during the newspaper crusades, and to my three children: Linda, Rusty and Velda Kay. They could have been victims of the lawless Ku Klux Klan insurrection.

Copyright 1991
By W. Horace Carter

Library of Congress Card No. 91-073311

Printed in the United States of America by Atlantic Publishing
Company, Tabor City, North Carolina

Published by
W. Horace Carter
Atlantic Publishing Co.
P.O. Box 67
Tabor City, North Carolina 28463

ISBN Number 1-879034-09-3

Cover Design by Robert Walker
Cover Illustration by Rick Coleman

Introduction

Virus of Fear has been written to create an awareness and a remembrance of the visceral antagonism of the prejudiced portion of the populace symbolized by its rhetorical flag-waving that made up the Ku Klux Klan in the South in the 1950's and was an unprecedented threat to society.

Remembrances of inflammatory diatribes by Imperial Wizards, Grand Dragons, Titans, and others, who solicited followers into an organization shrouded in mystery, can be a lesson for Americans today. Impassioned words fell on receptive ears. Applications and money poured into the coffers of the Klan in the Carolinas. Normal serenity evaporated as peace disappeared, anxiety gripped the citizenry and disaster destroyed the lifestyles of many who differed with the moral standards of the KKK. Violence by the redneck vigilantes ran rampant, shattering the axiom that a man's home is his castle.

Setting the KKK up as judge, jury and executioner, the Klan's hierarchy condoned and conspired with the radical elements in its membership to harass, kidnap, whip and abuse their neighbors for a myriad of alleged moral violations contrary to the way of life that they considered godly, American and proper.

While openly critical of the Jews, Catholics and blacks (traditional groups on the KKK hit list), the unmerciful floggings that swept over the coastal Carolina counties were indiscriminately inflicted upon Protestant Anglo-Saxons with the same viciousness. Reports from a native farmer who was charged by the Klan with living with a woman out of wedlock, said, "While two hooded Klansmen bent me over the fender of a pickup truck and held me with my bare buttocks exposed, I screamed with every lash of a leather strap tacked onto a pick handle. A giant of a man whipped me so hard and so long that my bowels moved. Then the whole mob laughed, and they told me to get out of there and take care of my family or they would call on me again. I staggered home half naked."

Floggings of men and women like this and scores of others over many months in Columbus County, North Carolina, and Horry County, South Carolina, from 1949 and into 1953, prompted my decision to fight this lawless brutality with my tiny young weekly newspaper, the *Tabor City Tribune*, in Tabor City, North Carolina. I started this little newspaper in 1946 with a few dollars saved while I was in the Navy during World War II, and while I was struggling to make a living for my wife and two small children. Every advertising and subscription dollar looked as big as a wagon wheel even before the invasion of the community by the Klan.

Having graduated from the University of North Carolina School of Journalism during the era when Dr. Frank P. Graham, one of the great liberal thinkers of this century, was president, I was imbued with a strong sense of justice for minorities and all others. The repulsive rebellion against law and order by the Klan, and its infliction of pain and suffering on whomever it picked to punish was not something that my conscience would allow me to ignore. I was not sure if such an humble little newspaper had any editorial power. I questioned whether my sentiments would have any deterrent influence on this mob violence, but I had to try even when my closest friends advised against it.

Financially on the rocks, I further jeopardized my chances of economic success and ultimately my life and the lives of my wife and children by fighting the infamous KKK on the front pages of the *Tribune* from the very inception of the Carolinas Klan.

Threatened physically and economically over those troubled years, the little newspaper survived. Klan members by the dozens were arrested and convicted of assault, kidnapping and conspiracy to assault and kidnap. Many went to prison. Others paid heavy fines. The editorial campaign of the tiny weekly newspaper was the winner.

Subsequently, the *Tribune* became the first weekly newspaper ever to win the Pulitzer Prize for Meritorious Public Service. Until this day, it remains the smallest newspaper ever to win that coveted journalism award. The medallion presented to me (I was the news, editorial and advertising staff) and the *Tribune*, symbolic of the award, is now displayed in the North Carolina Journalism Hall of Fame in Chapel Hill.

These pages tell of the near-weekly violence of the KKK, and our blow-by-blow crusade against them. I chose to call this book *Virus of Fear* because fear was the emotion that dominated the thinking and the conversation of coastal Carolinians month after fearful month. The viperous night-riders spread fear as devastating as the black plague, and for years it seemed they would escape punishment. It was evident that their claim of Klan membership by some local law enforcement officers was not idle chatter. Except for the professional sleuthing of the FBI, the Klan might have escaped arrests and convictions forever.

While fighting the Klan during those frightening years and now with the publication of *Virus of Fear*, it is not my wish to depict that effort as heroic. The purpose is to testify to the power of even the smallest of the press when sincere words, written at great risk, are designed to expose clandestine evil on its very doorstep.

There is no media so insignificant that it cannot cast a big shadow when it is right. And we were right.

Acknowledgements

The enthusiastic encouragement of my children, wife, friends Tim and Darlene Tucker and fellow outdoor writing buddy, Don Ecker of New York, prompted me to write this autobiographical account of my clash with the Ku Klux Klan forty years after winning the Pulitzer Prize. I long refused to write this story of the Klan and my crusade against the uprising because it was so personal—relating the events of the time seemed like I was grasping a chance to pin bouquets on my shoulder. I was finally convinced to tell the story and preserve the events of that era for my grandchildren if for no other reason.

And I would be remiss if I did not recognize the assistance of Jonathan Daniels, *Raleigh News & Observer* editor during the Klan crusade, for nominating the *Tribune* for the Pulitzer Prize and me for the Sidney Hillman Foundation Award.

I also acknowledge the time and effort of Roland Guidez of Chapel Hill, North Carolina, who nominated me for the U.S. Junior Chamber of Commerce award, "One of the Ten Most Outstanding Young Men in America for 1953" that I appreciated so much.

Also, my heartfelt gratitude to J. A. and Betty Herlocker, who constantly supported the crusade, while working as type compositor and bookkeeper, respectively, with our struggling newspaper.

Foreword

Looking down at his shabby prison garb brought a surge of resentment to Prisoner No. 1064 at the North Carolina Camp No. 303 near Wilmington.

Prisoner No. 1064 contrasted his present apparel with the gaily-bedecked, gold-crested purple robe that had symbolized his lofty position as Imperial Wizard of the Association of Carolina Klans until October of 1952. Prisoner 1064 was Thomas L. Hamilton, self-appointed guardian of the people, and leader of the hooded order of the Ku Klux Klan, that brought a three-year reign of terror to North and South Carolina in the 1950's. This prisoner was the man who spawned that KKK insurrection.

An odious fate had befallen this infamous leader of his so-called "invisible empire." Patient and determined efforts by the F.B.I., prodded by its director, J. Edgar Hoover, and other law enforcement agencies led to Hamilton's ignoble position on the North Carolina prison gang. Portions of the Klan story and the smashing of the organization had gained nationwide publicity. An editorial campaign led directly to Pulitzer Prize recognition for a weekly newspaper because it refused to cower to the Klan's pressure and threats. This is the story of the rise and fall of Carolina Klanism in the fifties, completely told here for the first time.

Hamilton's rise and fall is the crux of the Klan story itself. It is a story of hate, bigotry, racial prejudice, violence and even death. It climaxed with scores of savage night floggings. Fundamentally, it is the story of the man whose greed for power led to his downfall just as surely as similar traits had brought on the disintegration of those other empire builders from Napoleon to Hitler.

And it is my story too. The story of a country boy in a sleepy little town that found itself the hub of this nefarious activity. While I am no hero, it is my story because I chose to fight against intimidation and fear despite constant threats of reprisal. My story, because I do not believe in condemning a man because of his race, color, creed, religion, national origin, the kind of shoes he wears or the way he parts his hair.

Yes, it's my story, too, because my little weekly newspaper, the *Tabor City Tribune*, elected to oppose the rise of the Ku Klux Klan with every ounce of influence and clout that words could muster.

My story because I chose to crusade from the inception of the Klan against this self-appointed neighbor's keeper. I chose to fight these vigilantes in the face of danger and against the sincere advice of friends. I called this organization un-American and undemocratic while it still floundered in its infancy. I continued the crusade when it grew all-powerful on my own doorstep and in other areas, and sought to rule the courts, law enforcement, elections and other government agencies.

I chose to write one editorial after another against this band of hoodlums even when my family lay awake in fright. My two-year-old son was so conscious of the tension that he asked, "Daddy, when's the Klan coming to get you?" For the first time in my life, every door in my home was locked at night. Every gun was loaded and ready. Telephone numbers of trusted friends were boldly written on the phone booth wall; my wife could call for help quickly when the dreaded hooded visitors made their midnight knock on our door. There was no 911 service then.

It's my story, too, because I had to meet and greet acquaintances on the streets of Tabor City with a friendly smile, knowing full well that some were Klansmen who didn't know I was aware of their secret. It's my story because I lambasted this mob organization with knowledge beforehand that little protection could be expected from law enforcement officers whose own ranks were infiltrated with Klan members. I knew that even one of our three town commissioners in Tabor City was active in the night flogging of his neighbors and mine.

I knew that the general public was bitter towards those who criticized the secret band. I further knew my family's livelihood depended upon the revenue from advertising and subscriptions solicited from many of the very people that I was blasting.

I knew also that even those who were anti-Klan were equally opposed to my crusade. Many sincerely felt that Klan publicity was bringing shame and disgrace to the community in which we lived and made a living. They felt that I should ignore the lawlessness and keep it out of the newspapers. But I felt I had to continue calling a spade a spade.

Yes, it's my story and Hamilton's. Mine because of a principle based on the belief that God meant for mankind to practice brotherhood, charity, humility and love. And love only counts when you are loved back. It's Hamilton's story because he sought unbridled power, fame, adventure and financial reward outside of and contrary to the constitutional guarantees of a free American people.

Many crusades fail miserably. This one didn't. For that I am eternally grateful.

I believe that God was in my corner.

About the Author

W. Horace Carter now lives at Cross Creek, Florida, but spent most of his adult life in Tabor City, North Carolina, where he founded, published and edited the *Tabor City Tribune,* and was co-owner of Atlantic Publishing Company for thirty-three years. He was always a crusading editor for many humanitarian causes.

"As the late Bunn Hearn, legendary University of North Carolina baseball coach, once said about his team, 'We won a few, lost a few, and we had a few rained out.' That's the way it was with our crusades," Carter reflects today.

Certainly his three-year campaign against the infamous Ku Klux Klan was one of his winners, as it marked the first time in the country's history that night-riding, hooded Klansmen were convicted for kidnapping and flogging of their neighbors.

Carter graduated from tiny Endy High School in Stanly County in 1939, one of only 14 seniors. He entered the University of North Carolina School of Journalism that fall, the first male student from his high school to enter college and graduate.

After working his way through school with the University News Bureau and serving as editor of the student newspaper, *Daily Tar Heel,* (with a four-year interruption during World War II, when he was a Navy lieutenant) he was mailed his journalism degree in 1949. He had already founded the weekly *Tabor City Tribune* in a tiny tobacco-road town of two thousand people on the South Carolina/North Carolina border. Tabor City, with its decades-long record of violence, was widely known as "Razor City" and "Border Town" for its numerous cutting crimes and other lawless violence.

"We fought this violence and lawlessness from the first day we published. It finally subsided when all the roughnecks killed each other over a period of several years," Carter reminisces only half-jokingly.

Since becoming editor emeritus of the *Tribune* in 1976, Carter has written fifteen books, and more than two thousand magazine articles, mostly on fishing and hunting. His book, *Hannon's Big Bass Magic* won first place in the Southeastern Outdoor Press Association Excellence in Craft contest in 1988.

He served three consecutive terms as President of the Florida Outdoor Writers Association, and is past president of the

Southeastern Outdoor Press Association. He was a member of the Board of Directors of the Outdoor Writers Association of America for six years

He was "One of the Ten Most Outstanding Young Men in America for 1953," winner of the First Annual Southeastern United States B'nai B'rith Award in 1952, winner of the Sidney Hillman Foundation Award in 1953, and recipient of the Pulitzer Prize for Meritorious Public Service in 1953.

He is a Rotarian, Baptist, Republican. He has three children and ten grandchildren.

Author W. Horace Carter as he appeared during KKK Crusade.

Table of Contents

Chapter One
Hate Crimes:
An American Tradition

Across these United States today, hate crimes continue to rise. This bias against blacks, Hispanics and Jews has been embedded in people north and south, east and west in the New World since settlers arrived at Plymouth Rock and staked out homesteads.

It is not something new nor is it something that is disappearing. It is getting worse, much worse. Riots ran rampant in the North during the Civil War. One particularly lawless uprising involved an estimated seventy thousand white Irish Catholics in New York City. They ran roughshod over blacks in the city, hanging many while burning and looting their homes. As many as a thousand blacks were killed in that single melee.

Recently a fifteen-year-old cheerleader in Orange County California, was beaten with a baseball bat and her face cut horribly with a piece of plate glass. It will be years, if ever, before she regains control of her facial muscles. She was abused by four white men because she had one white and one black parent. As if she could help it!

Tranquility is traditionally expected in the Northwest, but this isn't always true. Victims of hate crimes involving race, religion or sexual orientation rose twenty percent in that Pacific area in 1989. Two cross burnings, one murder and 149 assaults were directly connected with racial or religious differences in a five-state block.

California's Los Angeles county recorded 378 crimes of hate in 1989. They focused upon rapidly-increasing assaults against blacks, Hispanics, Jews and Arabs.

In the the East, Maryland reported a growing number of

cross burnings, arson, assaults and threats against people of minority races and religions in 1989. The number of hate crimes in Maryland doubled between 1986 and 1989, reaching a total of 686.

John Devitt, a criminologist at Northeastern University, has released studies of 450 vicious hate crimes in Boston, Massachusetts. He has concluded that victims of hate crimes are hurt much worse than victims assaulted for other reasons. They are three times as likely to require hospitalization. All hate crimes are vicious.

There are fewer hate crimes committed in racially "pure" neighborhoods. But where there is a mixed population of economically insecure, hard-hat, working class Americans, blacks, Hispanics and Asians have frequent confrontations with each other and with the white populace that leads to serious injury and death.

Educated classes also get into the hate crimes act. Anti-Semitic assaults have occurred regularly on many college campuses. More than 7,000 such hate crimes were reported to researchers at the University of Wisconsin at Madison in 1989.

Prosecutors are getting tough with hate criminals. In Oregon, a jury ordered a leader of the White Aryan Resistance to pay five million dollars to the family of a Portland black who was beaten to death with a baseball bat.

There still remains a substantial segment of the people who are firmly entrenched in religious and racial bias, as the ballots clearly revealed in 1989, when David Duke, an acknowledged ex-Ku Klux Klansman, ran for the United States Senate in Louisiana. He won more than forty percent of the popular vote. He made this remarkable showing without the endorsement of the leadership of either of the national parties and won a substantial majority of the white vote.

A bill allowing increased immigration in the next decade has been passed by Congress and signed by President Bush. It will likely promote even more hate crimes that will challenge police and state legislatures as they try to cope with a tragedy that has been prevalent all over America (and the rest of the world) since the first white man set foot on this continent.

Chapter Two

The Undercover Klan

Before the KKK showed its ugly face and held its first Tabor City motorcade, recruiters had been busy signing up members and organizing throughout the coastal counties of Columbus and Horry. They had chosen sides in recent elections, and campaigned against candidates that they considered too liberal. While they were not of sufficient strength to swing elections alone at that early period of their reorganization, the votes that they did have, coupled with the normally ultra-conservative attitude of the area, helped to defeat some outstanding candidates for public office.

Hamilton and his cohorts made no bones about their dislike for Dr. Frank P. Graham, who had been appointed to the U.S. Senate and was running in the Democratic primary for reelection in the spring of 1950. Dr. Graham, one of the great men of the twentieth century, was defeated by the conservative element in the party that included the embryonic Klan. Dr. Graham, a long-time personal friend whom I idolized because of his wisdom and principles, was very much aware of the Klan activities, and their opposition to his candidacy.

After he was defeated, just ten days before the first Klan motorcade through Tabor City, he mailed me the following message that I ran as a front page editorial because it expressed my sentiments exactly, although he said it much more eloquently than I ever could.

This Is America
In spiritual faith and the American dream, America is being made safe for democracy without vulgarity. Differences without hate, and excellence without arrogance; where men become brothers in the sight of God, and in the human heart; where the opportunities of the children in the homes and schools are the chief concern

of the present progress, and the chief hope of a nobler society; where enduring progress in human relations is made through religion, education and voluntary cooperation in the minds and hearts of the people; and where the struggle for the fulfillment of our historical Americanism is the best answer to fascism and communism in the present global struggle against totalitarian tyranny for peace and freedom in the world.

In this America of our struggles and hopes, the least of these our brethren has the freedom to struggle for freedom; where the answer to error is not terror. The respect for the past is not reaction, and the hope of the future is not revolution; where the integrity of simple people is beyond price, and the daily toil of millions is above pomp and power; where the majority is without tyranny, the minority without fear, and all people have hope. This is America. God Bless America!

/s/Frank P. Graham

That was a marvelous message for all of us at that point in time as well as today. In the face of political defeat and knowing the KKK was experiencing a revival and had campaigned against him, he wrote this short, simple sermon that touched my heart then. It still does. He was a great man.

Chapter Three
How It All Began. . .

Wind devils picked up little clouds of dust along Railroad Street where the pavement was narrow and the bare earth was exposed. There was no curb nor any marked parking spaces, just a railroad iron firmly mounted two feet above the ground that kept cars from rolling onto the tracks. It was Saturday afternoon. The date was July 22, 1950.

Several barefoot farmers in overalls strolled down the cracked sidewalks that were littered with boiled peanut hulls. Boiled peanuts are still a delicacy in Tabor City and all of eastern North and South Carolina. Tattered awnings stretched out from the fronts of small businesses that lined both sides of the two-hundred-yard commercial district along Railroad Street. Feed, seed, clothing, hardware, furniture, and tire stores, along with greasy-spoon hot dog joints were clustered on this main street. Other retail firms in the tiny town of two thousand people were located on Fifth Street, a busy section in the spring, where two mule auction barns smelled of dung and sweat. It was there buyer and seller haggled long and loud over the price of a beast of burden shipped in over the Atlantic Coastline Railroad from Tennessee. The boxcar full of mules was shooed out onto the street and driven into stalls at the auction barns. Few farmers had tractors. That equipment was impractical for row crops, they reasoned, and they didn't have the money to buy one anyway. The price of a tractor seemed outrageous at the time—as much as seven hundred dollars for a Fordson.

The tasks of planting, cultivating, suckering, grading and harvesting the bright leaf tobacco, the local money crop, was exhausting. Growers had to have mule-power to pull the plows in the spring and the drags loaded with green tobacco when it ripened in July and August. A good, farm-broke Tennessee mule cost a farmer about forty dollars. It was a lot of money when tobacco sold for ten cents a pound or less. Cigarettes were fifteen cents a pack. Soft drinks were a nickel.

5

The mule traders negotiated prices and the terms, as forerunners of today's used car salesmen. With a down payment of ten dollars you could carry the animal home and pay the balance after selling your tobacco. There was a twenty percent interest charge for carrying the promissory note. Many buyers used the animal through the tobacco harvest, then brought it back to the mule trader, not wanting to feed the critter through the winter. Often they didn't have the funds to pay the balance anyway.

With the deal completed, there was frequently all the excitement of the Wild West when the buyer mounted his steed and tried to ride it home. Unaccustomed to a man sitting on their backs, these wild animals bucked, pitched and even wallowed with understandable fright. Often the more robust mules dislodged the rider who cussed up and down the street in exhausting pursuit of his purchase. For the casual observer, it was a fun time. For the farmer-owner of the half-horse, half-jackass, it was frustration and not amusing.

Once a stable for farm mules, this building has been converted into an outlet for used furniture.

Business was slow that Saturday afternoon in July of 1950 except for the mule traders. It was always slow in July when the money that farmers borrowed to plant and grow their crops was exhausted and they hadn't yet sold their tobacco. They bought only the staples: coffee, rice, sugar, flour, cornmeal, grits and maybe a carton of cigarettes or Black Mare chewing tobacco. Many hauled their groceries back to the farm on buckboards or buggies. Since this was a rice-eating community, it was not unusual to see a farm family buy several one-hundred-pound sacks of rice when the general stores advertised that "new crop rice" had arrived. Typically, many rural families ate rice three times every day. A meal was not complete without it.

Sales were almost always on credit. The grocer charged everything until the tobacco crop had gone through the auction. Some farmers draped a large sack of rice on one side of the bare back of their mule, a sack of various purchases on the other for balance, then climbed aboard and rode home late on Saturday afternoon. Shopping was done once a week or even once a month. Farmers from miles away along the Waccamaw River came to town only two or three times a year. The twenty miles of soft-sand road made the trip a torturous all-day experience that often didn't end until late at night.

A few of the more affluent farmers had dilapidated automobiles, but they were difficult to buy even if you had the money. Automobile production stopped during World War II. When they came back on the market, very few farmers or businessmen in the Tabor City area had eight hundred dollars to spend on a new Ford or Chevrolet.

It was the day for my semi-monthly haircut at a point in time when only women went to beauty parlors (mostly "city women" at that). Men who didn't have their hair cut at home visited the places with colorful red, white and blue rotating poles that marked the barber shop. Barbers made a good living by charging two bits for a haircut or a shave. These small-town shops were manly meeting places, a center of gossip, and indeed, a kind of unofficial news center. The barber chatted with the public and he knew what was going on. He was always quick to share the latest news with every client.

Noting that I still had the cowlick in the back of my hair that made it stick up when cropped too short, barber Frank Young, who doubled as chief of the volunteer fire department, was unusually chatty—almost hyper.

I was editor, publisher, advertising salesman, circulation manager and janitor of the four-year-old *Tabor City Tribune* at the time. I had started the tiny weekly after my discharge from the U.S. Navy in 1946 with my total fortune of four thousand dollars that I had saved while in the service. With a devoted young schoolteacher wife and beautiful five-year-old daughter, I rode in to Tabor

7

City over a washboardy dirt road that jolted the hubcaps off my three hundred dollar 1939 Pontiac with tractor-grip tires. The only other thing I owned of any value was a journalism degree. I did have an abundance of energy and ambition, along with a burning desire to be in the newspaper business—be it ever so humble. In my pocket I carried a classified advertisement placed in a daily newspaper by the newly-organized Tabor City Merchants Association, asking for an aspiring journalist to start a weekly publication in the aggressive little town that was fighting to counter its reputation for lawlessness. Located on the South Carolina border, it was widely hailed as "Border Town" and "Razor City" because of its record of violence. Doctors were kept busy on Saturday nights sewing up cuts and stab wounds from fights and frays in the rundown beer and white lightning honky-tonks that straddled the state line near the southern city limits of Tabor City.

Businessmen and the civic-minded residents believed a weekly newspaper would be a boost to retailers, while helping clean up the recklessness and lawlessness that continually marred the reputation of the town. Arrests and convictions of the criminals in the community, even in homicide cases, were few. Much of the lawlessness went unpunished. It was a nineteenth century Old West spectacle in the twentieth century. In truth, the Saturday night melees stopped only after the dozen or so drunken redneck troublemakers killed each other. That was a deterrent that always seemed to work.

After passing a greeting or two with Frank and a kibitzer or two who waited on the wooden benches, I relaxed to enjoy the tonsorial artistry of this veteran with the clippers.

"What's the news, Frank?" I asked my usual question.

There was an unusual pause. Frank contemplated his next words carefully, not wanting to divulge anything that might be either a self-imposed or agreed-upon secret. And there were other people listening, too.

"I think you better be up town about 9 o'clock tonight. You'll probably get a story for your next Wednesday's front page," Frank muttered, without elaborating.

"What can I expect?" I asked.

"Just be here," was his terse, almost rude reply.

I didn't realize it at that moment, but the events of that evening to which the barber referred, would change my life forever. The Ku Klux Klan was coming to town. And I would be a witness.

Chapter Four
Time for Decision

A few minutes after nine, I was shocked out of the world of fiction by the shrill wail of a siren.

"There must be a fire," I told my wife, tossing my book down and running to the front door. Looking in every direction, I saw no smoke, and in Tabor City when there's a fire you can see it from any vantage point. The town's that small.

The nerve-wracking siren continued to shatter the otherwise serene July evening. I still hadn't associated this disturbance with the tip from the barber that I should be uptown at nine. But no doubt this was a news item for the *Tribune*.

"I'll walk up the street to see what the problem is," I told Lucile, and I pulled on my old felt hat (in those days hats were a trademark of newspapermen, and I so wanted to be a "real" newspaperman) and headed up Railroad Street past Lewis Gore's Red and White Grocery.

The normal Saturday night shoppers were milling around the stores that remained open until nearly midnight to accommodate farmers who often worked until sundown before coming to town for groceries and other supplies. Openings and closings were directly dictated by the needs of the farm families. Retail stores catered to their whims and sought to make shopping convenient. Shopping could be done after a hard day's work on the farm so that the tobacco grower didn't have to sacrifice precious daylight hours to buy his groceries and supplies

In that era forty years ago all Tabor City stores were technically "convenience stores" as far as the rural residents were concerned. Merchants kept them open early and late to accommodate the hand that fed them—the landlords and tenant farmers in the outlying communities. Tobacco farmers held the keys to economic survival, and they were the kings of commerce. Many dates and decisions hinged on their whims. (Even fall school openings and spring closings were rescheduled so that children could work in the tobacco when the planting and cropping were the

9

busiest.) But there was an advantage in that even the poorest children could work on the family-size farms, and unlike those of today, none got high school diplomas who couldn't read and write, regardless of opening and closing dates.

As the shrill siren's squeal approached the business section from Highway 701 East, a hush suddenly fell over the street. It was as if an unseen hand was being held over the mouths of hundreds of shoppers. A slow-moving car was rolling up Railroad Street. The noisy siren sound was coming from that vehicle. It had other reasons for attracting attention. A brightly-glowing red cross, two feet high, was mounted atop the radiator. The burning dome light cast an eerie glow on the four mystery riders inside who wore white robes and peaked witch-like hats that covered their faces except for the two narrow slits that were eye holes. The masked figures stared through open windows at the startled bystanders. They seemed sinister and threatening. Large red letters scrawled across the windshield proclaimed "KKK."

Twenty-eight others followed the lead car almost bumper to bumper. All had dome lights burning to emphasize the ominous presence of the Ku Klux Klan. For the first time since Reconstruction Days when vigilantes harassed the carpetbaggers and scalawags who corrupted governments throughout the South, Tabor City was witnessing the resurrection of the mysterious terrorist group. Was this really the night-riding Ku Klux Klan? Why was there a need for vigilante justice in an era of peaceful democracy? Weren't our constitutional laws and government, even though flawed with corruption and graft by a few greedy politicians, (and even though communism had crept into high places in Washington) strong enough to defend and protect the oppressed?

Then it dawned on me—this was not the Klan of Reconstruction years. Perhaps, only perhaps, there was a need for vigilantes in that lawless period when duly-elected Southern governments were powerless, trampled by our Civil War conqueror for a time.

Today, in 1950, we were a country of men and laws, properly elected with due process guaranteed to the individual. Granted, life was not always just nor equitable, but it was the best the world had to offer. Could a few hundred disgruntled rednecks cure the flaws in our system? Or would they more likely further oppress the rights and freedoms of the citizenry they hand-picked to punish?

Albert Schilds stood in the doorway of his department store

in awed silence. Clayton Sellers stopped selling beer on the main street corner to watch. A drunk swayed on the sidewalk, then leaned against a utility pole, his mouth agape. Three Negro women (this was before the day when they preferred to be called "blacks." They asked to be called "colored" or "Negroes," not "blacks" or "niggers," as the majority of the people still referred to them) quietly merged into the crowd, wanting to disappear. One was Evergreen Flowers, a tall, stately Negress with a figure that turned men's heads. They obviously knew of the Klan's ancient history of intimidating and abusing former slaves. Weren't those days gone forever? Would they face the same harassment as their forefathers on the southern farmland?

The Klan motorcade turned down the dusty, unpaved street toward the "bottom," the colored section of town where thirty percent of Tabor City's citizens lived. The cars circled several blocks, came back out on Highway 410 and headed toward the community of Green Sea in South Carolina. Finally, the last tail light blinked out of sight. Not a word had come from the night riders. The cars never stopped, but their message littered the streets. Multi-colored printed flyers flitted in the evening breeze. I picked up one of the handbills and read:

THIS MESSAGE IS FOR YOU!
Beware of associating with the niggers, Jews and Catholics in this community. God didn't mean for all men to be equal. All are not equal. The white Protestants are God's chosen people. We are organizing all over your state and particularly in this community. Soon you will have a chance to do your part toward saving America from the Jews, niggers and integrationist quacks who are communists and nigger lovers. When the opportunity knocks on your door, come join us. Help save our freedom for you and your children in the Carolinas. There's not much time left. Hurry to help!
THE ASSOCIATION OF CAROLINA KLANS
Leesville, S.C.
Thomas L. Hamilton, Grand Dragon

Police Chief L. R. Watson seemed petrified as he stood on the curb. Like others, he had never seen a Klan parade before. It was a new experience for everyone. Grocer Lewis Gore came charging out of his store, his dirty butcher's apron flapping, to see what had captured the attention of his customers. His store was empty.

"What's up, chief?" Gore asked excitedly.

"Looks like the Ku Klux Klan has come to town. I heard

today that they planned a motorcade through here, but I didn't know just when. I'm sure glad they didn't start something. Ain't nobody on this police force except Ted Watts and me, and we couldn't do much protecting if that hundred or more Kluxers decided to cause trouble," Chief Watson voiced an obvious concern that would be vividly documented in Columbus and Horry counties in the horrifying months ahead. It was the first time I had ever heard the word "Kluxers." It would soon become commonplace and KKK beatings would be "Kluxing" of the victim.

I walked slowly back to my home. Watson was right. What could a two-man police force do if this mob had elected to stop, grab up Albert Schilds (one of two Jewish businessmen in Tabor City), and beat him up, perhaps demanding that he leave town and never come back? He was among the most civic-minded, humanitarian merchants in the county. And he was my neighbor and close friend. What if they had told Clayton Sellers to quit selling beer and the drunk to sober up and take better care of his family or they would be back to inflict their kind of vigilante punishment. Maybe Sellers and the drunk were weak moral characters, but could vigilantes set the standards and enforce them? Or, in this day of impending chaos, when integration was on everybody's lips, could the Klan tell Evergreen Flowers she could expect a flogging if she ever appeared receptive to a white man's invitation. Could the Klan determine the lifestyles of the immoral when the law failed?

All these possibilities flashed through my mind that evening following the Klan motorcade. I had heard rumblings that such dastardly, prejudiced activities had been going on in a distant corner of South Carolina, but I didn't believe it. Perhaps it was more than a rumor. It seemed much more plausible now.

Those much-feared Klan reprisals didn't happen the night that first motorcade slinked in unannounced without a permit. Its coming was not a secret to a selected few and it happened prior to the time that permits were required for demonstrations and parades in Tabor City.

Frank Young, my barber, knew about this procession. I surmised that others knew about it too. That might have had something to do with a larger than usual Saturday night crowd of shoppers in busy July.

The Klan would have come to town with or without a legal permit. They simply didn't respect the law. What could Watson and Watts have done about it? Even if they had called in the county sheriff's eight deputies and the two state troopers they could not have stopped a motorcade carrying at least one hundred Klansmen, many of whom, we later learned, were armed to the teeth.

During the unforgettable months that made up the next two years, we would see these very same observers on that gruesome evening flinch and cringe from the vigilante terrorists who flaunted law and order to nominate themselves judge, jury and executioner. The next few years were to be the most infamous and fearful the area had ever known; a time when even the privacy of homes and churches would be invaded by hooded strangers with a vicious whip used to inflict bruises and cuts on both men and women, blacks and whites. Even death would be laid at the feet of this brazen Klan.

Turmoil and widespread fear would soon engulf the coastal Carolina communities, traumatizing the people. Held in the clutches of fear for months, many people were reluctant to leave their homes at night, and indeed many families moved out of the area, never to return.

My duty as the only newspaperman in Tabor City stared me squarely in the face. I could not compromise my conscience. I must fight the Klansmen with all the power that my tiny press could muster. That meant that I too would be the victim of their wrath. I was no hero, but the die was cast and I would have to respond. I must fight this KKK resurrection with the same intensity that, as an impressionable young UNC student, I had once fought to keep Dr. Frank Graham on the War Labor Board. If and when they came to drag me from my home, their numbers would be such that they could succeed. In numbers they had strength. But I would not go meekly to their whipping post. Several of the hooded mobsters would be found face down in my yard unless their henchmen dragged them away.

I hadn't been a hunter all my life for nothing. I was a crack shot with a rifle. Even a novice with an automatic shotgun and buckshot could stop a few night riders. If it happened, I wouldn't be remorseful. A man's home is his castle, and only an imbecile wouldn't defend his life and his family. Man must kill in war. That Klan's intrusion was a declaration of war on my doorstep and as a matter of integrity and honor I would fight by whatever means the circumstances dictated.

The blueprint of what the future might hold for me and others flicked through my busy mind as I slowly walked home.

I stepped inside the den from the back door. Lucile was frantic. I had been gone much longer than she had anticipated.

"What's going on uptown? I saw this string of cars come by here with people wearing robes and hoods. Was that a Ku Klux Klan parade? What are they doing here?" she peppered me with questions, some of which I could not answer.

"Yes, honey, it was the Ku Klux. They didn't stop or do anything tonight, but it is a forewarning. Take a look at this recruiting circular that they passed out. I shiver at what could happen in a rural community like this. The people here are hardworking, fifth and sixth generation Americans. They are good people, but many of the adults never saw the inside of a schoolhouse.

"Few of the rural farmers here got past grammar school. They have heard about the pride of their Klansmen grandfathers in ridding many counties of the carpetbaggers a hundred years ago. Those adults out there now who did go to school have had the exploits of that Klan fantasized in the classrooms for generations. Perhaps some of that teaching was proper. I don't know. But now with all the talk of school integration, eating together in restaurants, sleeping in the same motel beds, building homes in white residential areas, and working the same public jobs as other people, there is racial tension that could play right into the hands of the Klan. President Truman's lack of popularity in the South adds to the frustration of many people who live around here.

"You also know that laws here in Columbus and Horry counties are not always enforced fairly. Perhaps they never will be. That leads to disrespect for the rules and the laws. It's such disrespect for laws on the books that gives Ku Klux Klan recruiters ammunition to attract the masses. They will sell bedsheets and pillowcase hoods by the hundreds right here in our community.

"I told you about the time when three men faced first degree murder charges in a term of court in Horry County. All three were acquitted. Then a black man was charged with stealing a hog. He got a year in prison. That's when I ran a front-page headline that read: 'It's O.K. to Kill a Man In Horry County, But Don't Steal His Hog.'

"On another occasion the late Harry Bell and I stopped in for breakfast at a Conway cafe one morning before daylight when we were on the way to Murrells Inlet to pier fish. The cook-proprietor was talkative. 'I killed me a nigger this morning,' he said with a strange grin on his face. I cringed at his nonchalance.

"Why did you do that?" I asked, thinking that perhaps he was joking or I misunderstood.

"'He sassed me. He was just a tenant farmer's kid, and he came to my house last night and wanted to borrow five dollars. I told him to get lost. I wasn't giving him any money. He was about half drunk, and he said if I didn't give him the money, I would sure be sorry. That made me mad and I told him to get off my property and not to ever come back. He looked me right in the face and said I was one whitey that he hated. I was a selfish son of a bitch.

"'That was too much to take from an uppity nigger that was a tenant on my farm. I picked up my rifle from the corner of the porch. The kid struck out up the road as fast as he could run, but he didn't outrun that .22 bullet. It hit him square in the back of his head. He was dead when I got to him. I pulled him out of the road and sent one of the hands to tell his ma where to find him. He was gone this morning.' The cafe owner told the story exactly like that. He seemed to be proud that he had upheld his honor or something.

"There was never an arrest, indictment or trial, even though that appeared to be a cold-blooded murder of a teenage Negro.

"With a citizenry that thought like that—justifying a sickening homicide—you could predict a successful recruiting drive by an organization like the Ku Klux Klan. Of course, the percentage of people who thought as this evil minded man was a small portion of the population. But there were enough of them to organize a powerful gang of night riders that would stop at nothing to intimidate and rule.

"A situation like that is conducive to Klan reorganization and even some good people may fall into the trap and participate. You know and I know that we will be traitors to the community if the *Tribune* doesn't fight this Klan every way we can. Our future depends upon it," I passionately made my case to my loving wife.

"We may not have any future if you start fighting them. Oh, I wish we had never come here to begin with!" she said, as fear for what lay ahead gripped her heart.

"'Cile, I'll do my best to keep you and the kids safe. But please stick with me. I'm starting my campaign against the Klan next week. I must," I said, as I held her close and listened to her sobs. A trying time was just around the corner.

A verse from Psalms crossed my mind, etched there perhaps from a childhood Baptist Sunday School teacher. "This is the day that the Lord has made. We will rejoice and be glad in it." I wondered if that could possibly be true of this day!

"Were it left for me
to decide whether we
should have a
government without
newspapers,
or newspapers
without a government,
I should not hesitate
a moment to
prefer the latter."

Thomas Jefferson

Chapter Five
The Crusade Begins

I searched my soul that evening and on into the next week. Was it worth sacrificing our happiness, shattering the tranquil life of running a little weekly newspaper in a small town and taking part in Red Cross Drives, church covered-dish suppers, and the Annual Yam Festival promotion just because I believed in a principle? Was it worth the risk that the printshop might be burned, our home dynamited?

I could be dragged from our house with the frantic screams of my family ringing in my ears. I might suffer a brutal lashing by a band of masked hoodlums or even death if I dared to oppose them. Is it the time to stand up for principles even before I am fully aware of what this Klan proposes?

I didn't want to sound pious or self-righteous, but I reasoned that if I were ever to campaign against this Klan reorganization, I should do it from its inception. That was now. I sat down in front of my used fifteen-dollar Royal typewriter and with my experienced hunt-and-peck style (typing was not taught in the high school I attended) I wrote this editorial:

THIS IS NO TIME FOR THE KLAN

Many of you saw and if you didn't see, you have certainly heard about the motorcade of Ku Klux Klansmen who invaded our community last Saturday night. They did no harm on that visit, but the long history of this infamous band of vigilantes guarantees that their very presence in this community will bring violence, despair, lawlessness and tragedy if they succeed in organizing and survive.

They are recruiting memberships now, and in the days ahead you will be pressured to join this hooded gang of night riders. They will assure you that your membership will forever be secret and no fellow Klansman will dare divulge your association. The Klan promises death to any who break its code and reveal the names of others.

This is a pie in the sky organization that assumes it can be powerful enough to police the state, and eventually the nation, perhaps in time gaining political control.

It behooves every citizen to think seriously before casting his lot with this secret membership gang. If you get hooked, it may be difficult to get unhooked. Think! If the KKK is worthy, why do the members hide behind a mask, meet in secret, and closet their by-laws? Klansmen of the past have talked religious principles while their actions were devilish. Would Jesus Christ seek membership in today's Ku Klux Klan?

The movement here is still in diapers. Turn your back on it. Don't get involved. Certainly, the time will come when you'll be mighty glad that you did.—W.H.C.

While the editorial was no great literary masterpiece—I have never claimed to be much of a scholar—it expressed my real feelings and my hopes for the rejection of the Klan's invitations. At the time I wrote it, I had no idea how prophetic one of the sentences was. When I conjectured that in time the KKK might seek to control the ballot boxes and elect its own to political offices, I did not know that such an effort would eventually be among this embryonic Klan's primary objectives—to elect sheriffs, judges, district attorneys and lawmakers who would be friendly to every type of Klan shenanigan.

The two-column, ten-point boldface type editorial ran down the middle of the *Tribune*'s front page on Wednesday. It was too important, at least to me, to run inside on the editorial page where it might be overlooked by many. I knew it would be read on the front and at that moment I made the decision to publish all future KKK editorials on the front page regardless of the length of the campaign. I had a feeling then that there was no quick fix. This would be a long, hard-fought struggle. Neither the Klan nor the newspaper would just roll over and play dead.

The ink was hardly dry on the newsprint before the telephone began ringing off the hook. At first it was only friends with a word of caution.

"You are sticking your neck out too far on this Klan mess. You better be careful. It's dangerous. They'll get you one way or the other. Before it's too late, you better pull in your horns," my good friend and advertising benefactor Shay P. Smith cautioned. He was the charter president of the Tabor City Merchants Association who had convinced me to start the *Tribune.*

On the street I ran into Ruey Hewett, another friend and respected businessman, who had my interest at heart.

"Horace, you can't take on the Klan like you have. They'll beat you to a pulp or burn you out. I have heard about this reorganization out in the country for several weeks. They are gaining membership like wildfire. I am a native of this section and I know the people a lot better than you do. They can be vicious, particularly when an outsider like you tries to give them advice. I'm your friend,

Shay P. Smith

but take my advice—stop the editorials. Just tend to your own business, and let them alone." Ruey was deadly serious. I had to pause and rethink my stand.

Tend to my own business, I reflected. Isn't the welfare of the people in this community my business? Isn't that the business of every newspaper, large or small, that's worth its salt? Isn't it my business as the editor of the only local newspaper to inform and discourage the people from advancing an organization that can only mean trouble, fear, intimidation and turmoil? Should I sit quietly by and let a community's peaceful way of life evaporate? I think not. I could not let my ideals be squashed by criticism. Maybe the era of such idealism has long since passed. Maybe I am a reactionary in the middle of the twentieth century.

I did know that Ruey was right about at least one thing— people resent being told what to do by a newspaper, particularly as to how they vote. The endorsement of political candidates by a newspaper is generally the kiss of death. Only the shoo-ins win when the newspapers endorse them. They win despite the endorsement, not because of it. Reaction to the endorsement often assures the other candidate's election. Casting a ballot in defiance of the endorsement is the way many Americans show their independence, their freedom of choice. They do not want to be led around by the nose. I'm not so sure that isn't the best for America. The hard-hat Americans in the South have always been fiercely independent, and proud of it.

I sure hoped that my chastisement of the Klan and strong warning to the people not to be victimized by the recruitment drive wouldn't backfire like endorsements of political candidates. I don't think it did, but within a few months after the first motorcade, unofficial estimates of KKK membership in the area of Columbus and Horry counties reached five thousand or more. The two-county population was about seventy-five thousand. If indeed five thousand were Klansmen, that meant that about one out of every fifteen people I met on the street owned a robe and hood. It might also apply to those I sat next to in church. I hoped not.

Another prominent citizen of Tabor City knocked on my door at home that Wednesday evening. She had a copy of the newspaper in her hand with the glaring headline about the motorcade and my KKK editorial

"Mr. Carter," she began, and I could tell she was more than just somewhat angry, "you should be ashamed for writing things like this about the Klan. You know it is a fine Christian organization that helps keep niggers in their place. You ought to be a member and help them instead of writing all this mess in the paper. I'll bet your granddaddy and daddy don't feel about the Klan like you do."

"I'm sorry, Mrs. Gore, that you don't approve of the stand I have made. But I think I am right, and I'm going to stick with my conviction come hell or high water," I said, a little nervously, and a blush burst all over her tanned face.

"You'll be sorry," she almost yelled, and she turned on her heels and bustled back to a car parked along the street with the motor running. Tires squalling, it sped away into the night.

At that moment I was not aware that women belonged to the Klan. In the months ahead, I was to see many of them wearing robes and hoods at recruiting rallies where a few made a pitch for new members, but none ever was unmasked.

Mrs. Gore was right about one thing. My dad indeed thought I was losing my mind by fighting the Klan. He remembered stories of the KKK of Reconstruction and considered it a savior for the South. It would be years before he finally understood and approved my stand. That was when the real twentieth century KKK was unmasked, exposing its true treacherous colors. Two of my great-grandfathers had died for the Confederacy. Both my grandfathers had passed away, too. But they probably would have been

KKK followers until they discovered the cowardly viciousness of this latter-day gang.

My last caller on that fateful Wednesday night after the first anti-Klan editorial was a typical Chamber of Commerce promoter who recorded community success or failure by the number of dollars he rang up daily on his general store cash register. Any day that sales were off was a bad day for him. Ted Ward chose the telephone instead of personally visiting.

"Editor, I have just read your editorial and looked at the headline about the Klan visit. You are just like all editors. You look for bad things to write about. This stuff you have printed today will give Tabor City another black eye just like the cuttings and shootings that have been in the news about this community for so long. People will not come to town. They'll go to Whiteville, Loris or some other town to do their shopping. Why do you editors always write about bad things?" Ward was raking me over the coals.

I hesitated momentarily before speaking.

"Mr. Ward, I know you are a deacon in the church and you have served on the school board, chamber board and numerous other noteworthy organizations. Are you not aware that almost fifty percent of the news in the *Tribune* is about those organizations?" I came to the newspaper's defense.

"Oh, yeah, I see those little items, but the bad things are what you always play up and sensationalize," he retorted with obvious disdain.

"O. K., Mr. Ward, suppose I run a front page story next Wednesday with the headline: Ted Ward Is Not Beating His Wife. That's good news, isn't it, and people will be happy to know about it?" I said only half joking.

"Oh, no, no don't do that. People will think I really have been beating my wife. Just forget about it," he said, the click of the phone hanging up ending the conversation. He didn't know that I had been told he was beating his wife. It would have been good news even if he had never laid a finger on her.

Fitful sleep didn't come quickly to either Lucile or me that night. Even the children sensed an uneasiness. But it was just the beginning. Things would soon get much worse.

Produce crops helped local farmers make a living.

Chapter Six
Threats Bring Fear

It was on Thursday morning that the Klan made its first direct and ominous contact with me. I had just started to get into my car to go to work when I noticed a sheet of notebook paper under the windshield wiper. Scrawled with a blue pencil were these words that hit me hard:

> You are a nigger-loving son of a bitch. What you said about the Klan is all lies. We are honorable men and women who are interested in saving America from the Communists and Yankee liberals who are ruining the country. Stop writing those lies about us right now or you'll not wake up one morning. We know how to deal with trouble-makers like you. I have sent a copy of your paper to Tom Hamilton. The Grand Dragon already knows you are a no-good liberal and he will see that you don't get away with lying about us.

I was not surprised that it bore no signature. That was standard Klan operating procedure. But it was certainly a real threat and the culprit had the audacity to pin it on my car only a few steps from my door. He was brazen and in the dark of night he could have set our house afire or blown it up. A house in Horry County had been blown to smithereens by a case of dynamite a few weeks earlier, killing its three occupants. That could have been a Klan reprisal. Nothing was ever proven. It made me realize how easy it would be to make us the next victims. More than ever I was fearful for my family's safety. These vipers were certainly creating an atmosphere of fear. It was a virus.

I hurriedly crumpled the paper, stuffed it in my pocket, and drove to the office. I would not tell Lucile. It would only make her more apprehensive and heighten her fear.

Other surprises were in store. Under the front door of the tiny *Tribune* office and print shop I found two other hand-written

23

threats. I had obviously riled the right people. Maybe that's what I had meant to do. Now we would wait to see how Thomas L. Hamilton responded when he learned from his henchmen that he was being criticized in bold, unrelenting print. Did even our little newspaper have clout? Was the pen really mightier than the sword? These serious thoughts lingered and I doubted.

Who was this Klan leader Thomas L. Hamilton?

It took a few days and a trip to Leesville, South Carolina to learn the answer to that question. He operated a small grocery in Leesville, a tiny town like Tabor City. Doing credit business in that agricultural community, he was not getting rich fast. He led a seemingly boring, hum-drum existence. At the age of forty-six, Hamilton was said to have illusions of grandeur, including political office and the accompanying power. But he was not considered real leadership material by even his friends in Leesville, who generally liked him and had known him since he moved from Georgia. In search of some type—any type—of fame Hamilton had hatched a plan to attain some status, no matter how despicable. After all, no one wants to live and die only to be forgotten. He would organize the local Ku Klux Klan and build a following that the public would see and feel at the ballot box and elsewhere. Could nationwide power be far away?

He might have borrowed some of his ideas from Bill Hendricks, a Florida building contractor who was the chief rabble-rouser in the Sunshine State, and was recruiting Crackers for Klan membership at that time. Hendricks even entered the political picture for governor in that state. Hamilton reasoned that perhaps a brawny, six-foot-two, two hundred-twenty-five pound grocery store operator could do as well in the Carolinas. If he criticized enough things long enough and loud enough, he would win some listeners and loyal followers, or so he believed.

Hamilton made a rather imposing appearance as I would soon discover when he preached his brand of hate through a loud-speaker mounted on the back of a flatbed truck at numerous public meetings throughout our communities. He was articulate, despite being uneducated, but his message was not professional. He made his weakest points stronger by yelling louder, a trait that incites the masses. Adolph Hitler used the same tactic.

On the surface, this self-appointed Grand Dragon would seem to be a pillar of the community. He was a 32nd degree Mason, a real travesty when you contrast the principles of Masonry with those of the Ku Klux Klan. He was a deacon in the Leesville Baptist

Church. He lived in a huge, picturesque colonial-style home, an indication that perhaps he had enjoyed a degree of prosperity in the days prior to 1950. His Leesville home would serve as Klan headquarters where he sold bedsheets and pillowcases to be used for KKK cloaks for ten dollars, and collected two dollar per month membership fees. At those rates, his money problems would soon be solved.

That was a thumbnail sketch of what Thomas L. Hamilton was when he ignited the Klan's resurrection in the Carolinas.

Tabor City at this time had no racial problems to speak of. The Negroes were poorer than most whites and there had always been some injustices. In spite of them the little town remained peaceful and quiet. There was no clamor for change, no animosity, no confrontations.

Hamilton knew how to garner a following of malcontents even when there was peace in the neighborhood. He would scream about the mink coat and deep freeze corruption in Washington that was making the headlines. Congress was talking civil rights, too, providing him with more emotional ammunition. Plenty of Southerners objected to that very concept, as did others north, east, and west. Fiercely independent, many Southerners visualized dictatorship in forcing them to do anything they did not want to do. Civil rights was distasteful to the masses at that time.

Armed with these national problems and the inherent attitude of much of the populace, along with the fact that the end of World War II had returned thousands of servicemen to the peaceful life of Columbus and Horry counties, Hamilton or any other astute organizer could win support. He did.

Hamilton was an excellent salesman. He quickly recruited leg men to travel over the coastal counties of the Carolinas, setting up klaverns that scheduled regular secret meetings. It was there that he established the initiation fees and system of membership dues.

Hamilton needed lieutenants in his recruitment. He remembered an old friend whom he had known in Georgia. Early Brooks, a former Fair Bluff, North Carolina, policeman was currently selling lightning rods from his home in Fair Bluff, a small town near the state line.

Brooks had peddled his merchandise to unsuspecting farmers throughout much of Columbus and Robeson counties in the Tar Heel State as well as into Horry County in South Carolina. The benefits of these rods were dubious to many, but highly acclaimed by salesmen in that area, who often convinced home owners that they would "draw the lightning right to your house and run it into the ground." I always remembered what my own father told such a salesman once when he was being pressured to put his hard-earned dollars into lightning rods.

"If it attracts lightning like you say, then I'll buy just one. Put it in the top of that tree over there in the woods a couple of hundred yards. The lightning will be drawn away from my house. I don't want something that draws the lightning to the house," Dad told the frustrated salesman. He soon left with neither contract nor money.

Hamilton knew that Brooks would make a fine recruiter because he was widely known in the farming communities. That was the life blood of the Klan. Brooks had learned about the Klan when he lived in Georgia. He was fascinated by the robed order. He fantasized about the romantic and adventurous legends of the Confederate era when the KKK punished murderers, rapists and thieves in the South. To revive this vigilante order was a dream of Brooks' that blossomed when he met the Grand Dragon in Fair Bluff.

Soon Hamilton appointed his old Georgia acquaintance the Grand Cyclops, a position equivalent to membership chairman. Every recruit who paid his initiation fee, which varied widely from as little as four dollars to as much as ten dollars, would be subsidizing Brooks' personal fortune with at least half the fee.

In addition, the Grand Cyclops headed the Fair Bluff Klavern, a group that quickly enrolled more than one hundred members from the village and the surrounding rural area.

Brooks was among the very best recruiters who worked for Hamilton's Klan drive. His pitch was swallowed by many good citizens who had never been in any trouble in their lives. They knew Brooks. They had confidence in him and his emotional spiel was convincing. They signed applications and soon began attending meetings with other ghoulish-looking Klansmen whom they could not recognize in their disguises.

They succumbed to the vivid tales told by Brooks, Hamilton and other Klan leaders. Some of their stories were tear-jerkers.

"There is rampant unpunished lawlessness and immorality here in this community that we must do something about," they preached. "We must protect our land from this corruption. Right here in Fair Bluff we have prostitutes selling themselves every Saturday night. Tom Simpson is beating his wife every time he comes home drunk.

"The three Gore children on Route 6 are going hungry because their daddy won't work. They don't even have shoes so they can't go to school in the cold weather. Bootleggers are making moonshine whiskey in every swamp around here, and no one is doing anything about it. You all know about how Raleigh Pierce is shacking up with that pretty neighbor of his. And the niggers around here have got to acting like they are big shots. We have got to do something about it. We got to protect our good people from these evils, because the law sure ain't going to help us." Such rhetorical speeches preached by Klan bigwigs fanned the flames of self-righteousness, prejudice and even hate to a vulnerable audience often looking for an opportunity to feel power and personal importance.

These community sins were not all imaginary. Certainly there were character defects in the citizenry in every community. New recruits in the Klan often had personal knowledge of the people who were being verbally attacked. Their vigilante spirits were fanned to the boiling point. Never did one of the speakers suggest compassion, understanding or humanitarian assistance. They did often refer to Christianity, but they did not apply those principles to the activities and punishment they would soon perpetrate on their helpless victims.

As he did with Brooks, Hamilton inflated the egos of many other Klansmen as he appointed a Great Giant, a Great Titan and a Grand Kleagle, all important in the undercover membership campaign that was exploding. Each such title holder had a different colored robe and hood, all tailored from high-priced silk or satin. These high-sounding titles, robes and hoods made many common men feel ten feet tall. The titles and distinctive robe colors were handed down from the historical Klan of Reconstruction days. Hamilton had done his homework. He had researched the original Klan's organization and these new Klansmen were anxious to prove their worth. They wanted action.

Circulars soliciting membership flooded rural mail boxes. Klan applications were easy to find. And disgruntled people filled them out by the hundreds, while others joined for financial gain or a chance to demonstrate their muscle and power. Some fantasized secretly that they could help eliminate many racial and social community evils under the guise of Christianity, the cover of darkness and the disguise of the masks and bedsheet robes.

Historically, there has always been a contingency of mankind that is intrigued with participation in secret activities that

Lucile and I at the office

border on the illegal and make one individual master over his neighbors.

This Klan would soon be involved in obvious lawlessness, far beyond any shadow of doubt, but in numbers it had great strength. It rapidly grew to more than five thousand in Columbus and Horry counties with hundreds of others scattered over the two states.

Its hierarchy openly boasted that many of its members were

public officials with much influence. They bragged that no jury of their peers would ever find Klansmen guilty of breaking any laws. On the contrary, they were sure that every jury would have some Klansmen on the panel. And obviously no juror would find a fellow Klansman guilty. Members felt safe in showing contempt for the law and years would pass before that concept was exploded.

Gangs would soon run rampant over the coastal counties, inflicting KKK justice while hiding under bedsheets and pillowcase masks. A special level of apprehension was reserved for Negroes, Jews and Catholics, legendary targets of the Klan in earlier uprisings. But even the native Anglo-Saxons would have the same fear. The Klan decided whose lifestyle was free of sin and promised to punish the others. A weakness for alcohol or women, laziness, or a temper that occasionally grew out of control were all nominations for Klan "floggings," the term that made the headlines frequently for three years. The Klan's cowardly abuse of these weak men and women and violent lawless punishment was just around the corner. Fear would grip the local population with an unbelievable stranglehold.

My mail would be plentiful for months. Anonymous letters with rough warning messages poured in. Most of those letter writers labeled me one of God's lowest creatures. I should have never been born, they insisted.

I thought about the crumpled warning I still carried in my pocket when I went home late that afternoon.

Was it really so derogatory? Biologically, I knew I could not be a son of a bitch. Everyone knew that. And as to being a "niggerlover," well, perhaps I was. From the time I moved to Tabor City, I sat with the Negroes every time there was a public meeting when both races attended. Often I was the only white on their side of the room. I was the first white man to make a commencement address at the Negro School, a rundown weather-boarded frame structure that had wall cracks big enough to throw a cat through.

My little newspaper was the first in southeastern North Carolina to run pictures of Negroes on the front page. The nearest daily, the Star-News in Wilmington, an independent newspaper that is now part of the New York Times chain, even routed out the faces of Negroes in group pictures in order not to have a Negro photograph in the newspaper. I had long editorialized that mankind should not condemn or hate any race, color or creed. There were individuals in all races and creeds that I didn't want to have anything to do with. But select your contempt of individuals for what they really are; don't criticize your fellowman because of his color or beliefs and temper your attitude with compassion. Brotherhood is essential to the survival of mankind. Maybe I was a "nigger-lover." If so, I was not ashamed of it. So be it.

"What was that paper on the car that you took off when you went to work this morning?" Lucile asked.

"It was just an advertising flyer," I lied. There was no reason to worry her about it. She was already under enough strain. Taking care of two children under those trying circumstances was enough of a burden for her to bear.

The worst was still to come.

Bird's eye view of Tabor City.

30

Chapter Seven
Editorials and Repercussions

My second editorial lambasting the Klan was splashed down the middle of the front page. It read, in part:

NO EXCUSE FOR THE KKK

In this democratic country there is no place for the Ku Klux Klan. Any organization that works outside the law is unfit for recognition in a country of free men. Its very presence here is deplorable and a black eye to our community, even without violence. With violence, (that is sure to come), it will be even more repulsive.

If you approve of the KKK, that's almost as if you rode in their midst. It will take a united front to combat this evil lawlessness. It will take a united, law-abiding people to genuinely oppose these hoodlums who have no respect for the laws of the land. While the Klan preaches Americanism, their very being and growth is the personification of Fascism and Nazism. It's these outside-the-law operations that lead to tyranny, through fear, intimidation and insecurity.

Klan Power is based on fear and it is motivated by hate. The Klan is not an organization of love, understanding and tolerance, rules that God would have us live by. There is no denying that we have some racial problems in this country. We do not have warfare. The primitive activity of the KKK will most certainly promote violence and warfare like we have never experienced in this community before.

Granted, there are always people in every neighborhood who live immoral lives year after year. Race is not a consideration in those situations, but the Klan has in the past inflicted its kind of justice on all people whom it considered immoral without judge or jury. It whipped them, cut their hair and otherwise harassed a populace whose life-style they opposed. We do not feel that any band of hoodlums has a right to inflict their kind of justice on those with whom they find fault. If there is lawlessness, then due process should eventually take its toll. When there is no lawlessness, even though moral principles are being abused, no band of hooded vigilantes has the right to take the law into their own hands. If the laws are not adequate, they can be rewritten. The KKK is not the lawmakers of this land.

The recent Democratic Party campaigns in North and South Carolina did much to stir up racial trouble and it played right into the hands of the Klan. The mud-slinging campaigns based on racial hatred were the most ungodly ever staged in the Carolinas. The campaigns over-stressed the racial issue. There's no real struggle between races in this community at this time. Integration will come to the South and the nation eventually. It will come by law, and the inevitable acceptance of people of different races and religions who, while reluctant, will come to understand that this is God's world. Peace among men is the biblical teaching that is stronger in this Bible Belt than anywhere else in the land.

The Klan talks big and praises Protestantism, while condemning Catholicism and Judaism. Yet, our forefathers established this country while searching for religious and political freedom without fear and tyranny. Would the Klan have us wish for another New World where we could escape to because America is wracked with prejudice and intolerance?

I would like to say that I wrote those brazen sentences without fear, but that wouldn't be true. I knew the editorial was not diplomatic, was hard-hitting, lacked polish and, in the minds of many of my journalistic peers, was crude. Yet I said exactly what I felt and I was determined not to pussy-foot around. I wanted the Klansmen and the community in general to feel the impact of these words. I had never been any great scholar, and I wasn't now. My clientele who read the *Tribune* weren't scholarly either. They didn't have to be educated to understand what I had written. This was not a time for fence-straddling neutrality, an unfortunate trait that far too many newspapers (large and small) have adopted to ensure their economic solvency and peaceful atmosphere.

I was mighty weak if I handled this touchy subject with kid gloves—massaging every sentence so as not to antagonize a single soul—I could just as well have stayed in bed. A focus on the evils of the Klan in a no-holds-barred attack would perhaps attract the attention of bigger, more influential newspapers in the metropolitan areas. That might help to break the back of the Klan. My little newspaper could never win without some larger organizations in the media taking up the cudgel and joining the fight. My strategy was to aim straightforward editorials at the Klan which, hopefully, would raise eyebrows around the country. The usual soft and carefully written editorials by the sophisticated professionals would have gone unnoticed.

That editorial and others that followed almost weekly did attract attention, not only of bigger newspapers and television stations (television was in the its infancy in eastern North and South Carolina), it was discussed in the F.B.I. offices. The State Bureau of Investigation (S.B.I.), local sheriff's departments and police forces also took notice. That was my hope and my plan.

But it also brought down the wrath of the Klan and their sympathizers on me. Intimidating phone calls poured in at home and in the office. The mail was heavy and threatening. I turned the letters over to the F.B. I.—for whatever they were worth—except one that was signed. I had a duty to print any signed letters that were received, no matter how critical. I was anxious to give even my most severe critics a chance to be heard as I believed (then and now) that every newspaper should give even its worst enemies a chance to present the other side. That is what I consider freedom of the press. The letter, including its misspellings, questionable punctuation and poor grammar ran as I received it:

Nakina, N.C.

Dear Mr. Carter:

    I am dropping you a few lines to let you know that I for one of many people in this section disagree with you on Negro's. I read your column of April 18. God made the white race superior to all people. The Mundolans were second, the Indians were third, and the Negro's were fourth, witch was as wild and dumb as a jack rabbit and the Indians wasn't much better so how can you or anyone else dream up the idea that God created all races equal. He made us all but he did it the way I said and intend them to remain so I'm not a member of the K K K but I thing they are doing some nice work. You and I and every body should be praising the K K K and NOT try to stom them down. Now Mr. Carter I don't mean any insults by sending you this letter or any hatred feelings but read your Bible and history a lot closer. They aren't any race in all the world that got as much right to civilization as the white race has. Now Mr. Carter getting back to your column. But what you thing of negro's is what we don't want our children to be teached. I think it will pay us all including you to live upto the Bible a lot more that what we do.

Yours truly
G.B. Benton
Nakina, N.C.
Rt. 1

Another letter that I kept and ran in the *Tribune* of August 9, 1950, under a four-column head on the front page came from John W. Hardee. I prefaced Hardee's letter with an editor's note in which I pointed out: "This is an independent newspaper with its columns open to everyone who doesn't mind putting his signature on what he writes. While we disagree with everything that Hardee writes, we respect his right to say it." That paraphrase of Voltaire expressed our attitude quite well. Hardee's letter:

Tabor City, N.C.
August 7, 1950
The Tabor City Tribune Editor
Tabor City, N.C.
Dear Sir:
I'm writing of your editorials of July 26 and August 2, 1950 concerning the Ku Klux Klan Organization.
First I would like to write you a book but I will stop by just hitting the top of the mountains. To me (the editorials) are two of the most fantastic editorials I have ever had the misfortune to read.
To set you straight, I am no member of the Ku Klux Klan Organization, nor do I have any connection with them whatsoever; but to me it is just a good, old-fashioned, Red Blooded American Organization. It is organized to support the good morals of Good American People.
According to your editorials, the Ku Klux Klan Organization was a Lawless Hoodlum Organization. If I have been informed correctly the Ku Klux Klan has as their Law and Guide the Holy Bible. But the law enforcement officers of our land as a majority is something to be proud of. Most any good, Red Blooded Christian American could frown on such a job; but it is composed of such people who would sell their own SOULS for a couple of bucks. The laws of our country should be based on the

HOLY BIBLE, and the law Enforcement Officers should be Christian-Hearted men but the majority of so-called Two by Four Officers of our land will take a small unbelievable sum and let the (moonshiner) make liquor in the bays until he is gray headed and he will never bother you.

I would like to just ask one question, is that law or lawless. I think the 3K's should start cleaning out our Law Enforcements, and probably start with our good So and So at the top of the list.

I think the Ku Klux Klan is a very good Organization with one exception. They are getting too far behind with their work. Someone may say this is a free country, we still have the Holy Bible on which to build our morals of good friendly living. Do you want a bootlegger or a red light district next door to you? Brother I don't and furthermore I am willing to fight for such rights.

Your figure of 99 and 44 one hundredths percent of the people (an over estimate and incorrect) were against the Ku Klux Klan Organization and what they stand for, but thank the good Lord that I am one of the 56 one hundredths percent.

Of all the works of the 3K's that I have learned, they all seemed helpful. This within itself is a profit to the community and the Nation.

Just one more item, I would like to mention. As you recall, Mr. Truman was going to do away with the Ku Klux Klan Organization in the South Land. But to be sure he was only pouring Gasoline on an Organization of Good Morals and Clean Living.

A Klan's Friend at heart

John W. Hardee

Route 1

Tabor City, N.C.

P.S. To the editor according to the big writing of editorials, now let's see if you have the gutts to put this on the front page of your paper as your editorials appeared. Last but not least, I am not ashamed of my name either and furthermore I don't believe it is so scribbled you can't read it. Thank you.

Distribution:

1 copy Tabor City Tribune

1 copy P.O. Box 231, Leesville, S.C.

1 copy file.

These letters, with all of their unusual capitalizations, misspellings and punctuations, at least proved to the community that we would prominently print every criticism that was properly signed. Over the years I have concluded that it might have been one reason why I wasn't killed, burned out or flogged during that uprising. The thugs always had a chance to be heard.

The letters also served as an example of the misguided emotions and attitudes of a near-illiterate segment of the people in the communities in which the newspaper circulated.

Believe me, when the Hardee letter was published, it threw another big scare into my wife and children. It even seemed like some of my best friends were avoiding me. Lucile sent the children to spend the night with neighbors just in case our house went up in flames.

In fairness to Mr. Hardee, bootlegging or moonshining was rampant throughout the area. Legal liquor had not yet been voted in. The law enforcement officers in Horry County seemed to turn their backs on the lawlessness. When Hardee referred to cleaning out the law officers and starting with the "So and So" at the top of the list, he apparently was writing about the sheriff of Horry County. That sheriff came into office poor and left a rich man. He left office at the height of the Klan uprising. He was replaced by John Henry, and a few years after the demise of the Klan, the *Tribune* launched another tough crusade against Sheriff Henry and his eighteen deputies. We charged them with corruption and accepting bribes for allowing illegal gambling, white whiskey manufacturing and alcohol sales. Federal officers collected twenty-eight affidavits from citizens substantiating the bribery charges. But the grand jury would not indict the officers and they remained in office for several months.

Like many of life's little blessings, we lost that battle, but won the war. Sheriff Henry did not get reelected and all of his deputies subsequently lost their jobs. Indirectly we won that campaign.

While it can never be an acceptable excuse for revival of the Ku Klux Klan and its lawlessness against the community, corrupt and inefficient law enforcement in that era in both of the border counties definitely contributed to the Klan's acceptance and rapid growth. Poor law enforcement was a tragedy, but not reason enough to embrace anarchy that the Klan promised.

I didn't have long to wait for another episode in the Klan's infamous uprising. Other terse warning would come in from the mob and before the end of August there would be a killing. The war was on, like it or not.

Chapter Eight
Violence Erupts

Unlike the uneventful motorcade that eased through Tabor City a month earlier, by Grand Dragon Thomas Hamilton's own admission "all hell broke loose" in Myrtle Beach on a sultry Saturday night in August. It began when a gang of robed Klansmen (now widely called "night riders") in vehicles slowly drove around Charlie Fitzgerald's dance hall and tourist court. Fitzgerald was relatively successful and affluent, something the Klan detested in all Negroes. The Klan was obviously looking for trouble. They found it as they sought to intimidate this "uppity" black man. The demonstration went awry, resulting in turmoil and disaster that shook the nation.

Charlie's Place, a recreation complex, was located in the black section of the segregated resort city. It had been visited by the Klan motorcade earlier that evening without incident. Later, Hamilton contended that word got back to his paraders that Fitzgerald had sent a message to the Myrtle Beach Police Department that "the Klan better not come back." He had hoped for some police protection. Grand Dragon Hamilton, after getting the Fitzgerald message from the police force that was friendly with the KKK, announced to his henchmen that he had received such a warning.

"You know that no red-blooded white American could take such a dare from a nigger," he incited the mob.

Immediately the motorcade turned around, retraced its path and began circling the block where the Fitzgerald dance hall and several scattered tourist cabins were located. Someone was trigger-happy. More than three hundred rifle and pistol shots ripped through the dance hall, sending the blacks inside into a panic. They quickly punched out the window panes and returned the fire. The blacks were outnumbered by at least sixty Klansmen in twenty-seven cars involved in the shootout. Klansmen soon knocked down the door and charged onto the dance floor, overpowering the Negroes still inside. A few had fled through a back door.

Hamilton claimed that he never entered the building, but admitted watching as "niggers began exploding through the windows with the frames still draped around their necks." His mordant smile when making the statement made it obvious the shootout had his approval.

Mad Klansmen inside severely whipped Fitzgerald. They beat his brother so badly that he required medical attention. Gene Nichols was shot in the foot. Charlie Vance suffered internal injuries from being pounded repeatedly in the stomach while his arms were pinned behind him. Cynthia Harrell was bruised and battered, requiring medical attention, along with thirty other black customers who were whipped in the dance hall.

Details of this unbelievable catastrophe encountered by Charlie that infamous night would not surface for weeks as no one in authority talked, even to the press. There were a few facts: at the height of the gunfire, a tall, gangling Klansman groaned and slumped to the ground a few steps from the front door. Blood quickly reddened his robe as he bled profusely from under his left arm. His cronies picked him up and rushed him to the Conway Hospital, fourteen miles away. He was dead on arrival. A .38 caliber bullet had hit his heart. Emergency-room medics removed his Klan cloak and were startled to find the victim was dressed in a policeman's uniform. He was quickly identified as James Daniel Johnson, forty-two, a veteran policeman on the Conway force. He was also a member of the Conway Klavern, one of four community klaverns recently organized in Horry County.

Johnson's death was an intimidating influence upon all who feared the Klan. The rumor mill had repeatedly emphasized that Hamilton had recruited many Klansmen from the ranks of law enforcement. He claimed he had even enrolled a number of Protestant preachers. The dead Klansman was proof that the Klan did have lawmen who were active in the KKK revival. Sympathizers and street corner kibitzers bragged that Hamilton really had recruited law officers and opponents of the insurrection from now on would be more careful with their criticism. It was months later when the public learned that several preachers were indeed in the Klan, along with members of their congregations who held leadership positions.

Klan cars left the Fitzgerald place and quickly scattered. But their abusive lawlessness and vengeance against Fitzgerald had only begun. Gagged and bound hand and foot the bleeding, half-conscious dance hall proprietor was stuffed into the trunk of a Klansman's car. The lid slammed shut and the car roared out of town. Charlie had difficulty breathing in the car trunk. He fought for air while shaking with fright. The car bounced along an unpaved country road and stopped. What would they do to him now, he wondered? And why was it happening? Hadn't he always cooperated with the police? He had never been in trouble. Was this his reward for being a successful Negro businessman? These and hundreds of other questions rushed through Charlie's anguished mind as the painful ride ended.

Trembling noticeably, Fitzgerald was dragged from the car trunk. Uncharacteristically, he begged for mercy as the masked Klansmen sneered. Half walking and half dragged, Fitzgerald found himself surrounded by a circle of ghoulish-looking thugs. He stopped begging and looked around. Was this to be a lynching? Furtively, he glanced at their hooded faces. There was no escape.

"That's the nigger who dared us to come back tonight. He's the man who shot one of our brethren. Our fellow Klansman died at the hospital. This nigger and a lot of others around here are not going to get away with feeling so important and talking so big. We are going to make an example out of him that he and others will remember. Where's the whip?" a muffled voice from the circle of Klansmen threatened. Fitzgerald was understandably terrified.

"Here it is," another Klansman answered.

"Lay it on him good and don't stop until I pass the word," the original speaker and obvious leader commanded.

Stroke after blistering stroke slashed Fitzgerald's clothes to shreds. At first he hollered and squirmed to avoid the cutting, bruising blows that seemed to continue forever. But more strong arms pinned him against a car fender. His bare buttocks and back bled profusely. He felt the warm, sticky fluid running down his legs and into his shoes. He lapsed into unconsciousness as the brutal flogging continued.

"That's enough of that," said the commanding voice. "Now who has a sharp knife?"

"Here's one," said a gruff voice from one of those who had been holding Fitzgerald down. He handed the mob leader a six-inch whittling knife.

"No, it's your knife. You get this honor. Cut off his ears," and the knife was handed back to its owner.

"We want the other niggers around here to know that this no-good nigger and no one else can get away with daring the Ku Klux Klan to do its job. Get to it and let's go home."

Consciousness returned to Fitzgerald slowly. He groaned and looked around. He was alone in the middle of a sawmill road in a swamp. The Klansmen were gone. His back burned with all the fury of skinless muscles exposed to the air. Hardening blood caked his legs and he could feel the discomfort of blood-filled shoes and wet socks. He popped a hand over his aching right ear. It was gone. He felt the other one. It was gone too. He looked at his bloody fingers. Although he had been a brave man all his life, Fitzgerald wept and then screamed, "Oh, Lord, what have I done to deserve this?"

At least he was alive. For that Fitzgerald was grateful and he began putting one foot in front of the other as he stumbled toward a lighted sky in the distance that must surely mark Myrtle Beach. He staggered out onto Highway 17. A passing motorist showed compassion and picked up the pitiful man. Fitzgerald asked to be carried to a local doctor whom he knew. The driver rushed him to the suburban home of the doctor. He helped him to the door and promptly disappeared. The good Samaritan wanted no part of this fight.

Fitzgerald knocked softly on the door. A light came on in a bedroom. The doctor opened the door and Charlie fell inside. He was weak, bleeding and whimpering softly.

"I'm hurt, doctor, please help me!" the pitiful, abused Negro pleaded. He was weak and had lost a lot of blood.

The doctor recognized Fitzgerald as being a patient he had seen previously.

"What on earth happened?" he asked the ragged man whose clothes were in shreds.

"I can't tell you right now, doctor, but help me, please," Fitzgerald pleaded.

The doctor treated Fitzgerald's most serious wounds and let him rest on the treatment table.

"Charlie, I'll have to call the sheriff and report this. You have been beaten badly and someone has to pay for it," the doctor said.

Charlie just nodded his head in agreement and closed his eyes.

Sheriff Sasser and a deputy came and arrested Fitzgerald. They hadn't seen a case like this in years. Fitzgerald might be in danger if they locked him up in the county jail, they reasoned. So they headed for Columbia and the state penitentiary where their patient and prisoner would be held for safekeeping.

This cowardly KKK flogging of Fitzgerald did not surface for weeks as Fitzgerald was held incognito, and the sheriff would divulge nothing. The press and the public only knew that he received medical treatment at 3 A.M. But Fitzgerald's unfortunate abuse is an important element in the Klan's dastardly assault on Charlie's Place and person that shamed a lot of people in 1950.

All but one of the vehicles in that motorcade bore South Carolina license tags. One was from North Carolina. Was it coincidence that almost all the cars in the Tabor City motorcade had South Carolina license plates? I think not. Investigators later concluded it was the same band of night riders. Fortunately, there had been no melee, no violent disturbance in Tabor City's Negro section. It, too, could have easily erupted into a killing. The firing of a single shot might well have started a pitched battle and subsequent wholesale deaths. The war we visualized was certainly possible. It would be avoided only if this band of hoodlums was arrested and punished in a court of law. That wouldn't be easy.

With Fitzgerald whisked off to Columbia, the press could learn little about the Johnson killing and the attack on Charlie's Place. Interviews were not permitted. People conjectured about who killed Johnson. In such a melee, one of his own Klan brothers might have fired the fatal shot. The mob was firing in a wild frenzy when Johnson died. No one ever determined who shot him.

Sheriff C. Ernest Sasser, whom Hamilton and other Klansmen severely criticized privately and publicly, (charging that he was involved with corruption and graft) for a time would not say where Fitzgerald was being held. But the word leaked out that he was confined in a hospital wing of the South Carolina State Penitentiary in Columbia. There was uncertainty about Fitzgerald's guilt in the shooting of Johnson. He was never indicted for that homicide, but he was charged with distributing lewd literature (pornography was an unknown word then) and served a prison sentence. Years later he returned to Myrtle Beach and went back into business on "The Hill," as the black section was known.

Authentic information about the Myrtle Beach shooting was scarce. No one would talk. It was like pulling the proverbial hen's teeth to find anyone admitting knowledge of the fracas and its subsequent tragedy. As far as the *Tribune* and I were concerned (and even if Charlie's Place was a den of iniquity as the Klan charged) he deserved a medal for fighting back when his business was invaded by hoodlums who threatened his safety and that of his customers. That feeling summed up the attitude of part of the public, accounting for the fact that no charges were filed against Fitzgerald for the serious crime of killing a policeman. If he had been

41

reachable, others might well have lynched him. Fitzgerald possibly was totally innocent of the homicide. No one ever knew. But someone killed a Klansman purposely or accidentally and that stuck in the craw of the KKK.

With the death of the uniformed policeman in the Klan robe, the chief of the South Carolina Highway Commission, Claude R. MacMillan, came under fire. Were any Highway Patrolmen members of the Klan? The word spread that they were and that they had participated in the Myrtle Beach fight. It prompted a quick denial from the commissioner. He stated emphatically, "If a patrolman ever takes part in a Klan parade or demonstration, it will be the last time he will ever wear our uniform or draw a paycheck." That was reassuring to those of us in the anti-Klan movement. Hamilton would never again boast that he had state troopers wearing Klan robes.

Meantime, Sheriff Sasser would release only sketchy details of this shooting and his so-called ongoing investigation. He claimed that an effort to check license plate numbers had found that many of the cars had been sold since the incident. He said that as a result he was having trouble verifying the names of the owners of the cars at the time the shooting occurred. His effort from the first seemed only half-hearted. The public believed he was afraid to pursue the investigation because it might cost him political support.

Five days after the Saturday midnight tragedy, twelve South Carolinians were arrested for allegedly participating in the ill-fated demonstration. Those charged included Grand Dragon Hamilton; Dr. A. J. Gore, a Conway optician; J. C. Creel, a Conway oil distributor and secretary-treasurer of the South Carolina Klan; R. L. Sims, a Florence beer truck driver; June Cartrette, an Horry County farmer; Bennett, Bill, Boyd and Roy Ford; and Edwin B. Floyd and Rarien Britt, places of residence and occupations unknown.

All the arrested Klansmen were charged with conspiracy to incite mob violence. Of this, the Klan was obviously guilty. At the same time, in Loris, South Carolina, a community just a few miles from Tabor City, Constable T. M. Floyd was relieved of his duties by Governor Strom Thurmond after he learned the constable was an admitted Klansman.

Thurmond went on the air to declare that he was entirely against this mob violence and promised that the state would do all in its power to discourage the Klan reorganization. While contending that he had been threatened if he went on the air, Sheriff Sasser made an impassioned radio speech immediately following that of Governor Thurmond.

Sasser stressed that he was opposing the Klan in every way and would work diligently to bring the criminals involved in the Myrtle Beach demonstration to the bar of justice. He said other arrests were pending, but none were made. Few people believed he was making much of an effort.

"The Klan is very anxious for me to resign, but I will not. I am going to continue this investigation to the very end," Sasser declared, as he sought to hold on to some of his political following in Horry County.

Sasser said that officers had confiscated hundreds of letters from the home of Grand Dragon Hamilton in Leesville, along with a sixteen-foot bullwhip, two crosses and several Klan uniforms. He also said that he found a letter signed by Imperial Wizard Sam Roper, of the Georgia Klan, (dated November 17, 1949) addressed to Hamilton that criticized him: "You have violated every oath and turned traitor to the cause of Klancraft."

Hamilton was quoted as saying, "I can assure you that all hell broke loose at Myrtle Beach, and we took over and had it under control." Later a form letter written by Hamilton was found that stated: "I believe a thousand applications could be secured in Horry County right now. Boy are they hot! They are on the verge of impeaching the sheriff. I have a flock of mail from that section of the state and they are one hundred percent behind what we did at Myrtle Beach." I could not help but reflect on that statement. Was it true that the people really favored this assault on a private business in the dark of the night by a lawless mob? If that were true, my anti-Klan fight had a long way to go. The people's attitude could not favor such vigilantes. Or could it?

Remarkably, despite the noise made by Sasser and the $5,000 bonds the Klansmen had to post for the charges against them in the Fitzgerald case, not one was ever indicted by the grand jury. The cases were all dropped and the perpetrators went free. Either Sasser's evidence was too flimsy or the grand jury had some members who were Klan sympathizers. No one ever knew which. Continually, we decried this travesty and lack of justice. But the Klan in the Horry-Columbus area seemed to be able to get away with anything. Yet just 150 miles away in the more metropolitan community of Charlotte, eight Klansmen were found guilty of burning a cross in a yard and were fined $1,000 each. There was simply more and better justice in upstate Carolina than in the rural coastal counties.

While the Klan crusade steadily took a toll on the *Tribune* economically from the very beginning, the real boycott and subsequent squeeze would come several months later. It was encouraging to get a rare letter of approval. One of those indicated that (at least a safe distance away from the area) there were those who agreed with our effort. Here is what one approving letter said:

> September 14, 1950
> Tabor City Tribune
> Tabor City, N.C.
> Dear Gentlemen or Gentleman:
> Enclosed you will probably find a check for $2 which may or may not be good at this minute. However, if it is good, please send the *Tabor City Tribune*, which gives us all the news without fear or favor, for as long as $2 will suffice. I simply can't wait to find out when the KKK is wiped out.
>
> > Yours truly,
> > Bill White
> > P.O. Box 926
> > Wake Forest, N.C.

I never knew whether it was sarcastic or sincere. I only knew that the annual subscription rate of two dollars was a bargain and that I needed the money. The check was good. White got the next fifty-two weekly issues.

Most of the barrage of letters that followed were abusive and extremely critical of our Klan campaign. One of those hand-written, barely legible missives that arrived was unsigned and typical of the mail we received. They minced no words as to what they thought of the newspaper and me. One read:

> W. Horace Carter, ED.
> Tabor City Trib
> Tabor City, N.C.
>
> Dear Mr. Iscariot—
> How does it feel to be thirty pieces of silver richer? You did just about what Judas did for $500 1950 years ago. Prices have gone up, but still "they crucify to themselves the Son of God afresh" for Jew money. God help you for betraying your own kind for anti Christ Jews and niggers.

I didn't have $500, and certainly no one had paid me

anything for launching the KKK crusade. What did the writer have in mind? That bothered me a little. I found the answer in the previous week's paper. A front-page headline announced: "W. Horace Carter Heads UJA." The Jewish populace in the county had asked me to solicit funds for the local United Jewish Appeal's annual drive. I accepted, as I did many such charitable drive chairmanships in that era when I was trying to make a living and show my interest in the Tabor City community. I had a lot of energy and I believed in many of the charitable causes. The anonymous letter writer apparently felt that I was reaping some financial reward from chairing the UJA drive. In truth, there was no pay at all for soliciting those funds. It was a humanitarian cause that businessmen of all religious beliefs annually supported in Tabor City.

When my Jewish neighbor and friend, Albert Schilds, read the letter, he was outwardly amused, yet he was fearful for me. He thought that maybe even my innocent association with the Jewish and Negro movements made me a villain in the eyes of the highly prejudiced Klansmen and their sympathizers. I shrugged it off. Much, much worse threats would soon stare me in the face.

"I wish I had never asked you to head the UJA drive," Schilds said seriously.

"Forget it! It was just written by some kook," I assured my friend that it was harmless.

There was considerable focus on the Klan locally after the Myrtle Beach disaster. The night riders were still active, Fitzgerald was imprisoned on a trumped-up lewd literature charge, the dozen arrested Klansmen had gone free without indictments and my continued editorial campaign kept the interest up.

As in all serious and even dangerous times, some humor seems to surface. A local cafe operator had been successfully recruited into the local klavern, but he had concealed his membership even from his wife. He didn't dare leave his Klan robe and hood at home. Instead, he hid the regalia in a copper steam kettle in the back of his cafe. He used those big kettles to steam-heat buns for his hotdogs and hamburgers.

During a busy lunch period, the kettle in use sprung a leak. One of the cooks carried the leaky kettle to the storeroom where he knew there was an extra steamer. He was startled to find a white robe and hood when he took the lid off the stored kettle. Not realizing that it belonged to his boss, he decided to play a joke on his cohorts and customers in the cafe. He donned the Klan uniform and pranced back into the eatery. Just as he did, the boss came through the front door. Horrified, he quickly dragged his helper out of sight, disrobed him, and struck a match to the sheet and hood in the back alley. The evidence disappeared quickly.

The embarrassed restaurateur never admitted to his workers that he knew who put the Klan uniform in his steamer. However, he later told me, "I want you to know that seeing that kid in that robe and mask walk through my cafe was scary. I made a mistake by joining that bunch to begin with. That was the last time I had anything to do with the Klan. I never went to another meeting." He seemed grateful that he wasn't part of the Myrtle Beach mob who had attacked the Fitzgerald place. He could have been in real trouble.

Through the worrisome months of the Klan re-organization up until that time, their recruitment and motives had remained undercover. They carefully picked and chose whom they wanted to invite into the klaverns. There was no open public appeal. But that was to change.

On Halloween night, some message carrier for the Klan attached a flyer to the front door of the *Tribune* office. The same bright red circular was scattered throughout several counties. It was the first indication of the Klan's continued activity since the Myrtle Beach episode. It said:

Public Speaking
The Ku Klux Klan will hold a public demonstration and cross burning in Horry county Saturday night, November 11, 1950 at 8:30 P.M. This public meeting will be held between Mullins and Loris, S. C. on Highway 917 approximately 8 miles from Mullins.

The public is cordially invited to attend.

Come and hear the Klan's side of the Myrtle Beach affair. Hear what the Klan is and what it stands for.

Speakers will be the Grand Dragon of Florida and the Grand Dragon from South Carolina.

This public demonstration is being sponsored by the

ASSOCIATION OF CAROLINA KLANS

Knowing I was on the hit list, it didn't make much sense, but I showed the circular to my apprehensive wife and told her my plans.

"One way or the other I am going to that meeting," I said to her. She couldn't believe it. But I **would** be there.

Chapter Nine
The Dragon Roars

Despite being lambasted in the press throughout the Carolinas following the gangland-style shooting at Charlie Fitzgerald's Myrtle Beach night club, Grand Dragon Hamilton actually gloried in his new-found notoriety. Organizing a powerful Ku Klux Klan would be much easier when his name became a household word, he theorized. It now was. And he never thought that building his movement would be easy and without obstacles. He knew it would not be a rose garden and as far as this erstwhile Leesville grocer was concerned, even bad publicity would help in his two-state recruitment, not to mention the sale of bedsheets.

Tobacco fields covered rural areas.

I called the announced public meeting a recruiting session. Hamilton referred to it as a demonstration. Perhaps it was a little of both, as at least ten thousand men and women flocked through the soft, sandy tobacco field on a cold, rainy November night to see and hear first hand this man who was making all the headlines.

Many of the huge throng attending were curiosity seekers. Others were sympathetic to the Klan cause and looking for ways to aid and abet the reorganization. Still others were anti-Klan but anxious to see just what they had to offer. They saw and heard much more than they had expected. It was not a normal stump speaking, a political tradition in Horry County. At these political rallies candidates for public office appear in person night after night for weeks prior to each election to plead for votes and support. It's an antiquated campaign system, but one cherished by the people then and now. I am not so sure it isn't really the most American way of politicking for votes in any democratic society.

But this Klan meeting was drastically different. Hamilton's platform was the flatbed back of a two and one-half ton farm truck equipped with a microphone. Everything else made it truly a Ku Klux Klan demonstration. It was a show designed to thrill and influence a segment of the listeners who might later slip a completed membership application into the hands of a Klansman. Certainly the underlying purpose was to solicit additional members and enlist public support. The demonstration probably succeeded in both objectives.

As dusk settled over the open field near Mullins, Klansmen began arriving fully cloaked in their KKK robes and hoods. The truck that would be the stage carried a twenty-foot-tall cross made from pine poles. It was wrapped from top to bottom with fertilizer sacks, then called "tow sacks" in reference to the fiber they are made from. A Klansman quickly dug a hole near the parked truck, and after dousing the wrappings with kerosene, he and others stood the cross in its hole. It was imposing—almost surreal.

An hour before the demonstration was to begin, other Klansmen began arriving. Some rode in on white horses. Some hauled horses in on farm trailers. A few robed, masked women began milling around with the handful of Klansmen near the truck. Some men pushed their hoods up enough to smoke cigarettes. One even puffed on a crooked-stem pipe.

Realizing the danger I faced, I tried to be as inconspicuous as possible. Standing unobtrusively with me were my brother-in-law, J. A. Herlocker, who was a strong supporter of my anti-Klan

crusade as well as a compositor in my printshop, and Bill Oakley, also a friend and linotype operator at the *Tribune*. If there were other newspapermen present they had merged into the crowd in similar fashion. I was with my "bodyguards." This was neither the time nor the place to be brave. I hoped I would not be recognized.

With the field rapidly filling with cars and pickup trucks, the Grand Dragon made his appearance in a bright green robe. With his hood pushed back on his forehead, Hamilton was easily recognizable—as he was at all public meetings. He was the only Klansman whose identity was never a secret. He relished his role as the front man. His underlings hid behind the masks, even when they occasionally made short speeches.

"Light the cross," he instructed, "and let's get the show on the road."

A bright, smoky flame raced to the top of the cross as the burning kerosene and sack material cast an eerie glow across the field. Like a regiment of soldiers, both men and women started walking slowly around the cross. Six rode white horses. The well-known hymn, "Amazing Grace," known by every rural church member in the area, rolled across the field. The spectators were quiet. "Amazing Grace" was followed by several Negro spirituals and light classical music pouring forth from the speaker system.

Hamilton tested the loud speaker. He raised his hands to the audience. A hush fell over the crowd. Then he prayed. He often prayed back home in Leesville where he was a deacon in the Baptist church. He was experienced in praying. The crowd was reverent and attentive but was anxious for what was to come.

While Hamilton had advertised the demonstration as a time and place where he would explain the Myrtle Beach motorcade and shooting death of Klansman/Policeman Dan Johnson, he quickly skimmed over that subject. He only reiterated his previous remark that "Charlie Fitzgerald said we better not come back to his place and you know red-blooded American gentlemen are not going to take a dare like that from a nigger."

He did make a point that obviously struck a receptive cord. "I have affidavits showing that people are paying off the law enforcement officers of Horry County for the privilege of doing illegal business. I will expose this corruption in the near future," he said. While he never elaborated, it was widely believed that many officers were being paid to protect moonshiners, white-lightning sales outlets and illegal gambling in the Myrtle Beach area. Hundreds of good people were interested in ending this alleged corruption.

Hamilton was smart enough to know he would gain sympathizers by noting the graft and threatening to expose the offenders. He never did.

He had plenty of other things to criticize. Newspapers were a focus of much of his tirade. "Churches that are controlled by do-gooders who actually want the colored to come to their services are about as bad as the newspapers," he told the crowd, his loud voice echoing across the tobacco field. Later, churches were to feel the wrath of the Klan when they were invaded by the masked mob during worship services in an attempt to intimidate the racially unbiased leadership and congregations.

Half of Hamilton's lengthy speech was severely critical of President Harry Truman, the public schools, colleges and universities, and particularly the United Nations. Hamilton screamed that the United Nations was a vehicle of the Jews of the world with "Jew Alger Hiss, the molder of the UN charter, using his position to undermine the United States and make it possible for the Jews to control the whole world. No United Nations flag will ever fly over a public school in the Carolinas!" Hamilton got a murmur of applause with that fiery remark, but most of his ninety-minute talk was met with near silence—except for an occasional burst of laughter.

"I had never been arrested in my life. I have never even had a parking or speeding ticket. But when Sheriff Sasser came for me after my friend Dan Johnson was shot in Myrtle Beach, they sent fifteen men, two with machine guns, to arrest me. I must really be a dangerous man." At that, laughter erupted near the podium.

"Can you believe that when they put me in jail, there was a nigger in the cell on my left and another on the right? I couldn't believe they would do that to me," he murmured. "I don't like living with niggers even in jail."

At one point he shouted, "You better be careful what you say about the Ku Klux Klan at this meeting. Many of us are out there mingling with you. The man or woman at your elbow may be a Klansman. We didn't all wear our robes tonight. So you better guard your talk if you know what's good for you!" I looked to the right and left. J. A. was on my right, Bill on the left. I knew for sure they weren't Klansmen. I wasn't sure about the rest of the ten thousand. Needless to say, I didn't challenge anything Hamilton said at the meeting. This was his shindig. My time would come the following Wednesday when the *Tribune* went to press.

Near the close of his demonstration (nearly one hundred

51

robed Klansmen had gathered around his truck/platform), Hamilton again concentrated his attack on the Jews.

"President Truman is supposed to be President of the United States, but he is really just a figurehead for the Jews. General George C. Marshall got a Hungarian-born Jew, Mrs. Anna Rosenberg appointed Assistant Secretary of Defense and that's a downright tragedy. Some Methodist churches are holding up services now until they can get some colored people to come to their church. Governor Thurmond had his picture made a few days ago with some 'pinks' (Communists). One of them was a Baptist who had written a mess about the Klan in one of the church's publications.

"Believe me, the Klan will fight every effort of the Congress to give federal aid to education. If they ever give the schools money, they'll take over and we will no longer have any rights as to who goes to our schools. (This statement later proved to be correct.)

"The Justice Department has labeled the Ku Klux Klan subversive. That means they are calling us Communists. The truth is, it's the Justice Department that is communistic and about half of Washington, D.C. is, too."

Among the twenty-seven organizations and programs that Hamilton lambasted at the speaking were the welfare departments.

"Women with a house full of illegitimate children are getting money from the welfare departments. But the widowed mother whose children are legitimate gets nothing. That's how things are going in this country," he noted. That remark hit a receptive nerve among many listeners.

"Two months ago we had two Klan organizations in Horry County. Today we have four. I ask all of you good people who are interested to get in touch with me and help carry on the Klan's great work." As the Grand Dragon concluded he got a little scattered applause.

While Hamilton had announced that Florida Grand Dragon Bill Hendricks, also called Imperial Wizard on occasion, would make a speech at the demonstration, he was not present. Hamilton said Hendricks was hospitalized and he played his recorded message. Hendricks blasted the newspapers first.

"There is no truth in your newspapers. It is a controlled press and the truth is suppressed. Radio stations and the movie industry are just as bad.

"Most Jews are Communists and they are seeking to

overthrow the United States. The KKK is fighting this menace to America," Hendricks charged.

Both Hendricks and Hamilton were viciously critical of the National Association for the Advancement of Colored People. "The NAACP is another Jewish-controlled organization that can get an audience with the U.S. Justice Department, but they won't give me a chance to be heard. They just label us subversive," Hamilton said.

Hamilton's other targets included the United Council of Christian Churches, U.S. Supreme Court, YWCA, the Governor of South Carolina, CIO's Political Action Committee, World Federalists and all "brotherhood" organizations.

The meeting concluded with a benediction, after which a massive traffic jam clogged the rural road for hours.

Tobacco barns dotted every field.

I stepped out of J. A.'s car in front of my house. I had ridden to the meeting with him in hopes that I had less chance of being recognized if I didn't drive my own car.

"Thanks for the ride, J. A., I sure appreciate you and Bill going with me," I said. "I don't believe I would have chanced it alone, and you two let yourself in for some possible harassment by being my bodyguards. I'm thankful nothing happened. We got some first-hand Klan philosophy tonight. I think I can write an editorial for next week's paper that will sink into the minds of a lot of readers. Maybe our going tonight will serve a worthy purpose. See you Monday."

Lucile unlocked the back door, obviously relieved to have me back home safe and sound.

"How did it go?" she asked nervously.

"There was no ruckus. No one recognized me in the dark. Hamilton just criticized the newspapers and about everything else. It was the first time I ever saw a burning cross and Klansmen riding white horses. That was quite a show. I'm glad I went and happy to be back home." I held her in my arms and tried to comfort her, although she was almost inconsolable.

I was sleepless into the wee hours of the morning as I wrestled with a whirlwind of thoughts that raced through my mind. How should I attack this Klan movement next in the *Tribune*? Should I attack it at all? My best friend had said, "You can't take it upon yourself to ride the Ku Klux. They'll drag you out and beat you to a pulp. If I were you, I'd tend to my own business and let them alone."

Tend to my own business? Isn't this Klan uprising the business of everyone who lives in this community? Isn't it the business of the only newspaper editor who gives a whoop about Tabor City? Is it my business to fight injustice wherever I see it? I believed it **was** my business when it threatened the serenity and lives of the people in my community. The KKK represents evil and injustice. There was no turning back now.

I eased out of bed, careful not to wake Lucile, and set my old Royal typewriter on the kitchen table. It was three o'clock when I began writing another front-page editorial. I wrote what I felt.

The next Wednesday, when the paper came off the press, my very best friend read the editorial, shook his head and allowed a somber look to surface. "You have put your neck in a noose," he warned.

Maybe so. We would see.

Chapter Ten
Neck in a Noose

Boldface ten-point type, two columns wide ran from the top of the *Tribune* front page to the bottom. It was my editorial rebuttal to the charges made against people and organizations at the Highway 917 Klan demonstration by Grand Dragon Thomas Hamilton. Saturday night's tirade against so many people was not easily forgotten. I did not forget it. Instead, I wrote these words that I hoped would make an impact on every reader:

> Contrary to the Grand Dragon's claim that his klaverns were filled with Christian, God-fearing Americans, that certainly isn't true. Many are neither Christian nor God-fearing. Rather they are prejudiced, adventursome rascals with little regard for the rights and privileges of others. While their membership is secret, almost everyone knows someone who is a Klansman in this community. Is the one you know a fine, outstanding citizen and Christian gentleman? The chances are your answer is "no."
>
> It is un-American to condemn a race or religion as Hamilton did the Jews, Negroes and Catholics. This melting pot called the United States is made up of a myriad of races and religions (Many of whose ancestors fled from Europe to settle in this New World). As with all races and all religions, there are some bad apples. But you cannot condemn a whole race of people for the sins of a few. Hamilton spent much of his time castigating the Jews in his Saturday night tirade. There are about nine million Jews in the United States. To call all of them Communists is asinine and preposterous. The proportion of Communist Jews to their total population is no greater than that of Anglo-Saxons who make up most of the Klan's prejudiced, self-righteous membership.
>
> Then, to charge that all the newspapers in this land are controlled by the Jews and Communists is reckless disregard for the truth. The daily newspapers of the Carolinas in the 1950's are independently owned by

outstanding local citizens with a high regard for accuracy and truth. They do not suppress anything nor are they controlled by anyone other than the local editors and publishers. As for our little weekly newspaper, everyone in the territory knows we print the news and write editorials based on the dictates of our conscience come hell or high water. We are not always right, but we surely try to be. As a man of wisdom once said of a larger publication, "The *Tribune* columns are written without fear or favor." (Author's note: *Needless to say, there was some question about the fear part of that sentence.*)

Furthermore, the columns of this little community newspaper are open to all, regardless of your beliefs as long as you will sign your names. We shall forever guarantee your right to speak your mind notwithstanding how it conflicts with ours.

The churches and schools of this community and nation are not being led towards communism, as Hamilton declared. That concept has been dredged up because the KKK is being openly opposed by ministers and educators. Anyone who criticizes their back-handed method of transforming the world is the enemy and communistic. Such is Hamilton's claim.

Only the Communist Party and the Ku Klux Klan have secret memberships. If all Klansmen are so pure and clean, as Hamilton declares, and if their activities are always within the law and the constitution, why doesn't the organization charter its Klaverns like other groups and quit hiding behind bedsheets, masks and secret membership? Why is it so mystic? Why were its activities historically carried on in the dead of night, as this current Klan's shenanigans will soon be?

Klansmen have something to hide. They are unwanted by real Americans here and elsewhere. Their very being is repulsive in Columbus and Horry counties. And they promise to be much more offensive in the days ahead when they decide whose moral behavior is acceptable and whose is not. That's been the trademark of the KKK from its inception following the Civil War and again in the 1920's when they organized an estimated five million people nationwide.

Please, won't you just go away?

At that particular moment I could not help but have great sympathy for the Jews in our community. While they were not being attacked individually, their race and religion was a main focus of the Klan. And that didn't make much sense.

In Tabor City, we had my friend and neighbor Albert Schilds who had come from Austria as a child. A hard worker and a thrifty man, he eventually opened his own department store. He was successful and the Tabor City community had never had a more dedicated, free-hearted merchant with compassion for everyone who needed help. He always gave far more than his share to every charity and was interested in the public schools, civic and business clubs. He voted at election time, but other than that, he avoided politics. He married in middle age and had two lovely daughters.

One of his long-time employees, Joe Simon, was also Jewish. Simon was active in the Civitan Club. He was a bachelor and was loved by all who knew him. He never missed a high school athletic event.

Our only other Jewish residents were Dave Simon and his family. He had a small clothing store and was struggling to make a living. An humble man, he was honest, hard-working and likeable. He had no enemies.

I thought about the other Jewish families in the area. In Whiteville, the Columbus County seat, there was Herman Leder and his brother Joe. As small children they left Austria early in this century, worked their way to the United States aboard a merchant ship, and arrived in South Carolina with a fortune totalling nine cents. They worked in a store in Conway, South Carolina for a few cents a day and lived in the upstairs storeroom because they could not afford anything better. After many frugal years of working long hours they opened a small store. From that humble beginning, Leder Brothers Department Stores were established over a large area of the coastal Carolinas. They were attractive, modern businesses that were welcomed in every town in the region.

Furthermore, like Schilds in Tabor City, the Leder brothers, from the moment that they were financially able, became leaders in every charitable movement in their communities. They married Jewish women from nearby counties and raised outstanding families of great character.

Other Jewish families in Whiteville were the Kramers, Manns, Leinwands and Moscows. Those families were like the Leders and Schilds, always active in civic and business affairs and they had unusual compassion for the underprivileged. In time, the Jewish community built a synagogue, a beautiful structure that was a credit to the area. It attracted Jewish worshipers from several counties.

The eldest of the Mann family was Joe. He served as commander of the American Legion post in Whiteville, and was later honored with an appointment to a state American Legion rank that he filled with distinction. He liked to sing and often entertained with a solo at civic and other community meetings.

The Robert Wolpert family in Loris, South Carolina, operated a store for two generations and were highly respected.

Also in Horry County, the Banner family was in business in Conway. They were stalwarts in their community's progress. They had a fine store that compared with the best in many larger cities. They never shirked their humanitarian obligations, a characteristic of all the Jews within the *Tribune*'s circulation area.

While the Jews made up only a tiny portion of the population in Columbus and Horry counties, their unselfish contribution to the less fortunate families and charitable organizations was proportionally much greater than their numbers. They helped significantly with every project.

The Jewish population had another distinction. Not one member of any Jewish family in either county had ever been in court for any reason—criminal or civil. They paid their taxes and lived exemplary lives for generations. Few in the communities in which they lived thought of them as being different from anyone else. These were the Jews that the Grand Dragon slandered and verbally abused at his public demonstration.

Our editorial had asked the Klan to go away. I knew that they wouldn't. Instead, they continued their rapid growth and as Thanksgiving and Christmas came and went, the dues-paying Klansmen chomped at the bit for action.

They wanted to show their power. Their despotic lawlessness, unlike any ever seen in the coastal Carolinas, was unleashed during the third week of January. Night-riding vigilantes took it upon themselves to be judge, jury and executioners by flogging helpless victims in three rural communities in a single week.

My three-column, forty-eight-point bold-type headline in the *Tribune* told the story. It read:

NIGHT-RIDING TERRORISTS BEAT
DISABLED VET, CRIPPLED FARMER
AND SICK, ELDERLY NEGRO WOMAN

I had predicted that worse things were yet to come. This was the start of the reign of terror. Hundreds of readers were shocked to hear of the brutality. Many hadn't believed the Ku Klux would really harass people in their homes. Some thought that I was reactionary when I suggested such lawlessness would follow the

KKK resurrection as it always had in the past in these same communities. But I was sure you couldn't organize a gang of troublemakers and appease them by holding meetings and talking about the price of tobacco. They would want to use those sheets and hoods for the bedevilment of others. They did.

Strangely, few people raised their voices to protest the terrorists. Not even the pastor in the Tabor City Baptist Church, where I taught a Sunday School class, would publicly criticize the Klan floggings. Businessmen didn't want to alienate customers—and Klansmen were customers. An ominous silence crept over the community following these beatings.

The virus of fear was spreading. Subscriber after unbelieving subscriber picked up the *Tribune* and read about the triple floggings that occurred right on our own doorsteps. Whom would they attack next? Could **I** be their next target?

When I reported on the triple floggings, I related the gory details as vividly as I could, hoping it would convince some so-called good people of the evils of this modern Ku Klux Klan. I prayed that it would. The night terror had to stop. We were truly at war with our neighbor—maybe the one who lived next door. Tragically we didn't know whether he was friend or foe.

Blacks were poorly housed in structures like this and Klansmen had little trouble smashing down doors to reach their victims, like Evergreen Flowers.

I continued my weekly crusade.

Chapter Eleven
Floggings in the Night

It was midnight on January 15, 1951, when armed Klansmen crashed through the front door of Willie and Evergreen Flowers' humble unpainted home in the Broadway section of Columbus County, twelve miles north of Tabor City. Willie, Evergreen and their ten-year-old daughter were asleep when "ten or eleven cars stopped in front of our house," the sickly mother later related.

Klansmen numbering forty to fifty poured out of the cars and approached the house. There was a loud knock on the door. Willie ran to a back room and found his old twelve-gauge shotgun. But he had no shells. He dropped the useless weapon on the floor, dashed out the back door and headed for his brother's house a short distance away, hoping to get help from relatives.

"I heard five pistol shots inside the house before I was out of the yard and I prayed that they hadn't killed Evergreen and my child," he said later. "Then I heard loud talking and my wife screamed. I ran to my brother's house, but he wasn't about to go back with me. There were too many of them Klansmen for us to fight. I just sat down and cried. Evergreen had been sick for weeks with consumption. She coughed all the time, We were black folks, but we hadn't done nothing to hurt nobody," Willie recalled the trauma of that night when his home was invaded.

After breaking down the door of the house, a dozen Klansmen dragged a cowering Evergreen and her weeping daughter Mavella outside. One trigger-happy night rider put five shots through the roof, believing Willie was hiding in the attic. Nobody had seen Willie race out the back door. Five empty cartridge shells were later found in the house by the sheriff to substantiate the shooting claim.

A car trunk was opened and Evergreen was shoved inside. Then she heard someone say, "Oh, hell, we can't get him. Let's just teach her a lesson and leave her here."

61

She was dragged out of the trunk and beaten—flogged was the term widely used at the time—severely. The aftermath of a gun butt's crashing on her head was an ugly gash. Several Klansmen held her while she was beaten with sticks and whips from the waist down, inflicting hideous bruises over much of her lower body. Her injuries were later treated at the Columbus County Hospital in Whiteville.

One Klansman used a razor to cut a cross in her hair all the way to the scalp and blood flowed down her neck and face. Throughout the ordeal she begged for her life while her daughter cringed and watched from the porch, where she was held by two burly Klansmen.

Finally they left. Willie came home and carried his wife and daughter to the hospital.

Not once during the flogging did anyone reveal the reason why this poor and helpless family had been chosen for such punishment. Conjecture was that these self-appointed moral authoritarians suspected Willie of infidelity, but the Klan never named a reason for the unmerciful abuse.

Frightened black neighbors would not discuss the incident. They would only admit to seeing some cars parked at the Flowers home and hearing some shots. They wouldn't identify anyone or any license plate numbers. One neighbor reluctantly said that the license plates looked like those from Virginia.

Newly-elected Columbus County Sheriff Hugh H. Nance, who investigated the flogging, said that the Virginia and South Carolina plates were the same colors that year. He believed the Klansmen were from South Carolina, but he could never get enough evidence to make an arrest.

It was the first of many floggings in the Tabor City area that went unpunished month after scary month.

On the very same night that the Flowers family home was invaded, a group of similar size (ten or eleven cars with forty to fifty Klansmen) knocked down the front door of the home of J. C. Gore and his uncle Sam, some fifteen miles away in Horry County. At about 1:30 in the morning robed and hooded invaders yanked J. C., a twenty-five-year-old disabled veteran from his bed. He had earned the purple heart in World War II. The Klansmen pushed him out into the yard and whipped him with a leather belt until he collapsed.

Other Klansmen stayed inside and flogged Sam, who had been crippled since a 1942 automobile accident. He was left crumpled on the floor.

Without so much as a single word as to why the floggings were being administered, the robed and hooded mobsters went back to their cars and drove away. The victims were treated at the Conway Hospital emergency room for multiple cuts and bruises.

The Gores were typical Anglo-Saxon farmers, natives of Horry County, who had never been in trouble with the law. Race was certainly not a consideration in this vigilante action. Again, like the Flowers incident, interested friends and relatives assumed that the KKK was judging moral conduct. But no one ever knew for sure.

Sheriff Sasser had said little about the Klan movement in his county since the grand jury had failed to return a true bill against the seven local residents charged in the shooting escapade at Myrtle Beach in the fall. He had claimed to be investigating and said he was serious about bringing Klan criminals to justice. So he again arrested the same seven defendants that he suspected in the Myrtle Beach case. He believed they were guilty of the Gore floggings, too. Once again, they all posted $5,000 bonds, as they had in the beach case, and none ever went to court. The grand jury refused to indict them for "lack of evidence."

Sheriff Sasser announced to the press that he was immediately deputizing scores of men throughout the county whose names would remain secret, but who would have full power and authority to investigate Klan shenanigans. With this secret law enforcement organization, he hoped to acquire information otherwise impossible to uncover. The citizenry generally was skeptical of the appointments, and if they were indeed deputized, none ever surfaced or made an arrest.

The brutal beatings of the unfortunate Gores aroused the public and Sasser was asked if he would request help from Governor James F. Byrnes. He said he would not at that time because he didn't feel that it was necessary.

In the meantime. Governor Byrnes, who had vowed before he took office that there would be no place for the Ku Klux Klan in South Carolina, said, "We do have a few people who want to take the law into their own hands and regulate the moral habits of others. If a man violates the law, he should be arrested by local officers. If they fail to act and a complaint is made to the State Law Enforcement Division, the offender will be arrested." The governor's statement was reassuring to many in Horry County who had little faith in Sheriff Sasser.

Shortly after the triple flogging, Tabor City and all of Columbus and Horry counties were flooded with flyers castigating

Sheriff Sasser, while praising the right of the Klan to organize and grow. It rang a bell in the minds of the older people. Would this uprising compare with the most powerful of all Klan movements, the one that bragged of five million members in the 1920's? That KKK had been strong in South Carolina. Could it regain that prominence nearly three decades later? Most people shuddered at the thought of such a Klan reorganization.

Founded by "Colonel" William Joseph Simmons in 1915 in Atlanta as a fraternal order for white Protestants who were native born, this second Klan (the first was begun after the Civil War) recorded only a few thousand members in Georgia and Alabama during its first five years. Then the colonel hired two professional promoters, Elizabeth Clarke and Edward Tyler, to help him recruit Klansmen. They succeeded in getting unusual newspaper publicity and the secret order's membership jumped into the millions within four years.

Quickly, the KKK began to dominate political life in several states. The Klan of that period was not only racist, it was also nativist, anti-Catholic, anti-Semitic and morally authoritarian. It found reason after reason for flogging hundreds of people scattered over many states.

In Horry County, there was a strong Klan from 1922 until 1925. Anonymous groups with traditional hoods and robes severely beat five residents and threatened at least twenty others during that period. It was a period of collective violence by ordinary people motivated in some strange fashion to influence life in rural Horry County.

Horry was a land of dense swamps and depended upon turpentine and cotton in its early years. The black population was small. Then there was a population explosion from 1900 until 1930 when farming changed to tobacco and lumbering. The number of farms jumped from 1,637 to 5,283 and the average acreage of improved farmland per farm increased from 7.4 to 33.2. The county's black population rose to 9,611 from 6,322. The native whites began looking for a rallying haven, listening for a cry that would bolster and preserve their superiority.

Three klaverns were active in that period in Horry. One was in the county seat of Conway, another was located between Conway and Loris and the third was at Little River on the coast at the North/ South Carolinas border. The klavern between Conway and Loris recruited at least two ministers, a constable and two county policemen. The Klansmen then paid ten dollars for robes and hoods as a part of membership fees. Few meetings were held, other than those flogging raids when they inflicted brutal beatings upon their neighbors in the community.

The strong Klan of the 1920's openly stressed opposition to Catholics, blacks and Jews. But in the South and Southwest its raids focused on intimidation of those within the community whose morals they sought to regulate.

An examination of more than 200 episodes of Klan violence in Louisiana, Texas, Arkansas and Oklahoma by Charles Alexander, reported in *Ku KLux Klan in the Southwest*, found that the victims were generally native whites who had violated the community's moral code. Prostitution, bootlegging, wife-beating and adultery were the most common reasons for Klan floggings. The community's desire for moral reform gave the Klan impetus.

In Horry County, seventeen of the twenty-five victims of the early Klan beatings were native whites suspected of immoral behavior. The first victim to suffer Klan justice was Mace Horn, a white farmer who lived in the Floyds Township. He was a prosperous man who often paid the fines and posted bail for convicted bootleggers. White whiskey manufacturing was a profitable business at that time. It was illegal because no taxes were paid on the booze and it was in great demand because of Prohibition. The Klan apparently suspected that Horn was a silent partner in the illegal moonshining ventures at Floyds and other remote sites in Horry County.

On a Sunday evening November 12, 1922, Horn was visiting his girlfriend. They were sitting quietly on a couch in her living room when three masked men burst into the room. Armed with pistols, they commanded Horn to come with them. Blindfolded and handcuffed, he was shoved into a waiting car that raced down the unpaved road, stopped several times (apparently at crossroads) and Horn heard his captors yell to others to "come on." He estimated his assailants carried him about fifteen miles before stopping the car and dragging him out. Voices all around him convinced Horn that there were forty or fifty people in the mob. A leader designated several of the Klansmen to stand guard while Horn was beaten severely. They pressured him to reveal information about a whiskey still in the community and a shooting in which his brother had been involved. He refused. One of his assailants used a razor-sharp knife to cut three notches out of Horn's ears. Bleeding, bruised and battered from head to foot, Horn was released in a remote section off Highway 9 near Nichols. They kicked him out of the car and left him to catch a ride back home. Shades of Charlie Fitzgerald!

Within a week of the Horn flogging, five other men received written warnings from the Klan. Sixty robed men took Bright Shelley from his home and carried him to a graveyard. He was told that he would soon be in a grave just like those around him if he didn't stop drinking, driving recklessly, swearing and mistreating his wife.

Other Klan raids focused on John Rogers and J. D. Anderson in connection with bootleg whiskey. Rogers, a constable (rural policeman) at Finklea Crossroads in South Carolina, was ordered to do a better job of enforcing Prohibition. Anderson was told to quit grinding meal at his grist mill. Meal is a primary ingredient in making "stumphole whiskey," as it was often called.

At the same time, J. C. Grainger and E. B. Sarvis received scrawled notes warning them that their way of life had been deemed unacceptable. They were warned to start attending Sunday School and church regularly or else.

All of the victims of that Klan scheme were farmers with land holdings of more than one hundred acres. The Klan didn't restrict its weird form of justice to only the poor.

Ten months after receiving the warning note, John Rogers was ambushed on a farm-to-market road near his home. A band of men, estimated to number about seventy-five, pulled him from his car, tied him to a tree and whipped him unmercifully with a buggy whip. They shaved off his hair and flowing beard. They also cut the hair of his companion Cret Huggins. She was a woman tenant on Rogers' farm. The Klan suspected the two were having an affair.

These incidents of floggings in Horry were all related to alleged immoral conduct. But on December 9, 1922, Daniel Duncan, a farmer with over five hundred acres of land in the Green Sea-Floyds section, received a warning for an entirely different reason. He was warned to remove a fence that was blocking an entrance road to a neighbor's home. A note signed "KKK" warned that if he didn't remove the fence "we will get you."

Duncan disregarded the notice. In January 1923, Duncan answered a knock at his door and was greeted by rapid gunfire. He saw no one as he ducked back inside unhurt. Two weeks later, on January 27, eight masked men fired twenty-four shotgun blasts at him as he rode by Grassy Bay Baptist Church in his buggy. His horse and buggy were peppered with the shot, but he escaped by flattening himself on the buggy floorboards.

The Duncan ambush that followed so closely the previous

five incidents in Horry County brought a loud outcry from angry influential citizens. They were disturbed over the breakdown in law and order and their insistence promoted local law enforcement officers to summon assistance from Governor Thomas McLeod. He promptly sent Constable W. W. Rogers to head an investigation that led to the arrest of eight men. He traced the shells that were used to ambush Duncan. The findings were that eight men, namely Monroe Hill, Albert Pridgen, M. C. Blackwell, Memory Pridgen, Stog Grainger, Lloyd Jolly, John W. Hill and Maybury Hill had fired the shots. Five of those charged lived in the same community as Duncan. Albert Pridgen was a Baptist minister. Three of the eight confessed to the crime and incriminated the others. John W. Hill was the ringleader. He had asked the organized Klan to help in the ambush of Duncan, but when he got no assistance, he formed "a little Klan of his own." All eight defendants were found guilty of rioting. Six were fined fifty to two hundred dollars and given suspended six month sentences.

Three weeks after the Samuel Duncan shooting at Grassy Bay Church, Sam Holden, a tenant on the Singleton Bay Farm in Socastee, received one of the dreaded notes signed "KKK." He was told to leave Horry County within twenty days. Investigators found that the warning resulted from an argument Holden had with neighbors who had hunted on his land.

On October 5, 1924, ten masked men took George Powers, the town marshall at Loris, into the country and warned him to stop his strict enforcement of Prohibition, particularly the confiscation of ginger. In Georgia and Alabama similar cases of terrorism involving threats to revenue agents and informants had made the news. Further investigation of the Duncan case revealed that another reason for his being ambushed was his willingness to tell officers where certain illicit stills were operating—generally a no-no in that era.

The 1920's Klan counted blacks and Jews among their sworn enemies, but Klansmen attacked few members of either group. In the Horry area, blacks and Jews received threats during the Klan's reign of terror. On May 19, 1924, ten masked men paid a visit to Max Goldstein, a dry goods store owner in Conway. They called him out of his home at three o'clock in the morning. Several of the Klansmen pointed guns at this head and told him that Conway was "white man's country." He was unwanted. Goldstein attributed his warning to the courteous service he gave blacks in his store. Authorities believed his ethnic background was the real reason for the threat.

Later that same year, an official of the Conway Lumber Company wrote a letter to the governor complaining about an anonymous note that had been sent to some of his black laborers who had been working a section of the county commonly referred to as the "deadline territory."

It was a long-standing tradition in that part of the county between Conway and Aynor that no blacks were allowed there, either to work or to live. Several years earlier, during the administration of Governor Martin Ansel, some residents of the area had tried to enlarge the territory by attacking black work camps that were operated by the lumber companies nearby. The governor and local law enforcement officers managed to restore order. Then in the midst of the Klan uprising in the twenties, black workers were again being warned to stay out of the "deadline territory." The warnings read:

> Gallivants Ferry, S.C.
> To you colored folks we have to carry out our line of business and you all no (sic) where you are and we have got a dose for you and if these don't move your bowels I thing (sic) the next will.
> Signed: The white hand
> (drawing of a bullet)

There was much talk at that time about the Klan's involvement in politics. In 1922, the Klan had a nationwide campaign to elect candidates friendly to its programs, an effort which had been highly successful in many places. Horry County had Klan and anti-Klan tickets in the municipal election of 1924. But the Conway Klan sent a letter to the newspaper denying that it sponsored a particular slate of candidates. M. R. Smith, a candidate for reelection, reported that there was such a list and that his name had incorrectly appeared on it.

The Klan issue divided the county. Conflicting views regarding the KKK were expressed in numerous letters to the *Conway Herald.* One anonymous writer who identified herself only as a mother, called on others to "pray for them (the Klansmen) and help them take the bitter cup from our boys and the examples that are being set for them."

Contrasting that letter, M. G. Anderson, a member of the school board, complained that he was being pressured by the Klan to accept a number of books that the KKK had contributed to the library.

The newspapers of that era seldom denounced the Klan. In one publicized case the *Herald* expressed complete approval of the Klan when its intervention in a case resulted in the reunion of an unfaithful husband and his family. Evidence of the Klan's community support is best understood in light of the fact that no arrests were ever made. The eight who were arrested in the Duncan case were not truly members of the organized KKK, but were a splinter group.

Incidents of collective violence in Horry County appeared to outsiders to be little more than unrelated neighborhood feuds. There was no real conclusion bringing a better understanding of why the violence erupted and lingered for so long. Common people had motives, trivial as they were, and many acted in a fit of passion at every provocation.

As the population increased and industries moved into Horry county, changes occurred. The influx of new people provided greater opportunities for "sin" and also brought pressure to farm more intensively. Industrialization, especially by the lumbering interests, brought blacks into sections of the county where few had ever stepped before. These early agents of collective violence, like the Ku Klux Klan and its splinter groups in Horry county, sought to preserve community values and customs in the face of drastic social and industrial change. As word spread about Klan violence and internal corruption, the respectable elements in the secret order dropped out. The movement died in Horry County and the violence stopped when the Klansmen realized that some of their leaders had the same weaknesses as the people they were trying to reform. One Klan leader had abandoned his wife and family, but later returned when his mother was near death. A group of one hundred Klansmen met him upon his arrival at the Conway train station, all wearing robes and hoods. They clubbed him with pistols as he got off the train and carried him into the countryside and beat him some more. Incidents like that weakened the Klan movement in Horry to the point that it vanished from view by the end of 1924.

I studied all of these records of the defunct KKK of the 1920's. Would it gain strength and again sweep the area with its collective violence, so despicable and widespread, as it did during that infamous time when Horry was only a few decades removed from total desolation? We were a hard-working, progressive people now. We didn't need vigilantes.

I knew the *Tribune* would never run a story of our own about the KKK reuniting a family as the *Herald* in Conway did. Instead, we would editorialize against this lawless mob with every ounce of

No offset printing . . .type came from linotypes.

Printing on hand-fed flat sheets.

strength we had. I hoped that we would not have to report other floggings of cripples, purple heart recipients and black women as we had just written.

I picked up a *New York Times* dated November 10, 1950, and read, "A new Klan has appeared in Horry and Columbus counties in the Carolinas. This Klan of the 1950's is concerned with race, not morals."

Just how wrong could they be? This Klan was no different from that of the 1920's. And time would certainly prove that point.

Chapter Twelve
Death Threats

I had just sat down to eat dinner when the telephone rang, further irritating jangled nerves that seldom relaxed from a steady barrage of phone threats, both at home and at the office.

It was two days after my story appeared with the gory details of the Thursday night KKK rampage. That cowardly attack in the dead of night had sent a sickly black lady, a crippled farmer and a disabled World War II veteran to the hospital with multiple bruises and cuts from brutal floggings in their humble rural homes. The story had made the KKK look bad.

With my nerves frayed from this avalanche of threatening calls, I picked up the receiver. I still remember every frightening word of that unforgettable conversation as if it happened last night.

"Is this Mr. Horace Carter? Are you the one that runs the Tabor City paper?" the deep, slow, almost ominous voice inquired.

"Yes, I am Horace Carter and I edit the *Tribune* here," I replied, all the time telling myself it was just another of those silly anonymous threats like many others that I had received almost daily for months. Those that came to my home phone worried my wife, but unknown to her, even more were received on the office phone. "What can I do for you?"

There was a short pause and the caller spoke in a tone that relayed the deadly seriousness of his message. Suddenly it felt like minnows were flouncing in my veins. I knew he was not playing games and that he had placed his call in an effort to help, not to threaten me.

"Mr. Carter, you do not know me," he began. "I am a medical doctor in Myrtle Beach. I have never seen your newspaper, but I have heard about the campaign you have been waging against the Ku Klux Klan there in your community and down here on the beach. You have angered the Klan leadership to such an extent that they're going to kill you, or at least they plan to.

"Strictly by accident, I overheard someone on my telephone just a few minutes ago contracting to have you killed. I had made a call to Atlanta in connection with my medical practice when two voices broke in on the line I was using. It was a freakish interruption, but I heard several minutes of their conversation.

"The call was apparently from a man in South Carolina to a hit man in Tampa, Florida. I don't know where the South Carolina man was, but the hit man he was talking with said that it would be a few days before he could leave Tampa. But give him a little time and he would do the job. He asked about where your house was located, its proximity to neighbors and the street. The caller told him the house was only a block from downtown Tabor City and that he had pictures of the house to give him.

"He told him that you were home most nights fairly early and the job ought to be easy. I don't know what price they have on your head, but the Tampa man specifically asked if the price previously agreed upon was still the contract. He assured him that it was and that the quicker he could perform his contract the better. They didn't mention killing, but I know that was what they were talking about.

"That's what I heard and I thought you at least ought to know about it."

Trying hard to believe this might be just another attempt to frighten me away from the crusade and even run me out of town, I asked, "How did you know to call me?"

"The South Carolina caller mentioned Horace Carter and Tabor City," he replied. "He said you and your newspaper were printing lies about his organization and that you had to be stopped. I called the Tabor City Police Department before I called you. They gave me your number."

The caller certainly seemed sincere.

"Thank you so much. Won't you give me your name? I certainly owe you a lot for warning me," I said.

"No, I don't want to get tangled up with the mess. There are plenty of Klansmen right here in my neighborhood and all over the county. If my name got scattered around about this phone call, I might be in for some trouble myself. I just couldn't sit here and ignore the message I heard. I think you are doing the right thing. I don't want you to get killed over it."

I thanked the caller again and hung up the phone. I must have been more than a little pale and shook up when I returned to the table and sat down.

"What's wrong?" Lucile asked expectantly.

"It's nothing. Just another threat someone from Myrtle Beach heard," I said, doing my best to lie with a straight face.

At that moment the front doorbell rang and I jumped. I suppose I imagined the hit man had made a quick trip from Tampa. Lucile went to the door. Night Policeman Ted Watts was standing there. He obviously had a mission.

"Mrs. Carter, is Horace at home?" he asked.

"Yes, come in," she invited.

"Hi, Ted, what's on your mind?" I asked as I pushed away from the table and greeted him near the door.

Ted looked at me and then at Lucile as if he wanted to say something very private. Lucile made no move to leave, so he looked back at me and asked:

"Did you get a Myrtle Beach telephone call a few minutes ago?" his somber face telling a story.

"Yeah, I did. Some doctor said he had overheard a phone conversation. The Klan was going to eliminate me. Probably some quack. Don't let it worry you," I said in a reassuring tone meant for my wife. "It might have been a Klansman calling who just wanted to scare me."

"Well, you are probably right. Just someone trying to unnerve you. He called the police station before he called you, and he told me about what he had heard. I thought I should check it out with you. I think you better be careful. Don't go out at night alone for awhile, and call us if there is any reason to be suspicious," Ted said, as he put his cap back on and headed for the door. "I'm going to tell the town board about this. They may want to station a bodyguard with you for a few days."

"That won't be necessary, but thanks, Ted. I appreciate your concern," I said, looking at Lucile, whose eyes were misty and frightened.

I held her in my arms a moment and we went back to the dinner table where the two children were rubbing food all over their faces.

"Don't worry about it, honey, that doctor may have been a Klansman just trying to scare us out of the crusade. Nothing would put more pressure on them than killing me or any other editor who is fighting them. That would really bring down the newspapers everywhere on the Klan. They wouldn't dare do that," I tried to console her even while I wasn't that sure in my own mind.

The next morning S. Porcher Smith, a longtime friend,

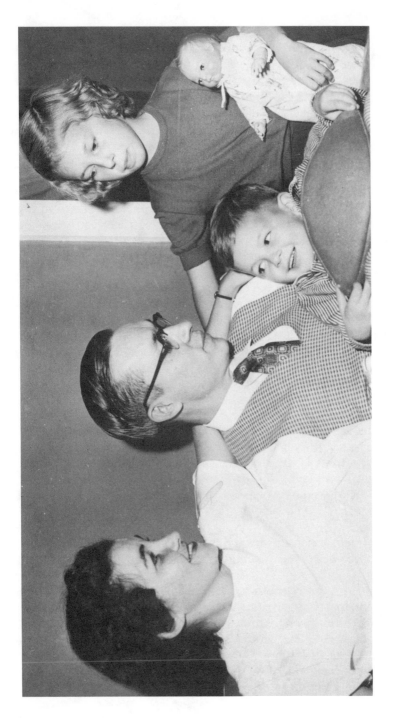

Lucile and I with Rusty and Linda.

fellow Rotarian and the charter president of the Tabor City Merchants Association, walked into the office. At that time he lived in Myrtle Beach and sub-let the back bedroom in the house where we lived. Some evenings he chose to stay in Tabor City, where his Carolina Department Store was located rather than drive the forty miles to the beach.

"Horace, you planning to do something to the house?" he asked. "I saw some fellow park on the street and make pictures a few days ago."

That got my attention.

"Did you recognize the man or the car or anything?" I inquired with obvious concern.

"No, but the car had a South Carolina license plate," he said. "He shot a dozen or more pictures while I watched from the window."

Suddenly it didn't seem like a bad idea if the police looked in on me for a few days. But with just a two-man police department, that wouldn't be easy.

A part-time policeman began a surveillance of my house every night for a week. The Town Board had decided the threat Policeman Watts heard from the Myrtle Beach caller was worth respecting.

The hit man never showed up.

The Carter home on Railroad Street.

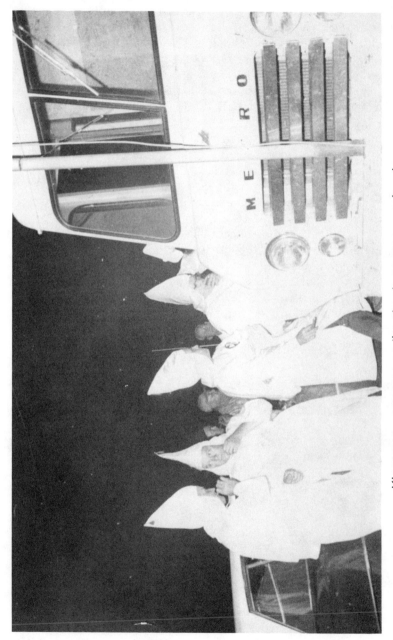

Klansmen were seen on the streets on many weekends.

Chapter Thirteen
Cryptic Messages

In mid-February I opened the office door one morning to find four mimeographed sheets printed in red ink face-up on the floor. I picked them up.

Three of the sheets had a rough drawing of a mean-looking wharf rat at the top. In no uncertain terms, the circulars sought to intimidate any Horry citizen who accepted one of the community deputy appointments that Sheriff Ernest Sasser had said he would name to rout out the secret membership and bring the vigilantes to justice. Under one of the crude rat drawings were the words:

> If you accept one of these deputy jobs, you are part of the gestapo that the scared sheriff needs to do his dirty work. You will be a rat just like the one at the top of this page. You will be another scalawag standing in the way of the noble work of the Ku Klux Klan in Horry County. Don't join the sheriff. Join the KKK and fight for your family and justice. Don't support a sheriff who allows bootlegging in every swamp and never does a thing about it.
>
> THE KKK NEWS

Other sheets were manila four-by-seven-inch cards, also printed in red ink. One said:

> Any citizen who accepts a community deputy sheriff appointment to help Sheriff Sasser is the lowest kind of rat. And you better think twice before taking such a job. The Klan will have its eye on you. THE KKK NEWS.

The last of the messages was critical of the newspapers of the area. One editor had referred to Sheriff Sasser as "the Klan-busting sheriff." (Not the *Tribune.* We knew better.) Another had called Sheriff Sasser "a hard-hitting sheriff." The Klan news bulletin sarcastically lambasted Sasser as a wealthy, do-nothing law enforcement officer.

The same day that Klan-printed missives were slipped under our door, Shepherd Strickland, a farmer in the Clarendon area, four miles from Tabor City, brought two handwritten warning letters to the newspaper office. Both had been slipped under his door on the same night.

The letters were written by different persons and on different types of paper, but the messages were similar. The letters, with poor grammar and spelling, read:

> We the KKK Clawn are warned you for the first and last time. If you don't treat your family like they ought to be treated, we will give you what you ned. We have heard that you have had a lot to say about the church of Christ. That will have to be stoped to. If it dont you know what will hapen. You have called them ever thing they arent and about them spells you have when you are drinken that will have to stop and also your drinking. They can tell that your belly was not made from drinken water. Your Enemys. KKK. The KKK leaders.

The other message was similar in content. It read:

> KKK
>
> Mr. Shepherd Strickland
>
> We the KKK's are warning you for the first and last time. If you don't let your famaly go to church we are going to give you what you need. You are the weorse man in the country. But the laws don't do eny thing about it. If this happen eny more we are going to take your hair off.
>
> We have know of your talking about them. You have called them ever thing. These people are not what you called them and we are going to take over from now on. The Church of Christ are the right ones. The People You Don't Like. K.K.K. The K.K.K. Reporter.

Shepherd said he believed the messages came from people in the community who didn't like him—not the Klan, but of course, that was conjecture. They never did anything, or at least if they did, Shepherd never told us.

The Klan circulars, along with rhetoric spread at their public meetings, were so critical of Sheriff Sasser that it seemed time to write an editorial on that particular subject. At day's end, we found the time to peck out these words for next week's front page:

78

BRING THE CHARGES TO COURT

This week the Ku Klux Klan circulated in Tabor City and elsewhere a circular headed "KKK NEWS" that charged Horry County Sheriff Ernest Sasser with embezzlement, corruption and graft.

This mysterious little mimeographed bulletin flung around many blind charges and went so far as to suggest that the county needs a Kefauver investigation (Author's Note: *Kefauver was making headlines at the time with his investigation of organized crime).* It charged in a kind of subtle way that the sheriff had sold out to the gambling interests. Yet, this guided missile that found its way under our office door carried no signature and can be regarded as just another piece of trash.

We have no complimentary remarks to make about Sheriff Sasser. But if this band of hoodlum mystery men have one shred of evidence to support their claims against the sheriff, why don't they bring the charges to the attention of South Carolina Governor Jimmy Byrnes? The governor has made no bones about it. He wants to and will take every necessary action to enforce the laws of the state and the nation, and if there is graft and illegal shenanigans going on here, he can and will do something about it.

If this band of night riders called the KKK are afraid to bring these charges up against the sheriff in the name of the Klan, and if they are righteous citizens with nothing to hide, they can bring the charges to the governor as private citizens. As citizens of Horry County they have the right to complain if they have reason to believe that irregularities are going on. But as long as the persons who supposedly have the goods on the sheriff persist in trying to cure the evil by themselves in a vigilante, backhanded, illegal manner, they will continue to make nothing but trouble.

This newspaper has made extensive efforts to track down some of the charges made against the sheriff by the Klan. We believe it would be to the advantage of the citizens of Horry County to establish or refute the truth in the rumors and KKK insinuations. We cannot say whether all these reports are true or false. We simply know that they are extremely difficult to prove and Sheriff Sasser remains innocent until proven guilty in a court of law. That's the constitutional due process on which much of the judicial system is founded.

We have talked with several influential citizens who say the Klan does have proof that illegal activities in

Horry County law enforcement are going on, especially in the bootlegging industry. If it is true, it is deplorable and we stand ready to help do something about it in a legitimate and above-board manner. Give us something to work with.

Hamilton and others continued to lambaste the sheriff. But no charges were ever brought before the court. His reputation for allowing lawlessness attracted many followers to the Klan who believed there was corruption and hoped the Klan might be a way of correcting it, but still nothing was done about it. How could one corrupt system hope to correct another?

Another humorous incident which comes to mind arose in the midst of all the threats and accusations. With the illegal manufacture of bootleg whiskey entwined in the Klan news every week, the public was well aware that it took sugar to make the stumphole booze. Sugar was scarce after World War II and was therefore strictly rationed. Federal officers investigated throughout Columbus and Horry counties, hotbeds of moonshining operations, tracking down the sources of the illegal sugar sales that went to the bootleggers. Without it, they were out of business.

One of the town drunks was named Charles C. Sells. Almost every week he was in city court charged with being drunk and disorderly. His name appeared in the *Tribune* record of court cases almost as regularly as the masthead. The Klan took note of his constant drunkenness and sent him several warnings to straighten up and take better care of his wife and children. The community generally was aware that Sells did have a drinking problem. That indirectly created a problem for another citizen.

One of the town's most prosperous and influential businessmen had the same name: Charles C. Sells. He ran the largest store in town, selling clothing, groceries, appliances, furniture and hardware. He was an active church and civic leader and was involved in local politics.

One Wednesday after the newspaper was on the street with another court story telling of Charles C. Sells being again found guilty of being drunk and disorderly, the influential merchant walked into the office.

"Horace, would you mind running a little note in the newspaper next week saying that the Charles C. Sells who is often found guilty of being drunk and disorderly is not the Charles C. Sells who runs the store with the same name in Tabor City?" he asked. "Some of my friends get the wrong idea." "I'll be glad to," I said, and I ran such a message the following week.

The paper with the clarification about Charles C. Sells, the drunk, not being the one who ran the store had hardly had time for the ink to dry when the alcoholic Charles C. Sells came into the office with the *Tribune* in his hand.

"Ho-Ho-Horace," he stammered, and you could tell he was about three sheets in the wind, "would you run this little piece in the paper next week?" And he handed me a scribbled note. It read: *"I would like for my friends to know that the Charles C. Sells who is always in city court for being drunk and disorderly is not the same Charles C. Sells who was convicted in federal court a few years ago for selling five thousand pounds of sugar illegally to the local bootleggers. Signed. Charles C. Sells."*

At a time when I was constantly on edge and fear ran rampant throughout the community, that little bit of humor was a welcomed moment and only vaguely connected with the KKK.

But the fight with the Klan was still on and the situation would get much worse before it got better.

Governor Herman Talmadge, one of the white supremacy politicians, had signed a bill that week in Georgia making it illegal to "wear a mask in Georgia, burn a cross or intimidate people." He was trying to avoid the shameful activities of the Carolinas Klan.

A few quiet months passed. Then there was another Klan motorcade crawling through the Negro section. It was May and the KKK was marauding again.

The Klan always came up Railroad Street.

81

Farmers were busy with produce crops.

This main square scene shows the center of activity.

Chapter Fourteen
Another Motorcade

Tobacco was growing. Plants had reached knee-high. The money crop looked promising. The Ku Klux Klan had been quiet for three months. There would be money in the pockets of tobacco farmers when the crop was harvested, cured, graded and put on the auction floors in July. To keep recruiting on the upswing, it was time to make a show. The KKK coffers had to be kept full if the Grand Dragon and his cohorts were to continue living high on the hog. The time was right for another motorcade and Tabor City was one of the towns the Klan wanted to impress.

The newspaper was not forewarned this time. Sirens screamed about ten o'clock on Saturday night. It seemed they always chose Saturdays for motorcades. I had already gone to bed. Suspecting that this was the return of the night riders, I dressed and walked up Railroad Street to the business district.

"What's going on?" I asked Deland Leonard who was standing in front of his garage/service station located at the corner of Live Oak and Railroad Streets.

"The Ku Klux just drove through town again. They have headed for the 'bottom' (the section of town where all the Negroes lived), but they'll come back through here," he said.

I had chatted with Leonard and other bystanders four or five minutes when a car bearing a red cross on the hood came into view on Lewis Street. It was followed by thirty-three other vehicles with dome lights burning, all filled with robed and hooded Klansmen. All but four had South Carolina license plates.

The motorcade never stopped. There were no shots fired. At least I never heard any. Some observers of the first motorcade had said that several shots had been fired into the air when the cars drove through the black section.

While the motorcade was peaceful, it did what it intended to do. It intimidated the residents of the black community and it advertised its continued strength to prospective Klansmen who might pay the ten dollars membership dues when their tobacco went to market. It was a recruiting device. Obviously the Klan's reorganization was continuing.

Several of the sheriff's deputies were parked near the tiny police station on the railroad at the "square." Ted Watts, the city's lone night policeman, was talking with them. I didn't know it at the time, but the sheriff's office had received an anonymous phone call two hours before the motorcade announcing the Klan's intention to drive through Tabor City. But they hadn't warned me.

Despite the peacefulness of the motorcade, I felt a duty to again lash out at this un-American invasion by lawless vigilantes. The spring of 1951 was a time when corruption and graft by dozens of federal lawmakers and administrators were headlined around the world. Many had accepted huge bribes, fur coats, deep-freezers, cars and a myriad of luxury gifts for votes and favors. President Harry Truman was being called an "associate of the underworld gang in Kansas City" and few Southerners had any kind words for the president.

Then and now I credit the sins of politicians in high places as being the prime reason for the rebirth of the KKK. I said so as I sat down and wrote this editorial:

The KKK. . .Another Step in The BREAKDOWN of GOVERNMENT

Never before in this country have so many people lost faith in our government and the men who have been elected to high office. Graft and subversion have crept stealthily into almost every phase of public life.

Taking advantage of this weakness, the un-American and subversive Ku Klux Klan is growing among the disgruntled, the troublemakers and the prejudiced.

Choosing not to openly carry on its activities in the light of day, the Klan instead hides its cowardly deeds in blackness of night. Its self-righteous infliction of punishment upon those whose morality it chooses to question, simulates comparable criminal deeds of big-city mobsters in the era of Prohibition. The Klan is little different from those lawless gangs.

If this gang of mystics truly has wholesome motives and advocates just reforms, why can't they shed their cloaks of secrecy and as sincere citizens go to the polls and vote for change. That has historically been the American way. Only the Communists are ashamed of their membership cards. Their motives are not honorable and American and neither are those of the Ku Klux Klan that rode down our streets Saturday evening.

We never knew a churchman who kept his membership a secret. Nor have we known a Mason, Rotarian, Civitan, Lion, Jaycee, American Legionnaire, Veteran of Foreign Wars or Farm Bureau member who hid his membership. These organizations openly work for the good of humanity. Why can't the KKK do as much?

The truth of the matter is that these disgruntled rascals enjoy a fanatical ego boost by using their power to disregard laws and principles. Much of their work is either illegal or fringing on the illegal. They promote bias among races, antagonism toward the law, and flaunt their vigilante justice that destroys the traditional American way of life.

Groups like the Ku Klux Klan are a challenge to democracy and if they continue to grow and go unpunished, freedom may perish and we will be ruled by fear.

A few days after my editorial appeared in the *Tribune*, Grand Dragon Hamilton walked into the office. For the first time we sat and talked face to face. It was a revealing conversation.

The editorial had brought down the wrath of the Grand Dragon who looked like the typical robust redneck that I pictured most Klansmen to be. He was upset that my little newspaper would challenge his fast-growing organization that was approaching five thousand local members.

He hit me with a threat that was unexpected. He didn't warn that the KKK would get me and my family one of these nights—as many warnings I received had said. Instead he struck where he knew it would hurt the most.

"If you keep on writing this junk about our organization, we will put you out of business," he threatened. "I can get most of your subscribers to cancel the paper any time I ask them.

"And all I have to do to put you out of business for good is to get my Klan members to boycott the businesses here that are advertising with you. The businesses won't dare to advertise if the farmers who are members around here go somewhere else to trade," Hamilton made his point.

"Well, Mr. Hamilton, you may be able to put me out of business," I answered. "I can't last long without advertisers. I need every two-dollar subscriber that I can find. But no amount of pressure you put on them will stop me from writing how I feel about the Klan as long as I have money to print another paper.

"The Klan fight is a matter of principle with me. I think you and your organization are a threat to the peaceful way of life of this community and I'll continue to write editorial after editorial pointing out the dangers of your vigilante justice. If you break me, and I have little resources, as you probably know, then you will have won this fight. Only then will I quit, if you continue operating in Tabor City.

"Keep this in mind, Mr. Hamilton, I came here with only $4,000 dollars that I saved while serving in the Navy in World War II. I don't even have that much now. So I came here with nothing and I can certainly leave here with nothing if I must. I can start a newspaper somewhere else. But as long as I am here, I'll fight you every step of the way. I believe in the rights of all Americans. That includes the underprivileged and all races. I could not live with myself if I turned my back on them and let the KKK run roughshod over them."

It was a stand that somewhat shook the Grand Dragon. I don't believe he thought I had the guts to stand up and oppose him face to face. I tried not to let him know that I had butterflies in my stomach and probably wouldn't be able to sleep for a week. My insides knew I was talking a pretty good fight, but there was fear aplenty.

I found the courage to face off with the Grand Dragon about one other belief. "Mr. Hamilton, there are two kinds of newspapers in this country that can truly be independent and call a spade a spade. They don't have to straddle fences. The paper that has a publisher with unlimited financial assets can have editors who write what they feel and stick to principles because they can afford to lose advertisers. The other newspaper that can be independent and write editorials based on principles and let the chips fall where they may is the one that has nothing. That publisher has nothing to lose. I am in that last category. I came here with nothing. I can leave here with nothing, but you cannot muzzle my typewriter. I'll write what I think is right and put the paper on the street as long as I can." Then and now these words described my philosophy about journalism.

Hamilton was dumbfounded with my audacity. Could a thirty-year-old farm boy stand up to him and his organization that had already flogged a number of people, shot up a Negro night club and severely abused its proprietor?

Could I oppose a group that attracted thousands to public

meetings and intimidated the grand juries enough to keep its members out of court?

"You are a bigger fool than I thought you were," he said, as he stood to leave.

"One more thing, Mr. Hamilton, I want you to know that I appreciate your going to the trouble to come here from Leesville to talk with me, even though it turns out we cannot agree on anything. Also, I want you to know that while I shall continue to criticize you and the Klan as long as you are breaking the law and molesting and intimidating the people, I will be glad to print anything that you have to say on behalf of the Klan. All you have to do is sign your letter and I'll run it exactly as you write it." I made it clear that, as humble as our little paper was, he had access to that free press.

"Fine! I'll write you a letter in a few days. Let's see if you will run it," Hamilton said, as we shook hands and he left.

My hands were shaking. I couldn't believe I had stood up to the Grand Dragon as well as I had. Make no mistake, I was scared. And when I think of it now, I'm scared again.

It would not be my last face to face confrontation with Hamilton.

I went back to work wondering if indeed, he would write the letter he promised. Three days later a letter arrived with no return address. It looked suspicious. The message inside was clear enough. It was written on a two-color letterhead with KU KLUX KLAN in red ink. It was the first, but not the last, Klan letterhead I was to see. No other newspaper had received a Klan letter at that time, either. It was impressive stationery and the single-spaced, typed letter covered two pages with Thomas L. Hamilton's distinctive signature at the end. It read as follows:

Invisible Empire
Association of the Carolina Klans
of the
KU KLUX KLAN

Office of the
Grand Dragon   June 21, 1951
Editor
Tabor City Tribune
Tabor City, N.C.

Dear Sir:

Recently in an issue of your paper you carried quite an editorial stating your opinions and your warped ideas with reference to the Klan. You stated in that editorial that the Ku Klux Klan was un-American and subversive. Now, sir, this statement by you in this editorial was untrue because nowhere can you find in the recent list released in Washington, D.C. where the Klan is un-American or subversive, but I can find the Newspaper Guild is Communist to the core. I think for you to be a real HE man you would sweep before your own door and clean your own backyard before you brand an Organization with an untruth. I dare you, Sir, to check the records in Washington and you will find that the Klan is listed as an Anti-CIVIL RIGHTS Organization; and I thank God that I can belong to an organization that believes in keeping the race of men PURE and SPOTLESS. Such men as you believe in mongrelizing America and by the recent talk I had with you in your office, I summed up in my mind that you are biased and leaning toward the group of people in America who are advocating the downfall of this great land of ours.

The Association of Carolina Klans has never been listed on any list from Washington, D.C. as a subversive Organization. You cannot make the statement that the Masons of Tabor City are wide open because the Masonic Lodge is a secret organization and its membership is held secret together with all of its workings and, Sir, you cannot class the Klan and the Masonic Lodge in the same category because they are two distinct Organizations carrying out their separate missions. No Klansman is ashamed to be a Klansman nor to claim membership in the Ku Klux Klan. Every man that I know in the Klan is PROUD of the fact that he holds something in his heart and that he is part of an organization that is fighting for the traditions of America. My integrity is worth more to me than all of the Newspapers in the World. I'd rather be a Klansman and know it than a left-winger and not know it.

The Klan does not have a membership of disgruntled men and women, but instead, it has as its membership a group of REAL-HONEST-TO-GOODNESS LOYAL AMERICANS who have awakened to the fact that a minority group in America is trying to overthrow their government. The Klan does not advocate or preach a doctrine of fear but instead we have people outside of the Klan who fear the Klan because they are doing a number of un-moral (sic) and illegal, nasty, un-Christian things and they are afraid that someone will get after them. I do not advocate taking the Law into my own hands nor will I be a part of an organization that advocates taking the law into its own hands. But, Sir, I do advocate digging into ever (sic) locality's local and state government and expose those men who are trying to use their office for greed and perversion. Then when the time comes to cast our ballots at the polls, we will be found not wanting.

The Freedom of America will perish and go down into oblivion unless every TRUE American awakens and joins in the fight to SAVE AMERICA.

The greatest medium in America to keep America American is controlled and is being suppressed by a minority group which has been able to remove from the American people that part of the Constitution that is so vitally needed at the present time. You could use your Newspaper, acting under the authority of Freedom of the Press, to a great advantage.

I trust that you have found that no man on this earth can supplant or take the place of the Lowly Nazarene our Lord and Saviour Jesus Christ. In Him is our being. In Him we MUST depend for guidance through the Holy Spirit. He is the one who will act as an intercessor with God Almighty for us in forgiving our sins and shortcomings while we are journeying through this life. A life which He requires us as individuals to do our utmost for Him and in His behalf. I would recommend Him to you.

Yours truly,
Thomas L. Hamilton

I read the letter carefully. How could he be so pious while beating up people and advocating social injustice? I would consider the points he made and run my rebuttal next week.

I was happy he hadn't made any reference to his threatened advertising boycott. That could send me and my family packing in a few weeks. It didn't happen overnight, but eventually the Klan pressure did get to our handful of advertisers and we struggled to make a living.

It was time to write my rebuttal.

"Welcome to Tabor City" sign did not apply to Ku Klux Klan motorcades. None of these was ever approved or announced in advance—they just suddenly appeared on Saturday nights and always moved down the main street, through the black section of town, known as "The Bottom."

Chapter Fifteen
From Kidnapping to Dognapping

After Grand Dragon Thomas Hamilton's visit and his critical letter, I felt a duty to defend the newspaper's integrity and my crusade against the lawlessness preached by the ever-pious Klan leader from Leesville. At the moment I did not foresee the consequences, but in some ways, it would wring the very blood from my heart. Even my beloved ten-year-old bird dog would suffer because I would not shut up. That was tragic. This rebuttal editorial appeared in the June 27, 1951 edition:

Dear Mr. Hamilton:

Thank you for your letter. As I told you these columns are open to you and every dissenter. That's our idea of freedom of the press, particularly when your message is unedited and appears exactly as you wrote it. It did, as you no doubt know.

I can't sit idly by and let some of your vague charges and insinuations go unchallenged.

You refer to the Newspaper Guild as being Communist. I can neither confirm nor deny that. I have never even known a member of the Guild. Certainly it has nothing to do with me and this newspaper and our crusade against the KKK. I dare say that there are few if any journalists in either of the Carolinas who belong to the Guild. Yet, they are all opposed to your Klan. You are saying you speak from an exalted pedestal representing righteousness, and all newspapers that are critical of you are wrong. You have an inflated ego if I ever knew one. All of us are wrong sometime. You are most certainly wrong in leading a lawless band of vigilantes with a warped sense of justice.

You take exception to my referring to the Klan as un-American. If the shooting incident at Charlie's Place in

Myrtle Beach is your idea of Americanism, we have certainly drifted a long way from the original definition. That's Al Capone and other gangster mobs in the big cities' kind of Americanism. To say that your Myrtle Beach motorcade had only peaceful intentions is also a little far-fetched. Why on earth were your Klansmen armed to the teeth and ended up firing as many as three hundred shots into the black-owned night club? People with peaceful intentions do not normally carry around such an arsenal and dozens of trigger-happy followers.

You say you thank God for an organization that believes in keeping the race of mankind PURE and SPOTLESS. I believe you will find that one Adolph Hitler preached a similar message to the masses and that ended in the massacre of millions of defenseless Jews in Europe. I wonder if Hitler thanked God for that privilege. Would that man of Galilee of two thousand years ago believe in gruesome floggings of men and women whose moral life-styles differed from his, even cutting off their ears? I think not.

You make a point that the Masonic Order is secret. That's semi-correct. I never knew a Mason who objected to anyone knowing he was a member. It's only some objectives and rituals that are secret. You should know. You are a Mason. That wasn't difficult to learn. You wear their ring and pin. I haven't heard of any Masonic Lodge perpetrating floggings on neighbors and taking part in shooting escapades. To compare the Klan with the Masons is ridiculous.

Your most asinine sentence is the one in which you say, "The Klan does not advocate or preach a doctrine of fear, but instead there are people outside the Klan who fear the Klan because they are doing unmoral (sic), illegal, nasty, unchristian things and are afraid someone will get after them." If your Klan doesn't punish people for this unacceptable conduct you mention, why should they have any fear of the Klan? How can you say "someone will get after them"? Your organization is like the Soviet Secret Police and the German Gestapo that seek to curb freedoms through fear. And you know it.

Regarding your stated intention of looking into local and state governments and exposing politicians and officials involved in greed and perversion, that is note-worthy. We have long advocated much greater participation at the polls for Americans who should be careful to elect the best candidates available. That is a responsibility of every citizen. I doubt that the KKK scrutiny of candidates would enhance the character of the people who represent us. They might even be worse.

You indicate that newspaper editorial policies are unduly controlled. By whom? There may be some metropolitan newspapers somewhere with a hierarchy that sets the editorial tone, but this tiny weekly certainly isn't dictated to by anyone. The policies we push are just as freely stated as those remarks of yours from the back of a flatbed truck in a tobacco patch. These Klan editorials come from my mind and my heart and, be they ever so humble, I have great faith that they are righteous, proper and not designed to be self-serving. You can believe it or not. It's the truth.

In your speeches and letters you speak often of Jesus Christ and the Bible. You have taken the time to recommend Him to me. That's a good Christian, missionary attitude. Of course, I need to be more Christ-like. I am a church member and Sunday School teacher, but that does not make me good. "There are none good," you have read or heard. But how can you profess godliness while terrorizing families, preaching dislike for Negroes, Jews and Catholics? Suppose the great biblical missionary Paul, a Jew, had preached only to his relatives. You, Mr. Hamilton, a Gentile would never have gotten the message. In all of his humility Jesus Christ was for all mankind everywhere and for all time.

It's traumatic that you sum up your message to me by saying that I advocate the downfall of this great land of ours. What a summation of falsehoods. You can't find three people anywhere who would back up those charges. On the contrary, people who know us best are fully aware that once and for all we urge good citizenship, participation in government on every level and honest efforts to maintain a strong democracy forever. There's nothing that we despise more than communism, left wingers and organizations seeking to break down law, order and democracy. I think your KKK falls right into that category and that makes me sick.

Yours very truly,
W. Horace Carter

A few days later an unsigned note in my mail box summed up one reader's lowly opinion of my rebuttal. It read: *"You devil traitor. You have sold out to the Jews."* If I had sold out, where was the money?

While that note was disconcerting—as all such

uncomplimentary messages have always been to me—it was not as unnerving as the telephone message at my home the same night. My wife picked up the phone and said simply, "It's for you."

A gruff voice on the other end of the line (that I believed was from out of town) was crisp and threatening. "Mr. Horace Carter, you can't get away with writing about us every week. It's all a bunch of lies. We are good people and stand for good things and you make us sound like cutthroats. You have been told before to shut up and leave us alone, but you keep right on harassing us week after week. I have been told that you are a quail hunter with a liver and white bird dog bitch that you call Bess. They say that a dog is man's best friend and you may feel that way about your dog. You wouldn't want her hurt would you? Well, stop writing about the Klan. If you don't, we will get your dog and maybe you, too." The phone clicked off before I could say a word.

"What's wrong?" Lucile asked when I turned around.

"Some nut says he is going to get me and Bess if I don't stop the Klan campaign," I replied. "Just another wild attempt to intimidate me."

While I minimized the phone call outwardly, it bothered me inside. I had raised Bess from a pup and she had given birth to dozens of fine pointers over the years. I had hunted with her all through college and she was all smiles and tail-wags when I came home from the Navy. When we moved to Tabor City, she came along. She was part of the family.

I called Bess a "country bird dog." She never ate a can or bag of bought dog food. She ate the scraps off the table, including chicken and fish bones which didn't bother her at all. Her stomach was attuned to bones. She was never tied or penned up. She stayed in the yard and was a lovable, harmless pet, always anxious to charge into the savannas and fields when bird hunting season opened each Thanksgiving. There was no greater joy than watching her find a covey of quail, pointing them for me and then retrieving those that I was lucky enough to shoot down. We were a team in the woods and I loved her unashamedly. I often felt a little sorry for her when she dashed into thick brier patches after a downed quail and came out with blood dripping from scratched and pierced floppy ears. Pointers' ears are not protected by long hair as are those of the setter breeds. I rubbed her head and neck the next morning, played with her ears a minute or two and lingered a little before going on to work.

Days passed and thoughts of the threat faded as I was

engulfed with work. The tobacco auction season was opening and this was a time when I had to sell advertising. It was the time of year when merchants and farmers settled up for the year. Almost everything was sold on credit. The bank and a few affluent merchants collected on the promissory notes and mortgages. The profits or losses were reckoned with and you could gauge whether you would survive economically until another fall.

I knew that the Klan would schedule many more recruiting meetings now because, like the merchants, they knew it was a time when the people had money and could buy sheets and hoods. As expected, a circular in the mail announced a public meeting in the Williams Township area on Highway 701 for Saturday night, August 18, on a leased farm field nine miles north of Tabor City. Grand Dragon Thomas Hamilton would again be the featured speaker.

I wrote a short, pointed editorial along with a news item announcing the meeting.

DON'T BE HOODWINKED BY KKK

The Ku Klux Klan is holding the first publicly announced meeting in Eastern North Carolina since the turn of the century. While these meetings have been staged by Grand Dragon Thomas Hamilton in nearby Horry County for several months and Klansmen have flogged our citizenry, this marks the first time they have come across the line for public recruiting.

Don't let this band of lawless hoodlums hoodwink you into joining their ranks and taking part in illegal, abusive punishment of your neighbors. There may have been a place for the KKK in Reconstruction days, but there certainly is no room for them in today's United States. You'll do well to ignore the urging of Hamilton and perhaps other speakers who would have you help finance their lawlessness.

If you must attend the public meeting, as many will as curiosity seekers if for no other reason, don't make the Klan stronger by becoming one of them. The Klan will end here in disaster and you don't want to be a part of it.

Ironically, a three-column picture on the front page of the *Tribune* was taken in the door of the newspaper office. In those days bright leaf tobacco was graded and cured before auction and the photo was of a six-foot stick of tobacco prepared for the auction. One end of the stick was held by Lewis Gore, a grocer. The other was held by Troy Bennett, who operated the small local bus terminal and snack shop. I didn't know it at the time, but Bennett was an active Klansman. He eventually was convicted for various Klan floggings and was given a prison sentence, but he died of a heart attack before serving his sentence.

It was some coincidence that we had run the anti-Klan editorial and Bennett's picture at the same time. The picture was promotional in nature and was run to convince tobacco growers to bring their crops to the Tabor City auction market rather than some other place. The editorial was my best advice to growers not to join the KKK.

It was my first attack upon the Klan since the infamous phone call in July. And I had forgotten about the threat. I again petted Bess on the neck when I trudged up the steps at day's end. She was appreciative as always.

But she was nowhere to be found the next morning. I looked around the neighborhood to see if perhaps she had been run over by a car during the night. She wasn't there. That was unusual. She never left the premises unless she went with me. She hadn't just strayed away. Could Klansmen actually have come into our yard and kidnapped my wonderful, lovable friend? That was the only logical conclusion.

Lucile was both frightened and horrified. "If they could come in here and steal Bess, they could have burned us out as they have threatened." And she was right.

I was chagrined over the loss of my dog for a long time. She was not easy to forget, and often I wondered just what kind of fate she had suffered because of me. I would miss her during hunting season to be sure, but Bess was more than just a dog. She was almost like an offspring and her abduction was no fault of her own. Gradually though, I missed her less.

More than four months passed quickly. My brother-in-law, J. A. Herlocker, who worked in the print shop and had attended some Klan rallies with me, was helping out one Monday morning by driving to Whiteville to pick up some advertisements. Five miles outside Whiteville on Highway 76, he saw a pointer bird dog trotting toward Tabor City on the shoulder of the road. She looked familiar. He stopped and yelled, "Bess!" Despite her absence of months, and a tired, worn-out look on her face, the old bitch scrambled into J. A.'s arms, licked him all over the face and lay down on his front

The Tabor City Tribune

SELL IN TABOR CITY
Four of the best
are yours Tabor City
has led Border Belt
in Leaf Prices.

IN THIS ISSUE
• Market opening Tuesday
• Ku Klux Klan Rides
Never
• Tabor City History
• Leaf Barn Burns

VOL. IV, NUMBER 54   TABOR CITY, NORTH CAROLINA, WEDNESDAY, JULY 26, 1950   5c A COPY, $2.00 A YEAR

Tobacco Market Poised For Opening Day On Tuesday

CARTER'S COLUMN
By W. HORACE CARTER

Ku Klux Klan Here On Saturday Night

This Tobacco was Smoked Before it Was A Cigarette

Tabor City Seeking To Set Price Pace

An Editorial
No Excuse For KKK

In this democratic country, there's no place for an organization of the caliber of the Ku Klux Klan which made a scheduled parade through our streets last Saturday night. Any organization that has to work outside the law is unfit for recognition in a country of free men. Saturday's episode, although without violence, is deplorable, a black eye to our area and an admission that our law enforcement is inadequate.

LIGHTENING STRIKES MILLS BARN: $800 DAMAGE ESTIMATED

YAM FESTIVAL COMMITTEE MEETS AGAIN

INDUSTRIAL SURVEY GROUPS NAMED IN EACH COMMUNITY

AMERICAN LEGION POST HERE THANKS PERSONS FOR SUPPORT

CALVIN BENNETT REPORTED MISSING IN KOREAN ACTION

Down The Main Drag

WANT A BOOTH

Local Baptist Church Schedules Conference

American Legion Meets Friday

Troy Bennett, Town Councilman/Klansman, and Lewis Gore appeared in this photo announcing the opening of the tobacco market.

seat. She went to sleep and he brought her back to the Tabor City print shop where I embraced her emotionally.

She was the picture of pity and determination. The claws on her toes were all worn into the raw meat. She was skin and bones. She had obviously been abused, starved and yet had somehow escaped from God only knows where. She had covered miles, maybe hundreds of miles, trying to get back home—and she would have made it even without hitchhiking the last twenty miles. Her sense of direction was unbelievable and it made me think of an incident my father had once told about a redbone hound that was moved from North Carolina to Missouri.

The hound resented the move and was unhappy. She disappeared. Six months later, she showed up in Palestine, North Carolina, a tiny village in the piedmont section where she was reunited with the family that had raised her.

Bess probably was not carried that far away, but she was well out of Columbus County. Yet, once she had the opportunity, she challenged the roads, rivers, swamps and other hazards to make her way back home.

I learned from the unhappy experience. That dog was determined. Even kidnapping and abuse never erased her vision and determination. She had won her battle against the ruthless Klan that abducted her. I would use her experience to strengthen my own resolve. Anybody who would inflict punishment on a man's dog was eligible for the dubious distinction of "meanest man in the world." I would fight back as Bess had, never relenting.

The upcoming Columbus rally was next. I would be there to see what Hamilton and his other speakers had to say. And it made me shudder to think the Klan might be succeeding despite our best efforts. Maybe a little newspaper like ours just didn't cast a big enough shadow to be a deterrent. But we would keep on trying.

The example Bess set would not be forgotten.

Chapter Sixteen
The Klan Heads North

Ninety-seven fully-robed Klansmen encircled a twenty-foot burning cross. A dozen Klansmen rode white horses around the burning cross and had considerable difficulty keeping their steeds calm near the fire amid photographers' flashing bulbs. The bustling crowd of curiosity seekers added to the nervousness of the horses.

A robust figure wearing a bright, flowing red robe and a hood that was pushed back on his forehead revealing his face, rose from his chair on the back of the flatbed truck that served as a podium, and moved to the microphone. This meeting of the Association of the Carolina Klans in the fall of 1951 had been well advertised and more than five thousand curiosity seekers stood in the stubbled former cornfield. Grand Dragon Thomas L. Hamilton had come to Williams Township in Columbus County, North Carolina, eight miles from Tabor City, to recruit men and women for local klaverns throughout eastern North and South Carolina. The former grocer made an imposing figure as he stood before the crowd at six-feet four, weighing about 230 pounds. He declared that he would outline what his KKK stood for and why every red-blooded American should fill out an application and purchase a robe and hood.

Florida Imperial Wizard Bill Hendricks started the program with a pious prayer after being introduced by Grand Dragon Hamilton. The muffled rumble of the crowd subsided as Hendricks raised his hand and began praying:

> Gracious Father Jesus Christ we come to thee with humility, ever thankful for thy blessings that have made us free men and women in a troubled world. We seek thy guidance and thy blessings as we read thy precious Bible and determine in our own hearts how we as white Americans can preserve our heritage and our way of life.
>
> We are grateful for our life, liberty and pursuit of

99

happiness, and hopefully as Christians we can save our democracy for our children and grandchildren even as government seeks to deprive us of our rights and freedoms.

Help us to face adversity with confidence and save us from persecution and laws that will rob us of our Anglo-Saxon ancestry by diluting our people into a mongrel race.

In Jesus name we ask, Amen.

After Hendricks' prayer Hamilton approached the microphone and began his own harangue:

My friends, it is evident as I look out over this great throng tonight that you too, like me, are fed up with the government and what goes on in America that promises to force us to go to school with the niggers and merge us into a society of half-breeds. That's one of the evils that has been thrust upon us in recent years and unless we as free, white, Christian Americans take steps to ensure against this lawless integration of the races in schools, restaurants, motels, churches and everywhere else, our children will grow up and lose their precious white heritage.

It won't be long before young white men and women will be dating and marrying the colored people in the communities if they take away our white public schools that the white people built and paid for all these years. These are your schools, but now the Supreme Court says we must let even the dirtiest niggers in the bottom sit right next to your daughters, eat at the same table in the cafeteria and dress in the same rooms in your gymnasiums.

Let me assure you tonight that the Ku Klux Klan is determined not to let this integration succeed in the Carolinas. We have organized to preserve the white race that believes in Jesus Christ and attends the Protestant denomination churches of our land.

We do not want members in the KKK from the Catholic or the Jewish people. We are fighting for the rights of white, native-born Christians. The Catholics would like to control the world and force all of us to be Catholics. If they had their way, we would not have any Protestant churches in the world. The Jews killed our Savior Jesus Christ, and Zionists world-wide continually plot to control the money of the world so they can make all the rest of us peasants and at their mercy.

President Harry Truman is determined to eliminate the pure white American race as he prods the U.S. Supreme Court to move forward to take away the rights of the white people who built this great nation. Now there is a movement to have the Communistic United Nations flag fly over the schools of the land. That's just another way to take away our privileges and rights as whites. It's another step toward mongrelizing all Americans into a race of mixed breeds with no loyalties to our white pioneering forefathers who established this land while seeking freedom from religious and governmental persecution in Europe. Truman and the courts are determined to take away those freedoms that have been so hard-earned. Let me, my friends, tell you here tonight that no United Nations flag will ever fly over the schools of this land where the Klan is strong. We will see that they come down as fast as they put them up.

Where the Klan is organized, we will see that immorality is not flagrantly flaunted in our faces. We believe in families and fidelity and those rogues who cheat on their wives, don't darken the doors of the church and let their children go ill-clothed and hungry will have to answer to the klavern leadership that will stand for no such behavior. The wife beaters in this community better straighten up and fly right or else pack their bags and head North or some place where they can get away with their abusive conduct.

Newspapers have been crying out against the Klan's reorganization and some seem to have gone crazy because we are succeeding despite their childish editorial opposition and ill-conceived crusades. These newspapers owe their business success to the Jews and they have to oppose us or lose their Jewish supporters. The Jews have a stranglehold on the press and there is no freedom of the press any more. If there was freedom of the press, these newspapers that are fighting us so hard would be on our side and helping us recruit. Let me pass along a word of warning to those one-sided editors and publishers. There will come a time when we will have enough Klansmen in these communities that those firms advertising in those newspapers will suddenly discover that their old customers no longer darken their doors. They will dry up on the stalk when Klansmen refuse to trade with the businesses that keep these newspapers going to press and lambasting us.

We can promote a powerful boycott that will bring

these newspapers to their knees and put them out of business. Those newspapers who learn this will survive. The others will soon close their doors. We are growing stronger. I have heard a few boos and catcalls here tonight. Let me tell you that I wouldn't be doing that if I were you. While we have a hundred or more Klansmen in uniform here tonight, there are thousands of other Klansmen here not wearing robes. That man at your elbow may be one of us and you'd better keep your boos to yourself if you know what's good for you. And if you have in mind identifying some of us and turning the names over to the sheriff, the FBI or some other law enforcement organization, remember that we have plenty of law enforcement officers on the Klan rosters. The man you report us to may well be one of us. That puts the reporter in a precarious position. I wouldn't do that.

I am the only Klansman here who doesn't have his face covered. You know who I am. I am Thomas L. Hamilton, the Grand Dragon, and I am proud of it. I intend to fight for the rights of white people everywhere until at last we are strong enough to survive the on- slaught of the federal government and organizations that are determined to destroy the real Americans of this land.

In South Carolina we have a good following of people in high political offices. They will help us in our determi- nation to preserve our rights and freedoms. We have not succeeded in attracting many of the political leaders in North Carolina yet, but we are determined to succeed in that effort. Once we have judges, sheriffs, legislators, solicitors and other people in high places, and jurors, we will not have to fear the courts that will cook up all kinds of false charges against me and other Klansmen. We will have a grasp on the power structure that will eventually save us from prosecution. We are gaining in political strength every day, as the world will see in the elections of the future. I don't believe any jury can be picked that doesn't have some Klan members on it. That's more protection for us. My friends, I thank you for your attention. I can see that most of you are with me in what we are trying to accomplish. Mixing in the crowd at the moment are fellow Klansmen with KKK applications. If you want to save the white race from the niggers, Jews and Catholics, take an application and let us hear from you. We will investigate your character and those with the proper credentials will hear from us in a few days.

Those who are without good character need not apply. Again, I thank you for coming and for listening. We need your help to save America and we need it now.

There were no arrests and no lawlessness as the two leading Klansmen in the country took turns lambasting individuals and groups that they charged were either Communist, un-American or a threat to the way of life of the white race in the United States.

Hendricks said the meeting was the first of many scheduled for North Carolina and "the Klan will again prosper in North Carolina as our effort expands to band all white, Gentile, Protestants together."

Hendricks was extremely critical of University of North Carolina President Frank P. Graham, a candidate for the U.S. Senate. He got his facts mixed up at one point as he referred to the University at Chapel Hill, North Carolina, as State College in Chapel Hill, SOUTH Carolina.

Among those pinpointed for criticism by the two were the CIO, Junior Chamber of Commerce, Eleanor Roosevelt, the Jews, the Negroes, politicians, Anti-Defamation League, National Association for the Advancement of Colored People, Bernard Baruch, Jimmy Byrnes, Cubans, Italians, Felix Frankfurter, Anne Rosenberg, preachers, lawyers, and the National Council of Churches

The nearest thing to excitement that happened during the two-hour tirade occurred when one of the Klansmen on the speakers' platform fainted. Hamilton asked if a doctor was present, but none stepped up. The unconscious Klansman was carried off the stage and was not heard from again.

The crowd shuffled toward cars and pickup trucks parked along Highway 701 as soon as the speaking ended. A handful of overall-clad farmers huddled near the speaker and reached for KKK applications. A few shouted approval of what Hamilton had said and shook his hand as he stepped off the truck. But mostly it was a quiet audience, both during the speeches and as they left the dusty field and headed for home.

There was interest from North Carolina law enforcement authorities as evidenced by the presence of seventy-two highway patrolmen and other officers. They recorded license plate numbers of all who attended, and later reported that some of the vehicles were from Maryland, Virginia, Illinois, Florida and Indiana, as well as the usual number from Georgia and the Carolinas.

Daily newspapers reporting on this initial North Carolina rally noted that the ninety-seven Klansmen marching around the cross and speaker's stand were out of step most of the time. We noted in our comments about the meeting that the abusive messages of these Klan bigwigs were out of step with reality in the twentieth century, and the United States as a melting pot for all freedom-loving people who fled from tyranny to the New World after its discovery.

Governor Kerr Scott was upset with the attempt at Klan recruitment in North Carolina and he minced no words as he spoke out against the KKK. "Neither communism nor the Klan is popular in North Carolina and we are not going to take any foolishness from them. The Klan is obnoxious. I'm opposed to people wearing robes and masks. It's not honorable to begin with if you are not willing to stand up and let yourself be known," he declared.

We ran those remarks from the governor on the front page of the *Tribune* after the cornfield rally, and asked him for additional quotes. He said, "The Communists want to overthrow our government. The Klan wants to take the place of our government. In the end it amounts to the same thing."

He noted that the Negro newspaper editor in Wilmington had been threatened by the Klan along with those of the *Tribune* and the Whiteville newspaper. The State Bureau of Investigation was looking into those matters, he said.

And then came the inevitable question—how does this 1950 Klan differ from the KKK of Reconstruction.

"There is no comparison," he replied. "In the South after the war it was a matter of survival. My grandfather was a Klansman and I was invited to join but refused. It was an entirely different problem then. We did not have law and order in those precarious days. We do now. In that period the Klan helped restore law and order. We don't have that problem now."

Another fall month passed. Hamilton called a second Columbus County meeting and challenged the president of the North Carolina Junior Chamber of Commerce (the organization had passed a resolution condemning the KKK reorganization) to debate issues with him at this rally. The Jaycees did not accept the challenge to debate, but suggested that Hamilton should sue them in the courts if he had been unjustly accused.

Hamilton mailed out flyers announcing the second rally and at the same time, a derogatory card was found in the mailbox of Wilton Hall, former U.S. Senator who published the *South Carolina Daily Mail* newspaper in Anderson. Hall's paper had been critical of Hamilton's Klan and the Grand Dragon's response was on the card that reflected upon the character of Publisher Hall. Sending it through the mail, as he did the rally circulars, was one of the first mistakes that Hamilton made in his Klan campaign. His defamatory card sent through the U.S. Postal Service violated federal law. The Grand Dragon was charged and brought into federal court.

Judge George Bell Timmerman, Sr. found Hamilton guilty and sentenced him to a year in jail or a fine of one thousand dollars. Although he denied writing or mailing the card, Hamilton paid the fine, the maximum penalty for mailing a message falsely reflecting upon the character and conduct of a person.

The noose was tightening. Hamilton and the Klan were under a microscope. They would have more and more trouble with the laws of the land, especially now that the federal government was involved.

Before September had ended, the Klan went to church in Horry County. But they were not there to worship. They were there to intimidate those whom they considered immoral and unchristian. Their unholy presence in the church for the purpose of harassing those of whose conduct they disapproved, was to again result in numerous arrests of both Klansmen and sheriff's deputies. It was a bizarre episode that occurred at least twice in the Klan's infamous rise to power when they intimidated rural church congregations by strolling down the aisles during worship services wearing their hoods and robes.

Close on the heels of that episode, the floggings resumed as the vigilantes lured men and women from their homes and inflicted serious bodily injury that would eventually prove to be their undoing. But they would prowl another year, harassing dozens of men and women, black and white in the eastern North Carolina low country along the South Carolina border.

The worst was yet to come.

Your Signature On These, Plus $10.00, Makes You A Ku Klux

Application For Citizenship in The
Invisible Empire of The
KU KLUX KLAN

I, the undersigned, a native born, true and loyal citizen of the United States of America, being a white Protestant Gentile person of temperate habits, sound in mind and a believer in the tenets of the Christian religion, the maintenance of White Supremacy and the principles of a "pure Americanism", do most respectfully apply for membership in the Ku Klux Klan through Klan

No._____ , _____, Realm of_____
        I guarantee on my honor to conform strictly to all rules and requirements regulating my "naturalization" and the continuance of my membership, and at all times a strict and loyal obedience to your constitutional authority and the constitution and laws of the fraternity, not in conflict with the constitution and constitutional laws of the United States of America and the states thereof. If I prove untrue as a Klansman I will willingly accept as my portion whatever penalty your authority may impose.
        The required "klectokon" accompanies this application.

Signed_____ Applicant

Endorsed by   Residence Address _____

Kl_____   Business Address _____

Kl_____   Date_____, 19____

The person securing this application must sign on top line above. NOTICE—Check the address to which mail may be sent.

NOTICE

The sum of this donation MUST accompany application, if possible.

Upon payment of same by applicant this certificate is made out and signed by person securing application, then detached and given to applicant, who will keep same and bring it with him when he is called, and then turn it in on demand in lieu of the cash.

DO NOT detach if donation is not paid in advance.

OFFICIAL CERTIFICATE OF DONATION

This certifies that_____
has donated the sum of TEN DOLLARS to the propagating fund of the

Ku Klux Klan

and same is accepted as such and as full sum of "KLECTOKON" entitling him to be received, on the acceptance of his application under the laws, regulations and requirements of the Order, duly naturalized and to have and to hold all the rights, titles, honors and protection as a citizen of the Invisible Empire. He enters through the portal of

Klan No._____ , _____, Realm of._____

Date_____, 19____

Received in trust for the
KU KLUX KLAN

By Kl_____

Captured along the way were numerous application blanks which the Ku Klux Klan used in signing up the infamous membership. The public has long known there was a $10.00 initiation fee but still wanders about what happens to the currency once the members has turned it loose.

Klan membership applications were available at public meetings.

Chapter Seventeen
The Klan Goes to Church

Mid-week revival services were interrupted on November 1, 1951, when twenty-four masked Klansmen invaded a gathering at the Cane Branch Baptist Church near Allsbrook in Horry County. It was the first time the public had heard about the KKK invasion of the churches. And then the truth quickly unfolded. At least three rural churches in Horry had been visited by Klansmen in full regalia that fall. Yet no one complained and it was not publicized. It was a well-kept secret for weeks.

Amazingly, to those of us opposing the resurrection of the terrorist vigilantes, the ostentatiously pious KKK had been invited to appear at the Cane Branch Church by the pastor, N. E. Tyler, and the moderator, Arthur W. Tyler.

No reason for inviting the Klan intrusion was ever given to the public, but unofficial spokesmen from the congregation surmised that the pastor and leadership approved of the visit, believing it might scare some of the "sinners" into repentance and a more moral lifestyle. The church pastor had openly endorsed the Klan activities in the area prior to the revival episode, while encouraging his members to join. Some did.

Hooded Klansmen marched through the front door of the church and walked up and down the aisles of the sanctuary for several minutes, while eyeing the awed congregation. Some sat down, apparently to listen to the revival message. Others got in their cars and drove away. It was a shocking display.

During the unconventional service, someone slipped out of the church and called Sheriff Ernest Sasser in Conway. When the benediction closed the service, county deputies were waiting outside with guns drawn. Sasser was not among them.

A little-publicized law had been passed during the last South Carolina General Assembly session making it illegal to wear masks on public property. Using that as a vehicle, the sheriff's force arrested fourteen of the Klansmen when they stepped onto highway property following the service.

All of those arrested were jailed overnight and released Thursday morning on $1,000 bond. The Klansmen, G. E. Cook, L. L. Gerald, Dr. A. J. Gore, Harvey Johnson, Rufus Bell, Waterman Johnson, Carl Lynn, Murrell Stanley, H. L. Booth, C. V. Bullock and Dewey Anderson, were all residents of the area and several had been involved in the melee at Fitzgerald's.

Ironically, on Monday (four days later), A. L. Tyler, a deacon in the Cane Branch Church, swore out warrants against the deputies who had arrested the Klansmen. The warrants charged the deputies with disrupting a church service and using obscene language. The warrants were issued by Horry County Magistrate W. F. Simmons against the deputies, indicating that the Cane Branch Church's approval of the Klan was localized. Deacons from other churches flocked to the rescue of the deputies and posted bonds for them a few hours after they were charged.

H. L. Bellamy, H. S. Morton, and H. P. Horton, of the Wampee Baptist Church, and H. G. Cushman, the Conway postmaster, posted bail for Deputy Bell. Jordan's bond was posted by W. A. Stilley, steward of the Conway Methodist Church, along with L. Y. Hodges and W. F. Hendricks, deacons of the Cedar Grove Baptist Church. Johnson's bond was posted by W. L. Robinson, deacon of the Conway Baptist Church, Pastor W. T. Johnson and Deacon J. J. Ray, of the Berea Baptist Church, and Pastor C. H. Tyler, of the Piney View Baptist Church.

Allen's bail was posted by J. A. Long, Lee Robinson, B. E. Richardson and T. O. Lane, deacons of the Conway Baptist Church.

Lewis's bond was posted by E. C. Wall, deacon of the Conway Presbyterian Church, and Joe Ivey of the Myrtle Beach Baptist Church, Frink Hughes, steward of the Myrtle Beach Methodist Church, and R. A. Johnson, C. L. Benton and C. H. Holcomb, Myrtle Beach businessmen. All bondsmen were well-known church and community leaders and this was a heartening influence for those of us fighting the Klan lawlessness who often wondered if we had the support of even the best people.

There was great significance in the response to the plight of the law enforcement officers. Their bondsmen came from all over Horry County and from many Protestant denominations. It was a message to the Klan that while congregations of a few small churches had approved of the intimidation and other activities of the Klan, the overwhelming majority of the populace was opposed to the lawless terrorists. They stood up to be counted.

This unity of the church leadership was of paramount importance to me and my crusade. Preachers and church leaders had acquiesced throughout the whole Klan reorganization and floggings. They seemed to dodge the issue, seldom condemning the KKK for obviously unchristian principles. Certainly the Klan was not practicing peace on earth and good will toward men. They were not turning the other cheek. They were not adhering to the biblical sermon on the mount or "do unto others as you would have them do unto you." The unity shown by bondsmen was especially meaningful to me since it came at a time when I badly needed encouragement.

Eventually the cases against the Klansmen were dropped, as were the charges against the deputies. But the incident did solidify Protestant opposition to the KKK. No further intrusions into church services were ever reported.

Maybe we were getting our simple message across. Maybe our editorials and a constant barrage of reporting shameful KKK terror was making progress. I certainly hoped so, as Thanksgiving approached. But while the Klan apparently decided it should stay away from church services where religious leaders were not susceptible to their propaganda, their determination to set the standards of moral behavior for the people continued. Clayton Sellers, who had watched the first motorcade pass through Tabor City, and Robert Lee Gore, were tricked out of their homes in the wee hours of the morning. They thought they were on a mission of mercy, but it was a clever ruse to abduct them. The Klan used the same deceit time after time. Their floggings were flagrant violations of human rights and the security of a man's home. Was it really his castle?

Klan's church invasion was talk of the town.

Prince Wanted an Arsenal

At the very height of the Ku Klux Klan uprising and when my newspaper was being threatened daily because of the vigorous crusade that we had launched, my longtime friend Eldred E. Prince of Loris, South Carolina, was getting a haircut in the corner barbershop when some of those waiting for the chair began a lively conversation about the crusade. Most of the talk was pro-Klan and vile and derogatory against the campaign.

Prince was never one to mince words or straddle fences. He openly came to my defense, declaring that I was fighting for the right cause and the Klan was a menace to the community and to society. He only got frowns and hostile gestures from the kibitzers.

When he returned home, he got to thinking that maybe some of those in the barbershop were Klansmen and that he might be dragged from his home and "kluxed" for what he had said.

"I had one shotgun in the house, but that didn't seem adequate. I drove to Whiteville to Gore's Sporting Shop and bought a 16-shot .22 caliber automatic rifle, a sawed-off shotgun and a pistol. I figured that with an arsenal like that I could at least leave some Klansmen in the grass if they decided my defense of the newspaper deserved a flogging.

"They never came after me," Prince remembers.

Chapter Eighteen
Cries in the Night

A noisy midnight knock at his front door awakened Clayton Sellers as he and his wife slept in their New Hope community home ten miles north of Tabor City. It was a breezy November night just before Thanksgiving and the Sellers had gone to bed early.

A twenty-eight-year-old automobile mechanic, Sellers was not surprised to find two men on his steps who asked for his assistance. They claimed to have run out of gasoline down the road and had heard that Sellers was the man to help them. Would he please help them get their car started? Sellers often helped stranded motorists in the middle of the night.

Sellers pulled on his clothes and, still barefoot, stepped outside, picked up a gas can off the porch and went to his pickup for a rubber hose.

"I'll try to siphon enough out of my tank to get you to a station," Sellers said, trying to accommodate the strangers.

He dropped a small hose into the tank and started to use his mouth to create enough suction to get the flow started. But he never finished the chore. A car screeched to a stop in front of his house. Two masked men jumped out and grabbed Sellers. The two strangers that Sellers was trying to help quickly fled. It became painfully clear to Sellers that he had been tricked out of his house so the Ku Klux Klansmen could kidnap him without the danger of getting shot.

Sellers was no weakling. He struggled and yelled as his assailants pinned his arms behind his back and then struck him over the head with a monkey wrench.

Sellers' aging mother heard the commotion and dashed out of the house. Seeing the masked men wrestling with her son, she grabbed for one of the face masks. The kidnapper quickly slapped the old lady to the ground.

Meanwhile, inside the house, Mrs. Sellers realized that

something was wrong. She retrieved a .38 caliber pistol from the nightstand and ran out to the porch. The assailants were dragging Clayton to their car as she came out. Not daring to shoot toward her husband, she fired five fast shots into the air. It did not deter the Klansmen. They roared off down the road with Sellers stuffed in the trunk.

Ordinarily in this day and age you would have expected Mrs. Sellers to call the sheriff's office for assistance—her husband had been abducted. But she didn't. Few people flogged by the Klan reported the incidents immediately. Sometimes they delayed for several weeks. Many were afraid to turn to the law enforcement officers because Grand Dragon Hamilton constantly claimed many belonged to his Klan. The delay might also have been prompted by the problems and behavior of the victims and families who didn't want to air their dirty linen in public. Many had a life-style that was frowned on in the community.

Sellers' mother and wife went back inside the house. They sat down, cried and waited. What was this all about?

Other masked men joined the kidnappers a few miles from Sellers' home. They tied Sellers' hands around a tree and proceeded to whip him with what he believed to be a machine belt or a strip from an automobile tire. He screamed and kicked as the punishment continued for more than an hour. Two burly men took turns beating him from his hips to his knees.

"What are you beating me for?" Sellers asked the masked mobsters.

"Because you hit your mother," one replied.

"I have never struck my mother in my life," Sellers protested, but his words did not stop the flogging that left him black and blue and with injuries that required medical attention.

In reporting the whipping more than a week after it happened, perhaps because the sheriff had been sent information by the emergency room at the hospital, Sellers said that he had never struck his mother. He and his wife had had a bit of trouble several months earlier, but they had patched that up and were living together amiably. He pointed out that his wife had tried to defend him from the kidnappers.

After suffering the severe beating at what he later described as "an out-of-the-way place," one of the night riders put a gun to Sellers' back and told him to "get gone and don't look back." He did glance around enough to know that there were a half-dozen or more Klan cars parked in the area. He staggered home to his worried wife and mother at dawn.

While the flogging of Sellers did not occur on the same night, Sheriff Hugh Nance learned about that incident on the same day he learned that a strikingly similar beating had been inflicted upon Robert Lee Gore in another midnight attack.

Gore's sleep was disturbed by a knock on his door in the Olyphic section of Columbus County, a farmland community near the South Carolina border about twenty miles from the nearest town. He answered the knock to find two strangers on his porch, possibly the same ones who had kidnapped Sellers.

"Our car has knocked off down the road a mile or so. Can you do us a favor and help us get it started?" they pleaded, asking for another mission of mercy.

Gore, a farmer, had mechanical experience like Sellers. He didn't exactly relish the midnight work, but agreed to help his callers. He went to an outbuilding and gathered some tools as the two strangers followed. He got into the car with them and they drove south across the state line less than two miles away.

They stopped the car near a parked vehicle and got out. Gore followed them. As they neared the car, all four doors burst open and masked Klansmen grabbed Gore. The two strangers headed back for their car and drove away.

The kidnappers blindfolded Gore, forced him across the front fender of the car and two men alternated beating him with a whip similar to the weapon used to flog Sellers.

Later, the abductors kicked Gore out of their car a mile from his home in Olyphic and dared him to report the flogging to the law. He kept quiet for more than a week, but at the insistence of his family he reported the abduction and flogging to Sheriff Nance. It was coincidence that both Sellers and Gore decided to talk the same day.

The floggings were almost identical. The sheriff was reasonably sure that the assailants were the same. And they had made a mistake that would eventually be their undoing. They had carried Gore across the state line, which made the flogging a federal offense. Nance asked the Federal Bureau of Investigation for help, and they quickly got involved.

F.B.I. Director J. Edgar Hoover hated the Ku Klux Klan. He assigned some of his finest agents to the Carolinas. They soon infiltrated the ranks of the Klan and their expertise in undercover operations began paying off.

Local and state officers were generally helpful and cooperative. But they are always under political pressure when thousands of voters are involved. And there were thousands of Klansmen. But they had no influence with the F.B.I. Hoover's men had a job to do and they did it.

My weekly "Carter's Column," which appeared the first week of the new year in 1952, praised the F.B.I., chastised the Klan again for its self-righteousness and challenged the good people in the Klan ranks to desert the cause while they could with dignity. Some did, and that brought the wrath of Hamilton down on me again in the form of a letter that reeked with hate.

Hamilton's vindictive letter minced no words.

Invisible Empire
Association of Carolina Klans
of the
Ku Klux Klan

Leesville, S.C.
January 21, 1952
Office of the
Grand Dragon

Mr. W. Horace Carter
Tabor City Tribune Press
Tabor City, N.C.

Dear Sir:

In the Tabor City Tribune Press under the title "Carter's Column," I read that you express your opinions and views about the people who are advertising in your paper and who subscribe to your newspaper—or should I say Trash Sheet? If there is one thing that the Organization of which I am leader stands for, it is freedom of the Press. Now Freedom of the Press, when used recklessly by some individual, whose mind is warped, and I have every cause to believe that yours is in that condition since the day that I had a conference with you, which was held through your insistence, by some of the statements you made at that time.

Now, Sir, since reading your column, and some of the other columns and news articles, I am led to challenge you to prove without a shadow of a doubt, where the Ku Klux Klan had anything whatsoever to do with the flogging or so-called flogging in your section of North Carolina recently. I further challenge you to prove where the organization has in any way tried to administer Justice on anyone—when that statement is made by you or anyone else it is a contemptable falsehood.

You further state in your column that in your way of thinking, the Klan is against the Constitutional Principles laid down by our forefathers. Your leanings and warped ideas seem to me that you could not give a fair interpretation of the Constitution. You further stated, in your column, about Fair Bluff—let me state clearly to you that upon a personal investigation, there was no connection there with reference to the Klan. When an individual and his family takes certain steps, it does not necessarily involve the Klan. If I were a resident of Fair Bluff, I would make you eat the newspapers you printed it in for telling an untruth about the people having so many guns in readiness. It is such untruths that stir up neighborhoods and cause violence. If your column was thoroughly analyzed, the right interpretation would be—that you advocate force and violence. You further stated in your column that the F.B.I. are nearing the day when wholesale arrests will be made. First, let me ask you a fair question—what is the matter with the elected law officers of Columbus County?

After the War Between the States, which was fought for the preservation of States' Rights the stalwart men of the South had to fight back oppression. History tells us that the carpetbaggers and scalawags and federal troops and agents were driven out of the Southland. The sooner that each individual State awakens and realizes its Constitutional rights, the sooner we will have less Federal interference and less agitation.

Now, Sir, you profess to be a teacher of a Sunday School class, professing and teaching the story of the Good Samaritan, yet when you print your column, you make the following statement: that you believe that the members of the Klan, in your area, are largely a bunch of disgruntled persons and low type individuals with of course some good people in their midst. Now, Sir, let me say, first, I have not had the pleasure of meeting all of the members of the Klan in your area, but those that I have had the pleasure of meeting and those that I know personally, I can truthfully say that you have made a **GROSS** mis-statement. I agree with you that there are some people in and around Tabor City who are telling that they are members of the Klan but I want to assure you that those people are not members of the Klan but are some disgruntled persons who are using that means of having something to hide behind. Sir, I dare you or any individual in North Carolina to find anything of an accusing nature against any man who holds membership in the Klan. Sir, they are the CREAM of the CROP in Tabor City and in Columbus County North Carolina.

Further in your column, you made reference to what a Christian gentleman said; I do not know who the so-called Christian gentleman is you had reference to and I care less, for my interpretation of the Holy Bible, God's plan and purpose, is to LIFT men UP. I have heard people, time and again make this statement with reference to the Church: "If so and so is connected with the Church, I don't care to belong to it." Remember-the shoe might fit your foot.

Constructive criticism is fine, but destructive criticism like your column does not make you any bigger in the eyesight of your people whom you must depend on to sell your papers and advertisement. Remember, you are a servant of the people and no matter what organization might be instituted or set up, you will always find some good therein. There is no individual living who does not have some good traits no matter how low or how bad he or she may get. I am always ready to act the part that Jesus Christ my Savior has implanted in my heart—that is to reach down and lift those who have fallen up, wherever it is possible to do so. My sole ambition, through the help of Almighty God, is in some way to help lift a Sinful and Perverted Nation back on its feet and into its rightful place.

God has a mission for each individual and he shoulders the responsibility that God has given him. America NEEDS MEN.

It was signed "Yours truly, Thomas L. Hamilton."

I did not correct any of the misspellings. I wanted the readers to see the letter exactly as Hamilton had written it.

After getting such a raking over the coals, I examined my column that had run on the front page. It was a pretty hard-hitting message, but I meant every word of it, even if it did bother the Grand Dragon.

These were the words that drew most of Hamilton's ire:

Our opinion of the Ku Klux Klan has never wavered. We still consider the organization a repulsive evil, and we are even more provoked now that a minister in Fair Bluff has been threatened by the Klan for preaching against them. It has so disturbed the preacher that he has left town and reportedly has suffered a nervous breakdown.

[Author's note: *He never returned to his pastorate after a dozen Klansmen invaded his worship service on Sunday morning and threatened his life if he continued to talk against them in the pulpit.*]

These hooded hoodlums are unfit and unworthy of administering justice upon anyone. The principles on which they exist are against the constitutional rights of Americans that were laid down by our forefathers.

Fair Bluff is now in turmoil because of Klan threats to a Baptist pastor and other church leaders. The night-riding bandits have stirred up the good people of the community to such an extent that the little town is now an armed camp that could explode into a violent confrontation with the least provocation. It's a dangerous situation.

All this fear is the result of the Ku Klux Klan, even though they deny the charges of threatening the preacher. Their very existence created the situation.

The day is fast approaching when the F.B.I. will bring the Klan floggers into court and to the bar of justice. There will be wholesale arrests and the secret membership will be exposed. Only legal action against the Klan will stop a violent and deadly confrontation. It will surely happen if the Klan continues to run rampant, flogging and intimidating people all over the area. We hope no massacre ever occurs, but that is certainly probable if the law does not stop the vigilantes.

We have long contended that the Klan membership is largely made up of disgruntled, prejudiced malcontents with only a handful of respectable people among them. That opinion is unchanged and was further strengthened last week when a local Christian man whom I know made a confession to me.

"I joined the Klan because I had been led to believe that it was good for the community. I went to my first meeting and looked around at my fellow Klansmen. I picked up my hat and walked out. I don't associate with people like that on the outside and I'm certainly not going to be one of them under a robe and hood," the friend divulged his mistake.

That's the kind of decision we would like a lot of Klansmen to make. Look around you! Do you feel at home with hoodlums? I think not.

Of course the Grand Dragon didn't like the column, but then I didn't want him to like it.

SACRED FREEDOMS
- Freedom of Expression
- Freedom of Assembly
- Freedom of The Press
- Freedom From Fear

The Tabor City Tribune

TABOR CITY
- Built by Farmers
- Patronized by Farmers
- Devoted to Farmers
- Interested in Farmers

"Tabor City — The Town With A City Future"

VOL. VI, NUMBER 21   TABOR CITY, N. C., WEDNESDAY, FEBRUARY 20, 1952   5¢ A COPY; $2.00 A YEAR

Public Pleased With Arrest of 10 Alleged Ku Klux Klansmen

The Hoods Were Off When This Picture Was Made

The 10 age Ku Klux Klansmen who were arrested last Saturday by the FBI seem to be slightly reluctant in having their pictures made after having been jailed in Fayetteville and charged with kidnapping and violations of civil rights. They are all out on bail on $5,000 bond pending a hearing next Wednesday or Thursday. Their faces and names were available to the public are left to right, front row, Bob Hayes, Early L. Brooks, Jesse Edmund, Fireman Fay Strickland, and Sherwood Miller. Back row, Horace Strickland, George Miller, L. G. Worley, Bobby Brooks and Bost Edmund.

Contract Let For Nakina Central High School

LEGION SEEKS BASEBALL FUNDS

INVESTIGATION TO CONTINUE ON OTHER WHIPPING CASES

Contract Let For Nakina Central High School

CAGE GAME

MRS. W. A. SARVIS' MOTHER PASSES

WILLIAMS CLUB TO GIVE PLAY

LOCAL SCOUTS TAKE HONORS

They Felt The Night Riders' Lawless Whip

AN EDITORIAL

A MEASURE OF SUCCESS

Thank God, there is still law, courts and justice in Columbus county.

It took a great investigation stretched out over many weeks and of a highly tedious nature but despite impatience that some of us might have voiced at times, law enforcement officers stuck to the task and have succeeded in filing charges against ten alleged night floggers and Ku Klux Klansmen.

They have yet to be proven guilty. But they will have that opportunity, unlike those many persons brutally beaten by night riders in Columbus during the several months that violence headlined the news from this area.

In a court of law with defense attorneys seeking by hook or crook to clear them of charges, these men will present their cases. Most likely there will be wholesale denials of any part in the specific flogging for which they have been arrested. But officers of the law will also have an opportunity to submit the evidence which they have so painstakingly sought out. Then a jury will have an opportunity to decide their fate.

We make no boast about it. If these men are guilty, and the FBI has every reason to believe that they are, we have no sympathy for them. They brought the predicament upon themselves without rhyme or reason.

RETURN FROM N. Y.

Chapter Nineteen
The Tide Begins to Turn

A dozen miles from Tabor City in the swampland along the Waccamaw River, the tiny rural community of Nakina made big news when three prominent farmers were hauled into court for threatening to "Klux" one of their neighbors if he didn't run a Negro tenant off his farm. Although they denied KKK membership, they used the organization's slang term when threatening floggings and the matter was handled like a Ku Klux project. What was encouraging was that, finally, a local state court had dared face the wrath of the night riders.

Dan Ward had a Negro tenant family on his farm. He liked the tenant and the sharecropper farming arrangement was attractive to the black family. Ward provided housing, farm equipment, land, fertilizer and seed while the tenant family provided the labor. The landlord and the tenant split the profits in the fall. But there were no other Negroes in the Nakina community and this prompted the "Kluxing" threat on Christmas Day that was first revealed by Ward in January 1952.

It was on Christmas morning that Ward was shaken by the appearance of three neighbors, Pink Jacobs, Russell Blackmon and Johnnie Ward. They knocked on his door. They had come to lay down the Klan law. One man was armed.

"You get that nigger off your farm by next Sunday or we will burn your house and barn and Klux you too. Move and move fast if you want to live." That was the way Dan and his wife Ella later recounted the Christmas morning threat.

Although unnerved by the threatening trio, Ward had the courage to do something about it. He went to the courthouse in Whiteville and swore out warrants charging the neighbors with trespassing and assault. The case against them was scheduled for January in Columbus County Recorder's Court.

In court, the Wards' testimony was substantiated by

Edison Simmons and James Callahan, who said the trio approached them and asked that they take part in "running this nigger out of Nakina." Trespassing and threatened assault were evident to the court.

Court Solicitor Robert Schulken took a strong stand against the defendants, telling the jury, "This, in my opinion, is the most terrible thing that has ever happened in Columbus County. When things come to a place where you can't say who is going to live on your own property, it's time to regard the matter seriously."

It was regarded seriously and all three defendants were sentenced to two-year road sentences. They appealed and were released on $2,500 dollars bond before eventually paying $1,000 fines and serving five years on probation. The tenant did not move.

It was a turning point in the Klan movement. Finally, the local court had dared to oppose the vigilantes—something I had never expected to happen until after federal cases were brought to court and convictions were obtained. But these three over-zealous guardians of the Nakina community overstepped their bounds in threatening a landlord and a respected citizen who considered it his American right to hire any tenant—black or white. The people were on his side and no vigilante organization can exist under those circumstances. However, the threat to the unwanted Negro tenant had other implications and repercussions.

Arthur Leinwand and his wife, a personable Jewish couple, had opened a small clothing store in Tabor City. Leinwand had been concerned over the constant Klan criticism of the Jews, but he never reported any threats to the press or the sheriff. He kept the threats and his fears to himself.

The same week that the Kluxing threat was made to Dan Ward, Leinwand walked into the *Tribune* office with copy for an advertisement in his hand.

"Horace, run this in next week's paper. I'm leaving town," he said. I was surprised. I knew he had a reasonably good business and it would be tragic for the community to lose him. His advertisement read:

GOING OUT OF BUSINESS
LOST OUR LEASE
WE HATE TO LEAVE BUT WE MUST SACRIFICE OUR ENTIRE
STOCK OF MERCHANDISE AND SELL DOWN TO THE BARE
WALLS. OUR MISFORTUNE IS YOUR GOOD FORTUNE. ALL
STOCK MARKED DOWN TO COST OR BELOW
LEINWAND'S
Tabor City, N.C.

A few days later his doors closed and he moved to Virginia where he again went into the retail clothing store business. Did the Klan activity force him from Tabor City?

At the same time, my good Jewish friend and next door neighbor, Albert Schilds, seemed obsessed with something. Suddenly he was hospitalized with a bleeding ulcer. He was back at work in a few weeks, but seemed weak and disturbed. If he had ever received a direct threat from the KKK, I was not aware of it. I only knew that the constant blatant criticism of the Jewish people was getting next to him. He never really prodded it out of his mind. The dangerous bleeding ulcer, a sure symptom of tension and stress, eventually killed him. I always wondered if the Ku Klux Klan hadn't been a leading cause of his demise. His wife continued to run the store for a few years before moving to Florida.

Klan rogues continued to harass the Fair Bluff community, located seventeen miles from Tabor City on the banks of the Lumber River. At first, Grand Dragon Hamilton denied his Klansmen had anything to do with the troubles. Later he changed his stand.

On January 30, he called the Associated Press from Whiteville, North Carolina, and announced that he was disbanding the Fair Bluff Klavern for "unklanish activities." He further said, "Some men have joined the Fair Bluff Klavern who have taken the wrong attitude and want to take the law into their own hands. The Klan does not approve of that kind of activity."

The downfall of the Association of Carolina Klans was imminent. But it still had some breath left in its unholy life.

Klansmen demanded a Negro tenant move out of the community.

Klansmen watch burning cross.

Chapter Twenty
A Flurry of Floggings

Peace had not yet returned to the Fair Bluff community when the KKK again reared its ugly head and shocked the village.

Eugene Purcell, popular young pastor of the Fair Bluff Methodist Church, had invited a Negro quartet to sing at a men's fellowship supper. On the night of the performance, several cars with South Carolina license plates stopped in front of the church with four robed, masked men in each car. When the black singers arrived, the Klansmen warned the pastor and leaders of the fellowship club to cancel the performance. Trying to avoid a dangerous showdown, the pastor and his group succumbed to the threat. They quickly escorted the Negroes back to their homes. It was flagrant violation of church and human rights. It was a traumatic experience for the pastor and the church. Tyranny stared the community in the face.

Alton Bullock, manager of the black quartet, said he had been approached by a stranger several days before the singing was scheduled. The man advised the quartet not to show up at the church. He did not take the warning seriously, but the Klan appearance at the church was enough to convince him that the warning was real.

Preacher Purcell's wife was pregnant and the incident wore terribly on her. The family left town to await its return to normalcy—and it would return.

The same week that the quartet was rebuffed at the Fair Bluff church, a stranger walked into my office and asked to speak to the editor. He was obviously disturbed.

I shook his hand. He never gave me his name. It was typical of even the best people in the community. They generally didn't want to risk the displeasure of the Klan.

"Mr. Carter, I read your newspaper," he said quietly. I know you have been fighting the Klan. I suppose you would like to know who the Klansmen are who are flogging people and disrupting our church in Fair Bluff. I can surely identify one of them for you if it serves any purpose."

"Yes, of course. I am trying to learn the identities of as many of them as I can," I replied. "Who do you know and how are you sure?" I was always interested in knowing whom the Klan had recruited.

"When they held the rally at Williams Township, I got a good look at a pair of brown, decorative leather boots that were worn by one of the Klansmen on the rostrum. They were different from normal cowboy boots. I saw those same boots in my church yesterday at the worship service. I was an usher and when I walked down the aisle with the collection plate, there sat the man with his legs crossed, wearing those same boots. I would have recognized them anywhere. He was Early Brooks who used to be a Fair Bluff policeman. He sells lightning rods now," the stranger revealed his observation. "I expect he was the instigator of the warning for the Negroes not to sing. I thought it might be of help to you and the investigators to know at least one of the troublemakers in our church. He may be the ring leader."

I thanked the informant. I knew that Brooks was the Grand Cyclops of the Fair Bluff Klavern and that he had been a leader in the Klan movement from its beginning. He was a longtime friend of Thomas Hamilton and they had known each other in Georgia. It was good to have this additional information. The F.B.I. might find it useful.

Brooks was eventually rejected by Hamilton after a power struggle, but he would get what he deserved—arrest and conviction for participation in and planning of numerous floggings as well as the church debacle. He was among the most vindictive of the Klan's leaders and was an outspoken foe of the newspapers that opposed the KKK.

Suddenly flogging victims seemed to pop out of the wood-work. While the actual beatings had occurred weeks earlier, several abused men told their stories to the sheriff during the month of February. The public indignation over the Fair Bluff church incident backlashed against the Klan. For the first time people were more inclined to criticize the vigilantes. That made it a bit easier for flogging victims to step forward and tell their stories.

L. W. Jernigan of Hallsboro had been dragged from his home and viciously beaten on January 1. Grier Pinkney Wright, also of Hallsboro, was thrown into a car, taken to a desolate clearing in the immense Green Swamp and beaten on December 29.

Dorsey Robinson, a Negro from Chadbourn, like the white victims from Hallsboro, had kept his flogging to himself, but he had suffered multiple cuts and bruises from a severe beating that he endured on the night of October 11, five months earlier. He had finally gotten the courage to report the flogging. It is amazing how people will reveal well-kept secrets once they are convinced the public will sympathize. When public sentiment seemed to be more with the growing Klan, many of even the most abused victims suffered in silence.

This was the time to talk. Two weeks later the first big Klan bust would make the national headlines. The Association of Carolina Klans and Grand Dragon Thomas Hamilton were in the throes of ignominious defeat. At last, the Ku Klux Klan would be unmasked. The surly collection of rednecks would finally face the ridicule they so richly deserved. They had escaped justice for two years as hoods and robes and the gloom of night hid their identities from a cautious and often frightened citizenry.

Willard Cole, my longtime friend, fellow crusader and Editor of the *Whiteville News Reporter.*

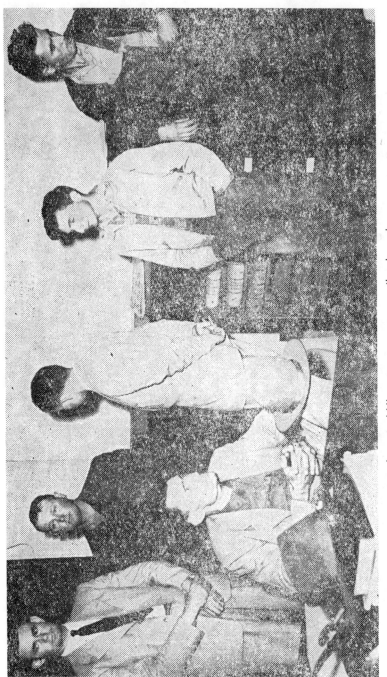

Arrested Klansmen were a motley bunch.

Chapter Twenty-one
F.B.I. Moves at Midnight

More than four months after Dorothy Dillard Martin and Ben Grainger were dragged from their bed, blindfolded, hauled across the state line and unmercifully whipped, their self-appointed judges and executioners would have their own sleep interrupted. The F.B.I. had done its job. Legal retribution in a democratic society would hold the trump card. Crestfallen KKK cowards would cringe and squirm when their deeds were exposed in the light of day for the world to judge.

Dorothy Martin, 35, and Ben Grainger, 40, were white Anglo-Saxon natives of Columbus County. Klansmen didn't approve of their common-law marriage. On the night of October 6, the Klan did something about it. It was to be their undoing. It doomed the resurrection of the Ku Klux Klan.

Knocking down the door, ten masked Klansmen burst into the bedroom, grabbed the frightened couple, tied towels over their eyes and pushed them onto the back seat of a car. They were then whisked across the state line into Horry County in South Carolina near Causey Crossroads. The Klansmen apparently were not aware that this mistake made their kidnapping a federal crime.

They charged the couple with not attending church regularly and living immoral lives. Grainger's clothes were jerked from his body. He was forced to bend over a car fender and was beaten with a piece of leather belt mounted on a wooden handle. The vicious lashing continued for twenty minutes or more, his assailants demanding that he agree to start going to church and stop living in sin with the Martin woman. Grainger suffered acutely and was so near collapse that his bowels moved, bringing a round of sadistic laughter from his assailants. He then slumped to the ground, unconscious. A bucket of water in his face revived him.

Flogged at the same time, but not as unmercifully, Dorothy screamed for mercy. She suffered from multiple bruises on her buttocks, but did not require the extensive medical attention that her friend did. About two in the morning, both were released on the roadside along Highway 9, ten miles from Fair Bluff .

Grainger was not the type who scared easily. He reported the flogging to the law despite warnings not to. The case was considered a crucial one by the F.B.I. and they asked that no public announcement be made of the whipping. The press agreed. The F.B.I. wanted to study the flagrant case without interference or pressure from the newspapers. And they did not want the Klan to know they were investigating. It went unpublicized from midnight on October 6, 1951, until the crackdown of Saturday night, February 18, 1952.

Synchronizing their watches to make sure an arrest of one Klansman did not lead to a tip-off of others, thirty-five federal agents and Sheriff Hugh Nance's Columbus County force swooped down upon ten Klansmen at exactly midnight. It caught all the Klansmen in the Martin-Grainger assault case by surprise. Handcuffs were clamped on the motley, dismayed floggers simultaneously.

Dressed in overalls and work pants, the unshaven Klansmen were jailed in Fayetteville and charged with kidnapping and violating the civil rights of Martin and Grainger—almost before they could rub the sleep out of their frightened eyes. Their bail was set at $5,000 each by U.S. Commissioner T. L. Hon. They were all locked up.

It was a forlorn crew. Early L. Brooks, the Fair Bluff Grand Cyclops and former town policeman who had killed a prisoner while holding that position, was among them. His eighteen-year-old son, Bobby, employed in Raleigh, was arrested in the state capital and joined his father in Fayetteville.

Horace Strickland, a former Tabor City policeman, was one of the arrested Klansmen, as were Ross Enzor, 43; L. C. Worley, 25; Pittman Foy Strickland, 29; George Miller, 19; Sherwood Miller, 26; Steve Edmunds, 26 and Bobby Hayes, 40.

The investigation of this case was a well-kept secret that might have been almost impossible today when the energetic, highly-pressured, competitive and motivated media leaves law enforcement with little privacy. That midnight raid took almost everyone by surprise even though there had been a general feeling for weeks that something dramatic and consequential was about to happen. The F.B.I.'s lengthy presence indicated progress and success were in the making.

Charged with kidnapping under the Lindbergh Law, the

128

terrible ten faced possible death sentences. That law made kidnapping a capital offense in the United States for the first time.

The announcement of the federal arrests was made in the wee hours of the morning by F.B.I. Director J. Edgar Hoover in Washington, D.C. When he sent the F.B.I. agents to the eastern Carolinas, he had instructed them to "find the criminals and bring them to court regardless of how tedious the job is and how long it takes."

The successful crackdown resulted from hard work, surveillance and interrogation of suspects, along with informants who had secretly worked their way into the Klan.

The Hoover announcement made the headlines of newspapers, magazines, radio and television all over the nation.

American Broadcasting Company's noted news reporter, Drew Pearson, announced the arrests of the Klansmen on his late-night news program. Having discussed the impending raid with the F.B.I. in Washington, he said that several agents had infiltrated the Klan ranks, gathered an abundance of evidence against the night riders and expected additional arrests to be made soon. He obviously had inside information that was not available to our little newspaper.

Sheriff Nance told us the following day, as the crackdown was now the main topic of conversation all over the area, that these arrests were indeed only the first. Every flogging case was nearly solved. Many other Klansmen would be fearful, cringing in semi-hiding, and awaiting the midnight knock on their doors by law enforcement officers. The tables had been turned. Their own invasion of private homes to inflict their kind of vigilante justice was over.

Citizens all over the southeastern Carolinas were suddenly elated over the arrests. In Tabor City, Mayor Al Williams said: "People in Columbus County are just like the rest of the nation. We feel that there is no place for this outlaw organization. Any group that tries to break up the democratic way of life is riding for a fall."

Chief of Police L. R. Watson added: "The fact that two former police officers in our county were among those arrested casts a reflection upon all the other officers. I am not sorry that they have been arrested, but I am sorry that they had any part to play in the Ku Klux Klan lawlessness."

P. C. Gantt, pastor of the six hundred-member Tabor City Baptist Church said: "I'm glad to see this organization broken up.

As I made many talks against the Klan I always had the support of my business partner, Mark C. Garner.

Maybe the community can now get back to normal." He was my pastor. It struck me as strange that he waited for the arrests to make any statement opposing the Klan. He had kept strangely quiet.

G. W. Crutchfield, pastor of the St. Paul Methodist Church in Tabor City, who had preached a sermon against the Klan insurrection and applauded the *Tribune* for crusading against them, said: "I am glad to see this lawlessness brought to a head. This definite progress is welcomed. Maybe now things will quiet down."

U. S. District Attorney Charles P. Green released a statement following the arrests: "I will present the evidence and seek convictions against these ten Klansmen. They will be brought to trial in Fayetteville in March. I do not know how much punishment will be recommended to the jury. But I am confident we have enough evidence to get a conviction." Later Green let it be known that he would not ask for the death penalty.

There was much speculation following the jailing of the infamous ten on whether the Klan would post their bail.

The question was answered quickly. C. L. Tart, a Dunn, North Carolina, lumberman, posted the $5,000 bail for seven of the defendants. Tart had a long-standing acquaintance with a prominent and influential Fair Bluff businessman who many believed prompted him to post the bails. He said he did it because he had business interests in Columbus County.

Bail for Enzor and Hayes was posted by J. A. Lovett, a Nichols, South Carolina, businessman. Mrs. Bessie Edmunds made bond for her son Steve.

I was overjoyed with the crackdown after two years of crusading that at times seemed like such a lost cause. I wrote an editorial for the front page. A news story told of the arrests of the Klansmen under a banner headline.

A MEASURE OF SUCCESS

Thank God there are still laws, courts and justice in Columbus County.

It took a great and lengthy investigation of a highly tedious nature, but despite impatience that some of us voiced at times, law enforcement officers stuck to their task and have filed charges against ten night floggers and Ku Klux Klansmen.

They have yet to be proven guilty. They will have their opportunity to defend themselves, unlike those many people brutally beaten by night riders here over many violent months.

In a court of law with defense attorneys seeking by hook or crook to clear them of charges, they will have their chances to present their defense. Likely there will be wholesale denials in the specific floggings in which they have been charged. Officers will then present the painstaking evidence that they sought so diligently to obtain. A jury will then decide the fate of the accused.

We make no bones about it. If these men are guilty, and the F.B.I. has every reason to believe that they are, we have no sympathy, no compassion for them. They brought the predicament upon themselves without rhyme or reason.

Our greatest hope is that those other Klansmen who have participated in the numerous floggings will soon feel the strong arm of the law reaching out for them too. Wherever they are and whomever they are, we want to see them ferreted out from behind their masks of cowardice to face the world and pay for the crimes they have committed against their neighbors.

Every night flogger is due severe punishment and law enforcement officers will not rest on the present laurels. Every effort is continuing and Klansmen will be flushed out of their hiding places and exposed to the world.

The *Tribune's* biggest and boldest headlines ever in the Ku Klux Klan crusade would appear just one week later. At last, the State Bureau of Investigation would also make its move. But the next seven days were traumatic for me. Sympathizers of the Klan were angry that I had editorialized against their brethren who had been arrested and jailed. They struck back. Again their hatred and vengeance would hit me close to home. It was another heartbreaking event.

Big Bruisers Wanted Fight

Twice during the dangerous Klan era, I was confronted on the Tabor City streets by a stranger who was obviously trying to provoke a fight. In each instance the troublemaker stopped me, looked me right in the eye and said, "Carter, you are a son-of-a-bitch."

In those days, to call a man a son-of-a-bitch in North Carolina was the equivalent of striking the first blow in a fight when court action followed. The bruisers who confronted me were obviously ready to be charged with starting the fight. What they were after was an excuse for beating me to a pulp. I was sure I would have come out second in both those near-fisticuffs.

I have to admit that both insults were hard to take and I was inclined to fight. But my better judgment told me I would not be up to the challenge. I would be seriously whipped.

I looked the rednecks in the face, folded my arms and said, "Both you and I know that I can't be a son-of-a-bitch. That's a biological impossibility." The off-the-cuff remark seemed to take the fight out of my would-be assailants. They muttered a few words and walked away.

I guess it was better to be a live coward in the eyes of those Klansmen than to be a dead hero. But it was hard to avoid fighting when invited to do so—a trait handed down from life in the Old West.

Chapter Twenty-two
Another Dognapping

It was after Bess had been kidnapped and penned up for weeks and before she escaped that I developed a special hatred for those persons who inflicted such cruelty on man's best friend.

Seeing how distraught I was over my missing bird dog, a close friend had tried to comfort me by giving me a fine Labrador retriever pup. He was a beautiful dog, as black as the dark side of the moon. I named him Chad, and long before Bess returned home, Chad and I became good friends. Like Bess, I let Chad run loose in the yard and often walked with him around the block at sunset after I came home from work. He quickly developed into a fine retriever. He brought back everything that I threw for him to fetch on the water or in the field. I am sure he would have been a great duck retriever, but I never had a chance to find out.

A day or two after I wrote the editorial applauding the F.B.I. for arresting the ten Klansmen and suggesting that they be given stiff punishments, my office telephone rang. It was quitting time and I had just headed out the door. I started to ignore it, but decided to answer. A man's muffled voice began talking before I had a chance to say "hello."

"I know you are Horace Carter because you are the only one in your office right now. I just drove by your place. I thought you would like to know you can't walk around the block with that damned old dog of yours today. I have him in the trunk of my car. You'll never see him again if you keep on writing all that trash in your newspaper about the Klan. It's a pack of lies, you no-good bastard. Just thought I would let you know where your dog is." The phone went dead before I could say a word.

I hurried home, hoping that it was some crackpot's idea of a joke. I looked around the house and called for Chad. He wasn't there. Chad loved everyone. Anyone stopping a car on the street could have beckoned to him and he would have jumped right in. Chad never met a stranger. He was everybody's friend. Now he was gone. I shuddered at the thought of his abduction.

"Lucile, have you seen Chad in the last hour or so?" I asked.

"Yes, I fed him at the back door not long ago," she replied.

"Well, he's gone now," I said, and then related the telephone threat I had just received.

"I guess we are still going to get killed or burned out," Lucile said. "There will never be a time around here when we are safe, even if the Klan is broken up. There will always be those sympathizers and relatives who may take out their vengeance on you, me and the children. If they can take our dog, they could have just as easily taken Linda or Rusty." She was frightened and she was right.

It was enough to make me consider my position all over again. I had put her and the children through incredible stress over two years of crusading. It wasn't anything like the peaceful life she had enjoyed as a schoolteacher in Gastonia, North Carolina, before we were married. But she believed that in marriage, the good comes with the bad. She knew I was determined to be a newspaper man before we said our vows and I was determined not to be just another newspaper man. I wanted to do my best to make Tabor City and my small corner of the world a better place to live. I knew I was succeeding in a small way. But I felt pain for her fear and suffering and now I also felt for Chad. The thought was inescapable—were the principles that I was fighting for worth the trauma and trouble?

"'Cile, I think I can feel your pain. You are the one who stands guard here night and day wondering what is going to happen next and whether the kids will be snatched away or our house destroyed. Maybe we should never have come to Tabor City. But we did. And you know and I know that I could never live with myself if I didn't stay here and finish this job you and I started. Isn't that so?" I pleaded.

She fought back the tears before surrendering the words that I will always remember.

"Oh, I am proud of you. You have known that all along. But it's hard to face the threats and danger and remain calm about it. I don't believe we will ever be safe here, but I'll do my best to support you with as little complaining as possible."

It made me love her more than ever. I could not fight this fight without the support of my loved ones at home. Her support was enormously important. And with Lucile again pregnant, making her even more vulnerable to the threats, I felt great sympathy swell within me.

Chad's disappearance was on my mind for weeks, but it did nothing to temper my crusade. I hoped he hadn't suffered, but suspected otherwise. It would be two full weeks before my fears materialized. I worked with renewed vigor.

State investigators were somewhat irritated that the F.B.I. had made ten arrests without asking for the assistance of the State Bureau of Investigation. The S.B.I. Klan Task Force from Raleigh speeded up their clock. A week after the first crackdown, the S.B.I., with Sheriff Nance alongside, arrested eight Klan suspects and threw them in the Columbus County jail in Whiteville. They were charged with another flogging.

They were charged with conspiracy to kidnap, kidnapping and assault in a case involving Esther Lee Floyd, a Negro girl from Chadbourn, on November 14, 1951. The men had driven to the home of Esther's parents. With drawn pistols they forced her father and mother into a bedroom, locked the door and pushed Esther Lee into a car. She believed they drove about 15 miles before stopping.

An unmerciful whipping ensued and stopped only when she pleaded that she was pregnant. They then shaved a cross in her hair and told her, "Go to Whiteville and tell everyone the Kluxers got you." She did, but that case, like many others, was not publicized until after the investigation was complete and the arrests made.

Eighteen officers participated in the S.B.I. raid and simultaneous arrests. Five of the eight arrested were Klansmen already facing charges in the Fair Bluff Martin-Grainger kidnapping. They were Early Brooks, Bobby Brooks, Bob Hayes, L. C. Worley and Steve Edmunds.

Three new Klansmen were charged in the Floyd beating: Douglas Grainger, 19, of Fair Bluff; Billy Horn, 25, of Chadbourn; and Leamon Ward, 40, of Chadbourn. Ironically, there was another Leamon Ward, a Columbus County commissioner and postmaster at Nakina, but the arrested Klansman was a different man and I pointed this out in the newspaper account of the arrests.

Police confiscated a leather strap two inches wide and six feet long from the Ward residence when the arrests were made.

These very first state warrants against the eight Floyd assailants were sworn out in County Recorder's Court, but a grand jury would later indict the Klansmen and change the trial to Superior Court. They were all held in jail overnight and eventually released on $5,000 bond each.

For the first time, officers from the S.B.I. divulged a well-kept secret—they had been investigating the KKK for about a year, coming to Columbus County even before the first recruiting rally was held at Williams Township.

The last week of February was a busy one for Klan-breaking news. Federal Commissioner T. L. Hon set the hearing of the charges against the ten arrested by the F.B.I. for March 3, and announced that they would be tried in March if true bills were returned by the grand jury in Fayetteville.

Fair Bluff was back in the news. Pastor Eugene Purcell, of

135

the Fair Bluff Methodist Church (where the Negro singers had been turned away) suffered a nervous breakdown. He tendered his resignation and moved in with his parents in Goldsboro. A well-liked man, he had pastored the church for three years. But now the Klan threats had broken him and robbed him of his enthusiasm for the ministry.

Grand Dragon Thomas Hamilton, thoroughly disturbed over the arrests of his henchmen, particularly Early Brooks, disbanded the Fair Bluff Klavern. He claimed Brooks had assumed too much authority and was the primary cause the Klavern was being disbanded. Maybe he was trying to protect his own skin by passing the buck to Brooks.

It was at this time that a blue-ribbon grand jury was convened in Raleigh to study crime in eastern North Carolina. Judge Don Gilliam charged the grand jury and several victims of Klan floggings were called to testify about the lawlessness.

The S.B.I. was somewhat miffed over the filing of F.B.I. cases and complained to the newspapers. Governor Kerr Scott pointed out that there was still plenty of work remaining in solving at least twelve other flogging incidents in North Carolina and that the state officers would get the credit when they brought those charges to court. It prodded them into a more intense effort.

For the first time in history, National Broadcasting Company newsmen and photographers converged on Columbus County. Documentary newsreels for theaters and television, then in its infancy in the Carolinas, were shot of victims, officers and even weekly newspaper editors. It was big time for our region, but we were not particularly proud of their reason for being there. At least NBC would let the world know we were fighting the menace.

Leo Derrick, editor of the *Columbus County News*, a weekly newspaper in Chadbourn, had not taken a big part in the Klan crusade, but he broke the Fair Bluff story about the threats to the Negro quartet. After reporting the arrests and the minister's nervous shock, Derrick found a note under the windshield wiper of his car at midday. It said, "You had your nose in the Fair Bluff Klan's work. So what do you think of things now?"

The unsigned message was a bit confusing. He never knew just what it meant. It drew his newspaper into the Klan campaign.

I received my usual threats that week, too. Under the office door were clippings of the paper from the previous week announcing the ten arrests. Scribbled with a blue crayon were the words "Carter's Trash." Written with a pencil across the picture of the Fair Bluff couple who had been beaten were the words "These two deserved it." Then there was the attached note that said, "Carter we don't waunt (sic) any of your trash sent through the mail." All the clippings were in an envelope with a Nakina postmark. That was confusing, too.

In that same issue of the *Tribune* I ran a picture of a Ku Klux Klan membership application. I captioned it:

"Your signature here plus a $10 check makes you a member of the Ku Klux Klan."

I also wrote another Klan editorial that week.

An Aroused Public

Our county and the Tabor City area have received a great deal of nationwide publicity in recent days. Unfortunately, this publicity has been bad. But it shouldn't be.

We are not proud of the circumstances that brought this publicity, we regret that an organization like the Ku Klux Klan could come into our area and recruit a following so large that it rates all the space in newspapers, magazines and the airways all over the nation.

Despite all the bad publicity that has brought us into the public eye, we are happy that against all odds something has been done about the night floggings of our people. It was painstaking, expensive and required great effort, but an aroused public felt the need for cooperation with the law and from that massive assistance has come these early arrests. Others are in the making.

Time magazine has called us a sleepy little Tar Heel town. That's a matter of opinion. We have never before had the name of being sleepy. On the contrary, we have always felt we were a lively little town and one that got things done when it rose to the occasion.

In the Klan resurrection, we believe we were far from being asleep. On the contrary, the newspaper and the better people of the town were alive to the need for eradicating the cancerous Klan that has no regard for human dignity. *Time* construed the infamous rise of the Klan with our community lackadaisical, sleepy if you will. That's derogatory, and as far as the Klan revival is concerned, unwarranted.

In the meantime, the Klan was being caught in a tightening vise in South Carolina. Finally, a flogging victim, upset that local law enforcement wasn't doing anything about her abduction, wrote to Governor Jimmy Byrnes and he called in the South Carolina Law Enforcement Division (S.L.E.D.). He demanded greater effort. It did the trick.

My dog Chad was still missing. I hoped he had died a painless death.

Carter and Cole named "Tar Heels of the Week" by *Raleigh News and Observer*

Chapter Twenty-three
More Floggings, More Arrests

At the same time that North Carolina investigators were arresting the eight attackers of Esther Lee Floyd, the South Carolina Klan was performing its first ritualistic beating of a person they considered immoral—they inflicted a "church whipping."

South Carolina Law Enforcement officers Lt. Roy F. Williams and Senior Investigator E. R. Peake handcuffed Lacy Inman and Roscoe Bellamy at Nixon's Crossroads shortly after sundown and charged them with kidnapping Fanny Brice at midnight on February 11, driving to an unknown location and beating her, inflicting serious bodily harm. The Brice woman was the mother of six children and she lived in the Nixon's Crossroad community near North Myrtle Beach.

Warrants against Inman and Bellamy were sworn out before Magistrate H. D. Crawford of Aynor in Horry County. Both the defendants had previously been charged in the Cane Branch Church intrusion, but no court action had been taken on those counts.

Mrs. Brice said her assailants were not wearing robes and hoods and she could identify them. She said they identified themselves as the Ku Klux Klan. She reported the whipping to the Horry County sheriff and when he failed to make any arrests, she scribbled a note to Governor Jimmy Byrnes asking for his help. He directed the South Carolina Law Enforcement Division to investigate, and the arrests were made promptly. It was a turning point in the Klan's hooliganism in South Carolina. These first arrests for kidnapping and assault followed closely behind the F.B.I. and S.B.I crackdown in North Carolina. Meanwhile, the S.B.I. continued to find suspects in other Columbus County floggings.

On March 5, Frank Lewis, former chief of police in Fair Bluff, surrendered to the sheriff in Whiteville. He had learned that there was a warrant out for his arrest. Three others were arrested the same day. They were: Henry Otto Edwards, 52, a Whiteville garage operator; John Honeycutt, Jr., 26, a Chadbourn produce dealer; and Ray Kelly, 43, a garage operator and mechanic.

All were charged in the abduction and flogging of Woodrow Johnson on December 8. Johnson had been called from his bed by a knock on the door and had reluctantly agreed to help the distressed strangers get their car started. Once outside his house, he was seized, carried to a remote spot near Lake Waccamaw and severely beaten.

Kelly was charged with having lured Johnson out of the house on that fateful evening. He was one of the unmasked kidnappers who pretended to have car trouble.

S.B.I. Agent James F. Bradshaw revealed that Edwards was the father-in-law of Johnson. He admitted being a member of the Klan in 1951, but said he became scared of the organization and had burned his card and robe. Honeycutt said he had sent a completed membership application to Grand Dragon Thomas Hamilton in Leesville, South Carolina. He said he didn't send any money and he never heard from his application.

With these arrests, the total number of North Carolina Klan defendants grew to twenty. Four of the Klansmen were charged in more than one case. There were sixteen different men under North Carolina indictment. All but two of those arrested were freed on $5,000 bond. Kelly and Edwards bonded out at $3,000 each.

S.B.I. Agent Bradshaw revealed after the arrests of this last four, that the twelve men charged in the flogging of Esther Lee Floyd would also be charged with a similar kidnapping of Dorsey Robinson, a Chadbourn Negro, on the same night. He was taken from his home and whipped.

Eight other flogging victims stood in the wings awaiting arrests of their kidnappers. They were Lee Tyson, Greet Pinkney Wright, Lawyer Jernigan, Robert Lee Gore, Clayton Sellers, H. D. Best, Evergreen Flowers and one unidentified victim, known only to investigators.

Meanwhile the first ten arrested by the F.B.I. had true bills (valid charges) returned against them by a federal grand jury in Raleigh. U.S. District Attorney Charles P. Green scheduled their trials for April 7, in Raleigh.

One of the counties adjoining Columbus was Robeson to the west. District Solicitor Malcolm Seawell was determined he would have no floggings by Klansmen in his territory. Researching historic Klan organizations, he uncovered an 1868 law forbidding membership in any "secret political or military organization." The little-used law was what Seawell needed to take action against sixteen known Klansmen. On March 7, the sheriff and the S.B.I. agents swooped down upon the Klansmen and brought them to Lumberton to face trial in District Recorder's Court on misdemeanor charges that carried fines ranging from $10 to $200 and imprisonment of not more than two years or both, at the discretion of the court.

Solicitor Seawell exercised a prerogative when he faced the sixteen accused. None had participated in any of the floggings. They were simply Klan members. Seawell offered them an option: Renounce the Klan and sever all ties to the KKK and he would drop the charges. It was a strange offer, but one that Seawell was sure would carry a message to Klansmen in his district— the Klansmen would not be tolerated whether they violated other laws or not.

L. F. Hardin, one of the men arrested, immediately denounced the Klan and denied he had ever been a member. He was freed immediately. All but five of the others denounced the Klan the following day and were freed. Five denied ever having been Klansmen. They faced charges in Recorder's Court the following week and all paid fines.

Another man, Paul Harrington, of Marietta, was later arrested under the ancient law after he had tried to recruit a highway patrolman into the Klavern. He repented quickly after he was charged, disavowing the Klan, and the charges were dropped.

Solicitor Seawell gathered the arrested Klansmen in a room prior to dropping the charges and made a speech. His speech was so dramatic and forceful that it had impact all over the area. He said:

"Some time ago the 'Supreme Vulture' of your society came to this county to sell the ideals of the Klan to the high school students and to others who might be interested. He was a native of South Carolina, a man by the name of Hamilton. He was ordered out of the Ninth Judicial District. He hasn't been brave enough to make an appearance here since then. In his stead, he has spawned you.

"Your position is different. All of you are residents of this county. As such you have had the advantage of our free public schools, the protection of our laws, the rights of our citizens. You have been free to come and to go—to do as you have seen fit within the framework of what is ours. No one has bothered you in your homes, your work, your religion; nor have you ever been persecuted because of your religious beliefs, your color or your morals.

"I just want you to know that the same laws that have protected you all of your lives are not your individual or your collective possession. These laws belong to the rich and to the poor, to the black and the white, to the Indian (there are many Native Americans in Robeson County), the native born, to the foreign born, to the Protestant, to the Catholic and to the Jew. It is going to stay that way.

"Let me make myself clear. I want you to know that if you, for the purpose of taking a person out to whip or flog, break into the person's house in the night time, it being occupied, or gain entry through fraud, I'll indict and try you for burglary in the first degree. In this state that crime carries the death penalty.

"We are not going to tolerate the Klan."

It was the greatest condemnation of the Klan by a public official heard anywhere during the Klan rise. It signaled the beginning of the end for Hamilton's floundered Klan in Robeson County. But the Grand Dragon tried to come to the rescue of those he had "spawned." He wrote Seawell a letter declaring that his Klansmen could not be convicted under the 1868 law.

Seawell replied, "If you are so sure that I cannot get convictions against these Klansmen for breaking the 1868 law, come on up to Robeson County and we will try you under that law to make sure that it works."

Hamilton never showed up.

With these Klansmen denouncing their Klan affiliation, and with Otto Edwards revealing that he had burned his Klan card and robe in fear, it was obvious that the members were having second thoughts about their affiliation. Suddenly, there was an exodus of families moving out of the area.

Years later, while fishing in Back Bay in Virginia for black crappies one fall morning, I started a conversation with anglers in a nearby boat.

"Where you fellows from?" I asked.

"Ah, you wouldn't have never heard of it. We come from a little town in North Carolina. We live here now," one answered.

"Well, I'm from North Carolina, too. I live in Tabor City down on the South Carolina line," I said.

"Tabor City! Now that is some coincidence. That's where we are from," they laughed with disbelief.

"How long you been living up here?" I asked.

"We left there and came here about five years ago."

142

"Why did you leave Tabor City? I think it is a fine little town and a good place to live," I said.

"It might be now. But when I lived there I joined the Ku Klux Klan. Then, before I knew what was going on, people were being arrested all over the place for beating people and stuff like that. I decided right then it was time for me to leave the country. I might get in jail next. And I haven't been back," my fellow fisherman said, laughing. I couldn't help but marvel at the coincidence.

It was indicative of the fear that swept over the land when Klansmen realized that the die was cast. They could no longer escape punishment as they had in Horry County where grand juries were consistently reluctant to indict their Klan neighbors.

On Saturday night, March 22, the Tabor City Merchants Association gave me an engraved wrist watch and named me "Tabor City Man of the Year." It was an humbling gesture, coming in the midst of the Klan crackdowns. My neighbors were showing appreciation for the hard fight that was endangering my family.

It once again made me think of my dog Chad that had been abducted, somewhat like the people who had been kidnapped. I wondered if he was still alive. Had he been abused? That was the sad thought on an evening when I should have been filled with joy.

Lucile and I were vest-popping proud following that presentation. Lucile might have realized for the first time that the Klan crusade was a noteworthy campaign and worth the fear and anxiety that we had both endured.

At midnight, I got another telephone call. I recognized the same voice that had called three weeks earlier, saying he had my dog in the trunk of his car.

"Carter, your damned dog got away this afternoon. I don't know whether he will find his way back to your house or not. But if he does, I want you to know he will not be there long. We'll get him again," the voice said before the phone clicked.

I went to the porch and called Chad for several minutes. He did not show up. I started back outside at dawn and I couldn't believe it when Chad jumped all over me at the front door. He was as happy as a dog in a meat house.

Chad looked like he had lost about fifteen of his sixty pounds. But even more pitiful, his nose and face were bleeding. I looked him over. All the skin around his nose was mutilated. His mouth had been wired shut—presumably to keep him from barking while he was in captivity. He had suffered plenty and was overjoyed to be back with the family. His captors had apparently held him only a few miles away. I cried as I hugged him and fed him all that he would eat.

Soon the children were up and lavishing their love on Chad. Even Lucile, not much of a dog lover, stroked his floppy ears. We had a memorable reunion. I was teaching a Sunday School class, so we were soon off to church, leaving Chad lying peacefully on the front porch. We waved to him and drove away. We were back home at 12:30. Chad met us at the garage. He was staggering.

"What's wrong, Chad?" I spoke to him as if he could answer. He just wagged his tail and looked at me pitifully.

"He's sick," 'Cile said, recognizing illness.

"You all go inside. I'll carry him to the vet," I said, and Chad climbed in the front seat.

The nearest veterinarian was in Whiteville. I got Chad there as quickly as I could, and as luck would have it, the vet was in his office. It being Sunday, that was remarkable. The vet looked Chad in the eyes and then down his throat.

"Your dog has been poisoned. Strychnine I believe. It smells bitter. We'll have to try to pump his stomach out," the vet said, as he began his effort to try to save my dog. "He probably ate a chunk of meat wrapped around a lethal dose of poison tossed out of a car." It was all in vain. The poison had already done its damage. Chad never woke up.

I carried him home, picked up a shovel from the garage and buried him in the woods. I felt like I should have erected a headstone. He died for something I had done. He was totally blameless. He wouldn't have hurt a flea.

Vengeance knows no rules. The innocent suffer along with the victims. It was a sad Sunday at our house. One that I have never forgotten.

Chapter Twenty-four
Court Convictions

The case against the original ten Klansmen indicted in the Martin-Grainger flogging case increased to eleven when Carl Richardson was named as another defendant by the special federal grand jury that had been called into session. He, like the others, was charged with taking part in the kidnapping and assault of the couple on October 6.

While indictments were handed down in Raleigh against the Klansmen, Judge Don Gilliam felt that justice would be better served by trying the cases nearer the homes of the defendants. He noted that many witnesses would have less travel if the cases were heard in Wilmington. So he moved the trials to the Port City and scheduled them for May 12.

The special North Carolina grand jury meeting in Whiteville continued to hear evidence and returned true bills against a total of twenty-seven Klansmen involved in forty-four flogging cases in Columbus County.

Six new defendants were indicted, including Jack Ashley, the police chief in Fair Bluff. Others implicated for the first time in a state court were Pittman Foy Strickland, Harvey Barfield, Mack Norris, Ernest Ward and George White. All were charged with conspiracy, kidnapping and assault. The kidnapping charge carried possible punishment of life imprisonment in North Carolina. Defendants were indicted for participating in the Esther Lee Floyd, Dorsey Robinson, Woodrow Johnson and Greer Pinkney Wright abductions.

Seven of the twenty-seven indicted by that state grand jury, had already been charged in federal court. Three of them were charged with as many as three of the night assaults.

Up until this point, federal and state indictments had been built around six different kidnappings and assaults. Seven other kidnappings and assault cases were still under investigation, including the floggings of Clayton Sellers, J. M. Russ, Robert Lee Gore, H. D. Best, Lawyer Jernigan, Evergreen Flowers and Lee Tyson.

Solicitor Clifton Moore would soon ask another grand jury to indict fourteen other Columbus Klansmen in three of the unsolved cases.

The first state cases went to court on April 29. The proceedings were immediately snarled by a defense motion to dismiss the charges because the grand jury had been illegally constituted. Judge Clawson L. Williams agreed that the grand jurors had not been picked on an alternating system as directed by a 1949 law. He quickly legalized the charges by dismissing the grand jury indictments and calling a new legal grand jury into session. Five hours later the Klansmen were indicted again—this time legally. The defense attorney's ploy had served only to delay the inevitable for a few hours. Judge Clawson's fast action in forming a new grand jury and proceeding with the Klan trials was indicative of the determined attitude of the court. The Tribune's banner headline saying "Defense Snarls K.K.K. Trials" was true only for a short afternoon.

Selecting a conscientious and impartial jury was a paramount consideration. The court feared appeals and overturned verdicts if every "i" wasn't dotted and every "t" crossed. Experienced, expensive defense attorneys would look for every flaw in the proceedings. Judge Williams thus agreed to an out-of-county venire of jurors and allowed the defense and prosecution liberal rejection rights. It was an exhaustive procedure.

Selecting a jury to hear the cases from a venire of one hundred fifty, then fifty more and yet another fifty from adjoining New Hanover County was troublesome. Eventually, after the defense excused seventy-eight and the prosecution released fifty-two, twelve white men were seated.

An ironic twist in the jury selection was the presence of Aaron Goldberg of Wilmington, as one of the defense attorneys. He did almost all of the questioning of jurors. Goldberg was Jewish, a group that was constantly lambasted by Grand Dragon Hamilton and the KKK in general. Some were surprised that he would have accepted such a case. Others wondered why the Klansmen would have hired him.

Finally, the long process of selecting the jury was over and the trials began Monday, May 5. Seventy prospective jurors were questioned before the eleventh and twelfth men were seated. Only one Negro, Richard Holland, was among the seventy jurors summoned. He was excused immediately. George T. Swain, a white Wilmington banker, was rejected when he admitted being a Klansman in 1922. John B. Allen, a wholesale grocer, was rejected when he said he was a Catholic—another group severely criticized by the KKK. W. T. Miers was rejected when he admitted he sympathized with the Klan in Columbus County.

State Senator Alton A. Lennon (later elected to the U.S. Senate) assisted Clifton Moore in questioning the jurors. Of the last seventy called, both the state and the defense excused fifteen each and Judge Williams used his discretion to excuse twenty-one. Each juror was asked if he were, or had ever been, a Klansman and if he had any kinship with Klansmen. They were all also asked if they had been threatened or contacted by anyone since their names were on the prospective juror list. All said "no."

The public observed the jury selection with great interest. Many people felt that the jury selection was equally as important as the evidence and they were aware of the Klan's expectations of avoiding convictions by stacking the jury. They had bragged at their public meetings that no Klansman would ever be convicted in the courts.

As the court convened, seven of the defendants threw themselves on the mercy of the court by pleading *nolo contendere* or "no contest," meaning that they pled neither guilty nor not guilty.

Seven other defendants, including Fair Bluff Police Chief Frank Lewis, Leroy and John Honeycutt, Jr., Ray Kelly, George and Steve Edmunds and Rex Conner, all of Columbus County, entered not guilty pleas in the Woodrow Johnson case. He was a Whiteville mechanic who was kidnapped and flogged on December 8, 1951.

One of the six defense lawyers was George Keels of Florence, South Carolina. His impassioned and colorful argument to the jury was a highlight of the trial. He stomped and pranced around the courtroom, his voice alternating between booming and subsiding to a whisper. He frequently bent over the jury rail, and in the face of a juror screamed, "Mistah Joo-rah, ah think the drunken Johnson wants to be a mah-tuh (martyr)!"

Other lawyers representing the Klansmen were Junius K. Powell, James R. Nance, Irving Tucker, Jr., and J. B. Lee.

Powell, a state senator, said he resented this trial that was "started by somebody who was publicity crazy. (He never identified the person.) It is a reflection upon the citizens of Columbus County" and then he traced the history of the Klan from the Civil War and

Confederate General Nathan Bedford Forrest, the KKK founder.

Three of the defendants took the stand in their own behalf and described in detail how the Johnson flogging supposedly happened. Fair Bluff policeman Lewis painted a clear picture of the fateful evening.

He said the Klansmen met in a dark room in the back of Henry Edwards' filling station about 7:30 in the evening. They formed in a semi-circle around Edwards who told them that Johnson was home and that he was drunk. Later the Klansmen drove to the Flynn Cemetery near Whiteville. One man was the spotter for another car that carried Early Brooks, Harvey Barfield and Lewis.

As the pickup truck passed Johnson's house, the driver pointed it out and sped away. The car stopped. Ray Kelly and Barfield went to the door and asked the forty-year-old mechanic for assistance. Barfield denied even being in Whiteville that night and had a South Carolina resident testify that he was in Nichols during the time in question. But Johnson identified Barfield as the man who grabbed his arms and put his hand over his mouth stifling his yelling as he was forced into the car. Johnson was blindfolded and taken to the Flynn Cemetery where the lashing began as soon as he stepped from the car. He was told he was being punished for drinking.

Klansmen were ringed around him as he was beaten, most of them wearing robes and hoods. When he was deposited near his home after the meeting, he was told he would be killed if he looked back. Johnson said his buttocks were badly bruised and he suffered a spinal injury that still bothered him.

Some of the attitude in the county toward the Klan was reflected by various conflicting testimonies by defendants and witnesses.

Mrs. J. E. Hill, sister-in-law of Ernest Ward, testified against Ward. S. D. McCormick, of Nichols, South Carolina swore that he saw Barfield in Nichols at the time of the Johnson assault. Judge Williams and the jury obviously didn't believe him, as Barfield was found guilty and sent to the road gang.

Ward testified that he stumbled into the Klan flogging while looking for a restroom. He conducted his own defense and he put Woodrow Merritt, his brother-in-law on the stand. When Merritt was asked about the reputation of Ward, he said, "I surely wouldn't say it is good."

All of the defendants were able to put witnesses on the

stand who tried to corroborate testimony and build an alibi, but none carried much weight with the judge and jury.

The Johnson trial was held during one of the busiest farming seasons of the year in the tobacco belt, but the courtroom was jammed during every session. There was widespread interest in the case throughout the southeastern counties.

The testimony against the Johnson case defendants ended at 4:45 Saturday afternoon. Three and a half hours later, the jury returned with a verdict of guilty of assault but not kidnapping against eleven of the Klansmen.

Judge Williams, in passing sentence said, "You are very fortunate that the jury didn't find you guilty of kidnapping. I don't see how you escaped that." Assault charges carried a maximum sentence of two years imprisonment while kidnapping was life imprisonment.

Lawrence Nivens and Brooks Norris were acquitted. Williams was tough on the convicted Klansmen.

Early Brooks, the erstwhile leader of the Fair Bluff Klavern, was sentenced to two years on the road gang. Lewis, Edmunds and Conner received two year road terms, suspended upon payment of $100 fines and three years probation—a reward for testifying for the state.

Brothers Leroy and John Honeycutt, Jr., were sentenced to two-year road terms, suspended upon payment of $1,500 fines and one-fourth of the court costs. Kelly and White were given two years on the road, suspended upon payment of $1,000 fines and one-fourth of the court costs.

Chaos broke out in the courtroom when Judge Williams passed sentence on Ray Kelly. When he sentenced him to two years, and before he had time to say "suspended," an old man near the back of the courtroom went into convulsions, his arms, legs and head jerking violently. He was making weird and unintelligible noises and two highway patrolmen moved near him, trying to restore calm in the court. He struggled with them briefly, then stood and shouted, "Hallelujah!"

Kelly's wife broke out in sobs, as did other members of the family. She then began dancing inside the bar and waving a white handkerchief over her head. When she reached her husband, she was wringing her hands and crying loudly. Kelly, a pudgy pulpwood worker, began sobbing too. When the weeping subsided, Judge Williams ordered everyone to return to his seat and he then proceeded to suspend Kelly's road sentence.

Solicitor Clifton Moore released a story to the press immediately following the sentencing of the Klansmen.

"Within the next few days, warrants will be issued for several other persons in Columbus County," he revealed. "These people have not been named in any previous flogging cases and they are fairly prominent in their communities."

He also noted that the reconvened grand jury in the Johnson case had renewed the indictments against Klansmen charged in the Esther Lee Floyd case. This Negro woman had had a cross cut in her hair as punishment for allegedly "going with a white man."

Dorsey Robinson, a black man, was Klan-whipped for carrying notes for the Floyd woman and "cussing in front of a white woman." Indictments against defendants in both those cases were reaffirmed by the new grand jury.

Most observers immediately felt that the court's success in this case would finally break the back of Thomas Hamilton's invisible empire. At least it was a good start.

While this first case against the Ku Klux Klan in the state court ended with convictions and moderate punishment, the trouble was only beginning for many of the same defendants and other assailants. The federal court case against the first ten of the Klansmen to be arrested would begin in Wilmington in three days. The vigilantes could expect more of the same and even worse.

We rejoiced in the convictions. Maybe this virus of fear would soon disappear. For my own sake and that of my wife and children, I surely hoped so. The *Tribune's* stand was partially vindicated, but there was still a long way to go.

I stepped up the battle with another editorial:

Justice as Prescribed by Law

When the Ku Klux Klansmen who heard their sentences pronounced in the county courthouse in Whiteville Saturday night used a leather strap on their neighbors, they administered outlaw justice as they saw fit. There was nothing illegal about the justice that Judge Clawson Williams doled out in Superior Court—the floggers got justice as prescribed by law. That's the only kind we believe in.

We find no sympathy for these night riders now saddled with two-year road sentences or heavy fines. They committed these criminal acts with their eyes open and deserve no more sympathy than a chicken thief or bank robber. In our eyes, not even as much.

In Judge Williams' court, these refugees from hoods and robes put their case before twelve of their peers. They had the benefit of an array of legal talent and could tell their story in its most favorable light. Yet they could not escape the gravity of their deeds and now they must pay the price. When they applied their interpretation of justice, Woodrow Johnson had no opportunity to select a jury from 250 unbiased men.

Many of those who now face stiff sentences in the Johnson case are also charged in several others, including the federal case that is now being heard in Wilmington. Some of them are going to spend a great deal of time in the future looking through bars at the outside world. Like criminals of all description, many Klansmen are repentant now, but it took a court of law to unseat them from the pedestal from which they administered brutal, arrogant punishment that they called justice.

From the first flogging and until today we have had no good words for the Kluxers and few for those who were flogged. There is no doubt that many of the victims were involved in affairs either illegal or immoral as society in this generation has determined. But we must remember that he who is sinless should throw the first stone. We maintain that the courts and the law are the only ones with the American right to punish its citizenry.

Our only compliments for those who have been whipped is that we admire their courage for reporting the beatings to the law. They did not fail in that regard and in doing so have made Columbus County a better place to live. The Klan is on the way toward total eradication in North Carolina. We doubt that it will ever rise again.

Those were bold words we wrote at a moment when we saw success on the horizon. They were confident words, too. I just hoped they would ring true in the end.

The
United States
Junior Chamber of Commerce

certifies that

W. Horace Carter

was recipient of the DISTINGUISHED SERVICE AWARD for outstanding community service during the calendar year of 1952. Through his loyal, faithful and unselfish efforts he has made a great contribution to his community, state and nation.

EXECUTIVE VICE PRESIDENT   PRESIDENT

This award made me the North Carolina "Young Man of the Year."

Chapter Twenty-five
Mood Changes

The mood of the people began changing after the conviction of Klansmen in Whiteville. Close-mouthed for months, the public spoke a little more openly after the thirteen vigilantes faced prison terms or heavy fines. The momentum swung against the Klan for the first time. That was important to me in this campaign. The people had to understand the evil of these "church whippings" that endangered the peace and tranquility of the Carolina low country.

Long reluctant to criticize the Klan movement, the people grasped the gravity of the court convictions and abandoned some of the fear as well as loyalty that had engulfed them during the Klan insurrection.

I understood why they were unusually noncommittal. Throughout the rural areas and country villages, almost every resident was either a relative, close friend or neighbor of one or more Klansmen. The natives of the area had moved into the swamplands since the turn of the century. It was covered with virgin forests and the first settlers made a living cutting giant cypress trees, known then as "ton timber" and floating the logs down the river to Georgetown and Charleston to market.

When the ton timber was exhausted, sawmills moved from the Piedmont section eastward. These lumber factories were located in deep swamps where loggers with mules cut the pines and hardwoods and dragged them to the mill. It was a tough way to make a living with mosquitoes eating away at man and mules in the watery wasteland. But for two decades, lumbering was the primary way of life with malaria and tuberculosis taking a terrible toll.

Lumbering put food on the tables and homes were built on the swamp fringes as trees were cut and new grounds cleared. Land cleared of timber could be bought for as little as one dollar an acre for a time.

Then came the cotton era. The sawmillers had become

farmers. Well into the 1930's, cotton was king. It was the money crop that fed families and paid bills. Then the boll weevil took over. There were no effective insecticides when the weevil first appeared. Cotton was doomed in the Carolina low country.

With cotton no longer profitable, farmers shifted to bright-leaf tobacco that they harvested and then cured with wood fires. Tobacco growing, cropping, grading, curing and tying was a family affair. Children, parents and grandparents all worked to put this great money crop on the auction warehouse floors. It quickly became the most profitable vocation the low country farmers had ever seen. Tobacco was hauled on wagons and mule-drawn carts to markets over rough and often muddy dirt roads to Tabor City, Whiteville, Fairmont, Lumberton, Loris, Mullins, Conway and other auction centers.

By this time, a second and third generation of Columbus and Horry rural residents had grown up, married, and carved out other farms from the jungles and built homes.

Many of those first settlers had been upstate neighbors and friends before they moved to the low country. The families were Spiveys, Wards, Wrights, Millers, Gores, Princes, Stricklands and Mills, among others. They had intermarried and almost everyone was related to others in the community. Many had the same grandchildren.

This close-knit relationship among rural residents played an important role in the Klan revival. It particularly accounted for the noncommittal voice of the people when the Klan was rampaging. Neighbors were not inclined to criticize neighbors. Relatives didn't want to offend relatives. And it was this closeness that for many months brought only silence from the leading residents of the area. They neither condemned nor condoned the Klan activity. They simply sat on the sidelines and tended to their own business. There was a special loyalty to friends and relatives that kept them quiet.

But now that the courts had established the lawlessness of the assaults and attacks, ministers were speaking out against the vigilantes and community leaders were being heard everywhere. The pendulum had quickly swung away from fear and embarrassment. Many community leaders spoke out against relatives and friends who had been hoodwinked or otherwise joined the ranks of Hamilton's Carolina Klan.

With the people now openly critical of the Klan, I felt like much of the newspaper's battle was behind us. I felt even better when news of forthcoming federal Klan cases to be tried in Wilmington was announced.

Three days after the thirteen Ku Klux Klan defendants were tried in state Superior Court in Whiteville and found guilty of assault in the Woodrow Johnson case, federal court convened in Wilmington with Judge Don Gilliam on the bench. The charges of kidnapping, assault and conspiracy to kidnap had been filed against ten local Klansmen in the case of Dorothy Martin and Ben Grainger.

It would take only two days for the KKK to see that the United States court would be tough on all vigilantes operating outside the law.

Early Brooks, ringleader of the Fair Bluff Klavern, had already been given two years in prison in the state court. Judge Gilliam gave him two concurrent five year prison terms to be served at the conclusion of his state sentence.

Brooks was one of the ten penitent floggers found guilty in the case. The eleventh defendant, eighteen-year-old George Miller, was found innocent when he testified that he had been mistaken by the Klansmen for his brother who was a Klansman. After he had heard the plans for the gory beating of Martin and Grainger, Miller was forced to participate because he knew too much. Judge Gilliam released him after his testimony, which was substantiated by others charged in the case.

Four other defendants were given three-year terms on each of three counts, the terms to run concurrently. They were: Horace Strickland, 29, a former deputy sheriff; James Robert Hayes, 38, whose car was used to carry the victims to the flogging site; Ross Enzor, 48; and Pittman Strickland, 29.

Carl Strickland, 60, the oldest of the Klan defendants, was sentenced to two years in prison on each of two counts, the sentences to run concurrently.

L. C. Worley, 25, the secretary of the Fair Bluff Klavern, testified for the state. He was sentenced to two years on two counts, but the sentence was suspended.

Sherwood Miller, 26, and Bobby Brooks, the nineteen-year-old son of Kingpin Early Brooks, were found guilty on each count and placed on three years probation.

Steve Edmunds, 26, was put on two years probation.

Standing before the bar to hear their sentences, all of the defendants were in shirt sleeves with collars open. They accepted the stiff sentences without immediate emotion, but several cried as they were handcuffed and led out of the courtroom. Many family members were hysterical.

Judge Gilliam lectured the Klansmen before he passed sentence. He said, "You men have been misguided, but you are responsible for your deeds and you must be punished. You must pay for your mistakes. The Klan is a combination of a lot of people who take the law into their own hands . . . a condition that would undermine our society if left unchecked.

"Grand Dragon Thomas Hamilton sold the gullible clay-road farmers of Columbus County a sorry bill of goods. He was interested in the Fair Bluff Klan only for the money he could get out of it." During the course of the federal and state trials, testimony indicated that Hamilton had pocketed a substantial sum of money from Klan dues and the sale of robes and hoods.

Testimony during the two-day trial ranged from Sheriff Hugh Nance to a parade of slow-speaking tobacco farmers in overalls who testified to the "good character" of the defendants. But Ben Grainger and Dorothy Martin's testimony about the severe beating was so convincing that the jury disregarded the character witnesses.

Seven of the convicted floggers served notice of appeal to higher courts following the sentences, including Brooks and his son, the Strickland brothers, Hayes, Enzor and Richardson. All the appeals were later rejected.

I got some special satisfaction out of the conviction of the defendants. In one of his nasty letters to the *Tribune*, Hamilton had categorically denied that the Fair Bluff Klansmen had had anything to do with the Martin-Grainger kidnapping. The court had found otherwise, which made my allegations against him and the Klan withstand the test for truth and accuracy.

While the Grand Dragon's underlings were preparing to don prison garb and start making little rocks out of big rocks in prison and on road gangs, the mastermind of the Klan reorganization and subsequent violence enjoyed the fruits of his recruitment. He remained free, but that would be short-lived. U.S. District Attorney Charles P. Green, of Raleigh, who led the prosecution against the ten Klansmen, was determined. He would not disclose what evidence he had, but said, "I may draw up charges against the Imperial Wizard Hamilton. I may seek an indictment soon."

To me, that sounded like the handwriting was on the wall. I was ecstatic when I returned home from covering the trial. But Lucile was not as overjoyed. "Don't you realize that now that these

Klansmen are going to prison that many of their friends and relatives will blame you for their predicament?" she asked. "They will reason that if you had kept your mouth shut and not hit them so hard in the paper that these cases might never have come to court. I wouldn't be surprised if we get calls tonight. They may still burn us out or grab one of the children like they did Bess and Chad."

I thought about that. She had a point. I considered taking all precautions, like hiring a security guard for a few days at the print shop. I would hate to lose what equipment we had, even if it was old and worn out. But I had no money to hire a guard. I decided to drop by the office a couple of times at night and ask the policeman on duty to keep a lookout for the next week. The danger would surely subside by then.

I hardly had time to consider the precautions before the phone rang.

"Editor, you are in for it now. Your writing about the Klan has got my friends in trouble. I don't know how their families are going to live on the farm without these men. There will be no one to plant and harvest tobacco. Some of those families will probably go hungry for a year or two. Doesn't it make you feel good to know you are responsible for bringing this hardship to these women and children? I think you ought to be ashamed," the caller said in staccato fashion.

"Well, sir, I have sympathy for those wives, mothers and children," I answered. "Certainly, many of the innocent suffer along with the guilty. That's tragic, but it is a fact that I cannot alter. I could not condone the ruthless abuse of men and women by the KKK. And I don't see how you could approve of such conduct if you are truly interested in your fellowman. I cannot agree with you, but I do sympathize with the innocent victims.

"I hope you and those suffering families will sometime realize that what we have fought for was right. The fight against the Klan has not been easy for me. It has cost me and my wife many sleepless nights. It will probably still be a lingering fear with us for a long time," I lectured the caller. It did not convince him. He had hung up long before I quit talking.

"I told you we would hear a lot more about your editorials. This may be the worst time of all for us," Lucile seemed almost angry with me.

"'Cile, we have fought the Klan for over two years. Some of the ring-leaders are going to be in prison for years. Both the state

157

and the federal governments are focusing on the Klan problem. I don't think Hamilton or any of his men would put their necks in a noose by going after us now," I reasoned.

My assumption was correct, but it did not stop the threats nor the fear that would trouble our family for many more months.

The thing that would break the back of the Klan all over the Carolinas would be the indictment and conviction of Grand Dragon Hamilton. If their leader wasn't around to keep his cohorts together, the Klan would fold. The first step in that longed-for direction was closer than I dared dream.

Before the end of May, Hamilton was handcuffed, jailed and charged with conspiracy to kidnap and conspiracy to assault in two Columbus County floggings.

My family had grown to three offspring and they were happy that Dad seemed to be winning the Klan fight.

158

Chapter Twenty-six
Water on the Dragon's Fire

Twice the Grand Dragon had been hauled into court and charged with participating in KKK lawlessness in South Carolina. But both times the Horry County grand jury refused to indict him. He went free. Those incidents shook my faith in the court system and it strengthened the Klan's image as a group operating above the law in the minds of the populace. People began to wonder if Hamilton had so many friends in high places that he could flaunt his lawlessness and get away with it.

But now his time had come. He could no longer evade justice. He would have to pay a price for his philosophy. People everywhere tensed for the showdown.

Testimony in the state and federal courts by Grand Dragon Thomas L. Hamilton's henchmen proved to be his undoing. His own Klansmen provided the initial evidence and Solicitor Clifton Moore wasted no time in preparing warrants for the Leesville grocer. It would extinguish much of the fire in his drive to create a powerful invisible empire in the Carolinas.

It was late on Friday afternoon May 23, that S.B.I. Chief James A. Powell handed warrants to Special Agents James F. Bradshaw and John W. Lowdermilk and directed them to arrest the Klan's top man. The warrants charged him with conspiracy in the severe flogging of Evergreen Flowers, a Negro woman of Chadbourn. She had been beaten with sticks and branded with a cross in her hair by forty or fifty Klansmen. The warrants charged that Hamilton played a part in the planning of the flogging. The Flowers family had moved out of the community soon after the beating and was now living in Cerro Gordo.

That beating took place January 18, 1951, at a time before Moore realized that the Klan even existed in Chadbourn. But as evidence unveiled in the trials of Hamilton's underlings indicated a few days earlier, they had organized, were growing rapidly and made a fatal mistake that doomed them when they assaulted Evergreen Flowers. It was the beginning of the end for the Association of Carolina Klans.

With warrants in hand, and accompanied by Sheriff Hugh Nance, the S.B.I. agents drove to the Grand Dragon's home, (he had recently promoted himself to Imperial Wizard) in Leesville and knocked on his door. His wife claimed that he was out of town on business. Officers wondered if it was monkey business. He had been scheduled to make a Klan talk in Darlington, but that appearance had been cancelled. The sheriff and agents decided to wait him out.

Somehow, Hamilton had been tipped off that warrants for his arrest had been issued and were about to be served. He had quickly left Leesville and gone into hiding.

Saturday morning came. He was still gone. Fugitive warrants were issued for his arrest. The vigil continued.

At 2:30 on Saturday afternoon Hamilton walked into the office of George Keels, a Florence, South Carolina, attorney who had frequently defended Klansmen in state courts. He had represented Harvey Barfield, who had been sentenced to two years in state prison. Hamilton, knowing that he was being sought, decided to surrender. Keels called Clifton Moore to inform him that his client would give himself up as soon as they could drive to Whiteville. They would leave immediately.

Hamilton walked into the solicitor's office two hours later. On his last visit to Columbus County, five thousand people stood in a field to hear him defame Negroes, Catholics and Jews. This time fewer than a dozen were on hand to see him arrested. What a contrast! He no longer rated a position on a pedestal.

Charged with conspiracy to kidnap and conspiracy to assault, Hamilton was released on $10,000 bond that was signed by Mrs. Roger Bullock, of Fair Bluff. She was a resident of the Cane Branch section of Horry County, where the Klan recruitment and activity had been so successful.

Nattily dressed in a navy blue suit and wearing spectacles, the pudgy forty-four year-old grocer did not breathe his typical fire and brimstone at his arraignment. The Klan chieftain, minus his white-robed guards was subdued, unspectacular and looked very much like any average businessman.

Another of his attorneys, Waldo Hyman of Florence, accompanied him to Whiteville. Hyman would not talk to reporters. He did

160

shake hands with two county officials and after the bond was posted Hamilton and Hyman drove out of town. Hamilton waived extradition from South Carolina and posted an appearance bond to guarantee that he would be back for trial in Recorder's Court on June 10.

In addition to the Flowers assault, Moore linked Hamilton to the Woodrow Johnson abduction. The Whiteville mechanic had suffered a severe beating in a cemetery for the supposed crime of drinking. His testimony in Superior Court had convicted a bevy of local Klansmen who had participated in the flogging. Moore told the press that he believed Hamilton would be connected as a conspirator in at least one other Columbus County flogging case. In fact, he would eventually be connected to many.

Hamilton had been charged three times prior to this arrest. The Horry County grand jury twice had turned him loose. But he had paid a fine of $1,000 in federal court in Anderson, South Carolina, when he was convicted of sending malicious messages through the mail that were injurious to newspaper publisher Wilton E. Hall. Hall's newspaper had opposed the Klan and Hamilton had violated the libel laws in mailing flyers critical of the news stories. He paid the fine rather than serve a year in jail. It was later learned that Klansmen contributed money to pay Hamilton's fine.

Since the first beating was reported in Columbus County late in 1951, the S.B.I. had been anxious to file charges against the Grand Dragon. Their opportunity surfaced when witnesses and defendants in the earlier trials connected the Klan chieftain with those beatings.

Ray Conner of Cerro Gordo, who entered a no contest plea in the Johnson case, was the first to bring Hamilton's name into the court record. He recalled that Early Brooks had read a letter from the Grand Dragon at one of the Klan meetings that said "some Fair Bluff women have written to me saying that a horse trader would have her (Flowers') husband arrested and then go out with her while her husband was in jail. I want this taken care of immediately." Conner's recollection of the letter started Hamilton's downfall. It was damaging testimony.

Steve Edmunds, the rotund, twenty-six-year-old tobacco farmer and a star witness in the state and federal Klan cases, testified that he had filled out his Klan membership application and personally handed it to Hamilton along with a $10 initiation fee. According to Edmunds $8 of this was for a robe and $2 for the first quarter's dues. These transactions were usually done in cash and were hard to trace.

Another link in the chain of evidence against Hamilton was forged by Walter A. Murphy, the F.B.I. agent in charge of the Charlotte office. Murphy testified in federal court against the first ten Klansmen arrested. He reported that after Early Brooks had been arrested, Hamilton had promised him $4 from each $10 Klan membership fee collected.

Like Edmunds, Fair Bluff Police Chief Frank Lewis, now sentenced to prison for his part in a flogging, said he was lured into joining the KKK when Hamilton made his vitriolic speech at the first cross burning in Columbus County in August of 1951. Lewis had now renounced the Klan and helped implicate other Klansmen involved in the abductions. He was among the most repentant.

Referring to the cross burning when Hamilton stood on the back of a truck surrounded by hooded figures and delivered his speech of hate, Lewis said, "I wish I had picked up a rock and knocked him off that stand."

In my conversations and correspondence with Hamilton he always contended that the only beatings that the Klan condones are those that occur "at the ballot boxes." He piously proclaimed that "disgruntled persons, not Klansmen" were guilty of carrying out the floggings in the name of the Klan. He always insisted that the KKK was taking a bad rap. But the testimony of witnesses was rapidly branding that contention of Hamilton's as a lie. The truth obviously wasn't in the Grand Dragon.

Other Klansmen were quick to talk now as they sought to save their own skins. As a result the Grand Dragon's part in the terror unfolded almost daily.

Under interrogation, several Klansmen said they had no idea where the money went after they paid fees and dues. Most of it went directly to Hamilton, who testified that he used it to assist various charities. No charity was ever identified. No accounting of the funds was ever released.

Federal Judge Don Gilliam, after hearing testimony against the Klan floggers, said, "I think this Grand Dragon in South Carolina is more interested in the money he is making out of the Klan than he is in the floggings."

This remark unmasked the Grand Dragon. Hundreds of Klan sympathizers in the community realized for the first time that the KKK movement was a money game that enriched some of its leaders. The revelation had to come from a source like the judge to convince many Klan followers that what the newspaper had contended for months was the truth.

Attorney James R. Nance of Fayetteville, who defended Klansmen in the federal case, added, "I agree. I have the idea that this Hamilton is building up the invisible empire for his own economic benefit."

Although the Klan's boss was under arrest, the pressure continued for other KKK members. State officers were investigating twelve other cases. More state arrests were imminent. And the F.B.I. was probing for facts in other cases.

Hamilton's June 10 trial in Recorder's Court was postponed, but the Klan stayed in the news.

Up until this point, Klansmen in the immediate Tabor City area had escaped indictments. That ended on June 20, when the grand jury in Whiteville returned true bills against twenty-five men, including two from Tabor City.

Troy Bennett, a member of the three-man Town of Tabor City Board of Commissioners and manager of the bus terminal, and Sid Scott, a local mechanic, were charged with participating in both the Flowers and Johnson floggings. At the same time, twenty-three other Klansmen were indicted.

The new indictments included Hamilton, who was charged with conspiracy in four cases. The evidence was climbing against him. That grand jury report was released by B.C. Powell, foreman, who lived in Fair Bluff, a hotbed of Klan activity. It again showed that the people had turned against the Klan lawlessness even in areas where the vigilantes had been strong at one time. Columbus County jurors took firm stands against the Klan activities once they were presented the evidence.

Solicitor Moore announced that still other arrests would be made in the twelve unsolved cases. Tabulation of court action against the Ku Kluxers at that point showed that there had been one hundred indictments, seventy-eight by state and county officials. Fifty-four different individuals had been charged.

Town Commissioner Troy Bennett resigned from the board without giving a reason and entered a plea of no contest in the court proceedings set for the following week in Whiteville. He was found guilty, but died of a heart attack before he could serve any time.

Two days later, the S.B.I. and the sheriff made additional arrests. This time, two former Tabor City residents were charged, along with sixteen others. The Tabor City men were Russell

Hammacher and Ernest Hardee. Both had moved to Fayetteville when the Klan investigation heated up.

The court calendar for July 22 was filled with dozens of Klan cases, including that of the Grand Dragon. The drama escalated.

Life was a little more pleasant for me at home after those court proceedings. At last, Lucile saw victory ahead. She smiled more now even while carrying our third child. Maybe this newest offspring wouldn't have to live through another crusade. Maybe, just maybe, the Ku Klux Klan movement was over

Even on the streets, the gloom of the night riders' heyday seemed to have passed. People were forgetting their suspicions and fears. Klansmen were going to jail. That would end the reign of terror. At least, that's what we all hoped.

Farmers were busy with tobacco.

Chapter Twenty-seven
Hamilton Humbled

Even to the end, the Grand Dragon protested his innocence.

A few days before Hamilton's trial began in Whiteville, he told a gathering of South Carolina followers, "Only God and me know that I am innocent." Both knew better at the time, of course, but hoping to influence the court verdict, Hamilton entered a plea of "not guilty" to charges of conspiracy to kidnap and assault.

Eight Klansmen who participated in the Evergreen Flowers assault took the stand for the prosecution before Judge Clawson Williams in a special term of court called just to hear the Klan cases. Hamilton sat stoically as they testified—but then he seldom showed emotion. It was almost as if he were resigned to a bitter fate.

Klansman T. L. Enzor summarized the case against Hamilton when he testified that Hamilton said: "I want to make the Klan strong enough so it can control the state politically." That was obviously Hamilton's objective.

Solicitor Clifton Moore asked Enzor which state Hamilton was talking about. Enzor replied, "Hamilton said things were pretty in South Carolina and he could make the Klan work pretty in North Carolina, too."

Other Klansmen told of Hamilton's burning ambition for power and his dream of building an empire. All testified he was the guiding hand behind the floggings and violence that wracked the Carolinas for many months.

Sid Scott, one of the Tabor City residents indicted, said he was told by Hamilton, "If we get enough Klan members, no Klansman will ever be convicted of anything."

It was the testimony of former Tabor City policeman Horace Strickland that put the bee on Hamilton and led to his conviction. He said that the Klan boss told him, "Do a good job of the beating of Evergreen Flowers or you will have to go back and do it all over again."

Strickland also testified that Hamilton set the night and hand-picked the Klansmen to take part in the assault. According to Strickland, they were supposed to beat up Evergreen's husband, Willie, but he escaped and his wife was beaten instead. They took Evergreen outside the house, tore her slip off and used it for a gag. She crawled under the house after she was whipped and several pistol shots were fired into the house by the Klansmen before they drove away.

In the hot courtroom, the only emotion Hamilton showed was occasionally pulling on his tie and shirt collar as the parade of Klansmen piled up damaging evidence against him. No longer enjoying his exalted pedestal and directing an invisible empire, Hamilton realized quickly that his not guilty plea had been made in vain. Upon the advice of his attorney, he suddenly changed his tune.

"Your honor," Hamilton's attorney addressed the bench, "my client would like to change his plea to guilty of conspiracy in the Evergreen Flowers case."

"Is that true, Mr. Hamilton?" Judge Williams asked the defendant.

"Yes, your Honor, I am changing my plea," the Grand Dragon replied somewhat tentatively and nervously.

At long last, the public would know that the truth never had been a character trait of the Grand Dragon's. He was a master at deceit and his true colors were finally revealed.

Moore made a statement to the court that put an exclamation point on the whole Klan affair: "The outcome of this case upholds the dignity of the law and should be a warning to any group which seeks to violate the statutes."

State Senator Junius K. Powell, who was assisting the prosecution, said, "It is my judgment that the end has come to the Klan movement in this state and Hamilton's admission of violence and conspiracy will have a deadly effect on the KKK everywhere."

Judge Williams asked Hamilton to stand.

"I need a little time to think about your sentence. I'll make my decision next Wednesday after I hear the other KKK cases on the docket. You'll be free on bond until then," he said.

The *Tribune's* front page headline read:

Hamilton Enters Guilty Plea

It was the story I had longed to write for two years, but even this was not the very end of this chapter of the Klan's demise.

The other cases were heard quickly. There was little doubt of the guilt of the defendants. Twelve other night-riding Klansmen were found guilty.

My impatience had never been more overwhelming as I awaited Hamilton's judgment day. I sat in that silent, crowded courtroom when the Grand Dragon stood before the judge. Several hundred overall-clad farmers were in the audience taking a short reprieve from tobacco harvesting to hear the judge pronounce sentence on the once high-flying, exalted Imperial Wizard.

"Mr. Hamilton you have pled guilty to conspiracy to kidnap and conspiracy to assault one Evergreen Flowers. For that crime I sentence you to four years in prison. Two years on each count. One sentence to begin when the other ends.

"You have your life before you. After you pay this penalty for the crimes you have committed, I advise you to live your life in an honorable manner," Judge Williams was stern as the Klan boss turned a little white and was silent.

Hamilton was still unemotional as he sat down to hear the sentences passed on many of his cohorts.

Troy Bennett, the Tabor City Town Commissioner, was next to face the judge. He was almost certain to be sentenced to the chain gang. He asked the judge not to sentence him to a road gang, saying that the physical exertion would be fatal since he suffered from a heart condition. Williams gave Bennett the benefit of the doubt, ordering him to provide the court with medical evidence. He later provided a doctor's report verifying his weak heart. Bennett died suddenly of heart failure before the judge could pass sentence.

Sid Scott, the other Tabor City defendant who had testified for the state against Hamilton, received an eighteen-to-twenty-four month sentence, suspended upon payment of a $250 fine.

T. L. Enzor was given two years on the road, also suspended upon payment of a $500 fine.

Joe Hardee was sentenced to four years on the road, two years on each of two counts.

Howard Gore received eighteen months, suspended upon payment of a $500 fine.

J. D. Nealey was found not guilty.

Jule Richardson and Ernest Hardee received two-year and eighteen-to-twenty-four month sentences, respectively, suspended upon payment of $500 fines.

Russell Hammacher, formerly a Tabor City resident, was sentenced to twelve to eighteen months on the road.

Jenrick Hammonds, Roy Carter and James Hammonds were given eighteen- to twenty-four month sentences, suspended upon payment of $250 fines.

Those were the sentences Judge Williams could dole out on that memorable July afternoon. But fifty-one other defendants were on trial at that special session. All but three were found guilty along with the Grand Dragon and paid fines or served prison terms. This was in the era when prisoners didn't sit around and watch television. They wore stripes, were watched by a shotgun-toting guard and performed hard labor maintaining the road system of North Carolina. It was no picnic to serve a sentence on the chain gang. And even the fines Judge Williams set on the defendants were not easy to pay. This was also before runaway inflation hit the world. Money was scarce.

Back at the *Tribune* office, printing foreman J. A. Herlocker hunted through the type cabinets for the largest, blackest letters he could find. He came up with some bold two-inch-high wood type. Bringing the word "Hamilton" to my office, he asked for my approval for the banner headline that would read: "HAMILTON GETS 4-YEAR TERM." It was just right.

Obviously a little cocky now and certainly with a feeling of self-satisfaction inside, I grinned and said, "Really, J.A., I was saving that big type for the second coming of Jesus Christ, but in that you found it, let's run it." And we did. It was the biggest headline we had ever run in the *Tribune*.

There would be only one other occasion to bring out that big, bold type—when we won the Pulitzer Prize for Meritorious Public Service. That demanded sensationalism too.

I got home in the wee hours of the morning. The newspaper was late getting off the press and on the street because we had waited for Judge Williams' sentencing of Hamilton and other Klansmen.

Lucile was still up when I walked in, my clothes, arms and hands smeared with ink. I had worked beside the printer and pressman to get the paper set on the linotype, made up, run, folded, addressed and in the mail as I always did on press day. It was before the day of lithography. The news copy was set tediously on two linotypes. The headlines were picked up a letter at a time from California type cases. It was years later before we could afford an Elrod that molded the headlines from hot type, somewhat like the

168

linotypes set straight matter. Then, because we could not afford a flatbed rotary press that printed from roll newsprint (they cost about $25,000), we fed sheeted newsprint through a big old Whitlock, two-revolution press—four pages at a time. We had to hand-feed the printed sheets through a noisy folding machine before gathering the eight or four-page sections and addressing them with a wing mailer for our mail subscription list. We had a measly fifteen hundred paid subscribers, but it took a lot of hard work by all of us to set, compose and print even a twelve- or sixteen-page paper.

Lucile, of course, knew about the four-year sentence that Hamilton would have to serve. I had called her from the courthouse a few minutes after the sentencing.

She smiled a little and seemed genuinely pleased with me and my hell-bent crusade against the Ku Klux.

"Well, it looks like you have won in spite of me and everyone who tried to get you to stop writing about the Klan," she said. I thought I detected a bit of pride for me in her eyes. I surely hoped she was proud.

"I don't know about winning, I answered. "We have certainly gained an advantage now that Hamilton is going to be put away. But there may still be some dangerous days ahead. Yes, I am happy with today. We may have won. Certainly, the worst of the fight should be over." I hugged her emotionally and thanked her for enduring through all kinds of trials and tribulations with me.

I philosophized a bit as we lay in bed talking.

"You know, success in this world is not measured by what you have, but what you have done. Hamilton may have made some bucks with his scheme to gain power by creating a strong following of devoted rednecks, but he cannot be proud tonight when he sees so many of his members going to prison and paying heavy fines. If he were given a report card right now, his service to mankind would be so skimpy that he would come up with all 'F's.'

"Maybe my report card wouldn't put me on the honor roll, but I believe the teacher would write in a passing grade." 'Cile laughed. She really was proud of me, even though I had caused the family a lot of anguish.

Happiness is a terribly inept word to describe what I felt that evening when I had finally dragged my tired bones to bed.

The Tabor City Tribune

HELPED TO HOLD · G. Finer · Carolina

"Tabor City — The Town With A City Future"

VOL. VII, NUMBER 1 · TABOR CITY, N. C., WEDNESDAY, JULY 30, 1952 · 5c A COPY; $2.00 A YEAR

HAMILTON GETS 4 YEAR TERM

Tabor Tobacco Market Opens Monday

At exactly 12:50 today, Judge Clawson L. Williams sentenced Thomas L. Hamilton to four years on the road, two years on two counts of conspiracy with one term to begin when the other ends, at the KKK trials at Whiteville.

Hamilton took the sentence

LOCAL FARMERS ENDORSE WOOD CORN PLANTING PLAN

...rads and a circus at-
...ll be in Tabor City
...day Yet, Monday, Aug-
...auctioneer begins that
...e selling of his and the 1952
...t of e...
...of e...
...d Pro...

...A fence, a watering place and a...

City, N. C., area, and several oth-

This is the headline we had long waited to write.

Chapter Twenty-eight
Hamilton's Last Charge

On September 1, 1952, ten convicted Klansmen began serving prison terms and twenty-four paid $15,850 in fines and received suspended sentences. Four others were temporarily free on appeals. They would join three others and have their cases reviewed by the Federal Court of Appeals before starting their eighteen- to twenty-four month terms on the chain gang.

Grand Dragon Thomas Hamilton asked for a delay in starting his four-year term, and Judge Clawson Williams graciously granted the request. The time was allowed to be with his wife, who was recovering from a major operation. He remained free on the $30,000 appearance bond signed by Mrs. Roger Bullock of Fair Bluff.

On October 1, Hamilton walked into Sheriff Nance's office in Whiteville, was promptly handcuffed and taken to the prison camp in Wilmington. He began serving his sentences, but not before one final battle cry. He still was full of self-centered defiance of the law and showed little or no remorse.

Hamilton had not yet given up his Klan allegiance—even as the bars swung closed. He handed out a press release that provided the *Tribune* with plenty of front-page copy. Our headline read:

Hamilton Implies J.K. Powell Represented Both Sides in Columbus County Ku Klux Klan Trials

Powell, the state senator from Columbus County, was prominent in the North Carolina Democratic Party. As an attorney, he frequently represented KKK clients who seemingly had impossible cases to defend. He was liked by some people and despised by others as a shyster lawyer.

Powell had assisted Solicitor Clifton Moore in the prosecution of forty-six Klansmen and had been paid a $5,000 fee by the state for his work.

Hamilton's news release contained a copy of a letter that he had written to Powell asking him how he could represent Klansmen and the state at the same time. He raised the question of a conflict of interest, saying that while Powell was paid by the state to prosecute the Klansmen, he was sending bills to Klan defendants.

Hamilton said that "without fear of contradiction" a survey he conducted proved that the people of Columbus County were on his side and that his investigation and data would cause some people in the county to fear and tremble. He continued his attempt to intimidate even as he was being locked up for conspiring to have people beaten up for "crimes" that he and the Klan considered unchristian and immoral.

South Carolina neighbors of the Grand Dragon appealed to the governor of North Carolina for leniency for Hamilton, but it was to no avail. Governor Kerr Scott was no friend of hoodlum lawlessness. He simply ignored the petition.

Hamilton's letter to Powell that he released to the press was postmarked Leesville, S.C., and was dated September 27, 1952. It read:

> Dear Sir:
> It has come to my attention through a clipping in the *Charlotte Observer* that certain statements were released by you or the Honorable Clifton L. Moore, solicitor of the district. This dispatch was captioned 'Whiteville, North Carolina.' I cannot gather who is responsible for the false and fallacious statements made against me in the press, namely that I had approached you and tried to get you to represent me. In fact I had never laid eyes upon you until I met you in the courthouse at Whiteville on July 21, 1952.
> I feel that any attorney who is secured by the state to represent the state should be paid by the state. But it is a little puzzling to me that a man who is employed by the state to act as state attorney can represent certain people (Klansmen) that he is trying to convict. Information has come to me from certain people in Columbus County saying that they have received statements from you for services rendered. How could you prosecute and render services at the same time??? One of these days, in the not too distant future, the facts of the Klan trials in North Carolina will be revealed so that the people of the great State of North Carolina will have a true conception of what really happened.
> Since I was convicted I have had the opportunity to talk with some of the most influencial (sic) and highly-respected citizens of Columbus County and from my talks with these people I have been led to believe and to

172

KNOW certain things with regard to my case there in Columbus County. I have had the opportunity to go into Columbus County during the last sixty days to talk with various people and I have found in talking with them that the press in Whiteville, N.C. was certainly false. At no time have I had any difficulty in getting WHITE or BLACK to the door at any hour of the night. It so happens that most of the residents of the rural areas that I talked with were Negroes and without exception they would come out to the car and direct me to the place I was asking about. I made this survey for my records. We are running a complete investigation in Columbus County and one of these days we will have data and material as well as evidence that I feel will cause some people in the county to fear and tremble. My survey of the people, who are the backbone of the county, I find that without fear of contradiction they are on MY SIDE.

TRUTH BEARETH AWAY THE VICTORY AND TRUTH WILL ALWAYS TRIUMPH.

Before reading this statement that was released to the press, I was led to have the utmost confidence in you for your position and standing, representing the people there in Columbus County and I feel that you should through the press straighten this falsehood out so that you will continue to have the respect of your people.

At no time when I spoke in Columbus County on two occasions did I quote a misstatement or tell the people of North Carolina a falsehood. Every speech that I made in that state I could back to the hilt. I do not know and personally I do not care about the opinions of some people in North Carolina. In your state as well as in other places I have led a fight of TRUTH and RIGHT. When the time comes for me to give up the ghost, Sir, that will still be my fight. I know that there are disgruntled people in North Carolina who wanted things to go their way and would not stop under any conditions until they had carried out their point.

I am reminded of Ephesians 6:11. "Put on the whole armor of God, that ye may be able to stand against the wiles of the devil." I realize the truth contained in that verse and I am led very forcibly to fight harder for the CAUSE OF CHRISTIANITY.

Under the guidance of the Supreme Architect of the Universe and under the Banner of the Lord and Savior Jesus Christ, may Peace and Prosperity be yours.

Sincerely,

Thomas L. Hamilton

Attorney Powell responded with a terse statement the following week. He never really publicly denied the charge that he had billed Klansmen for services rendered while prosecuting them in the court. But he did clear up one of Hamilton's charges when he wrote:

> This will acknowledge receipt of your letter of September 27. You are correct in your statement when you say that you never personally approached me to represent you in your trial here. However, I was approached the first time on the day you were here to post bond and the other time you made bond. We were under the impression that the persons approaching us were either your friends or represented you.
>
> I trust this clears the matter up for you.
> J.K. Powell

While Hamilton's charge of a conflict of interest was never pursued, it did cast a shadow on the state senator who had considerable political clout statewide.

Hamilton soon disappeared from public sight. Imprisoned at State Camp 303 off Castle Hayne Road near Wilmington, the Grand Dragon became just another stripe-wearing convict. Superintendent John Williams said, "All I know is that he is a prisoner and it's my job to see that he works."

In writing about the imprisonment of this gang leader who made such pious statements in his letter to Powell, I couldn't help but wonder just what really was locked up inside this man. Was he really the great Christian crusader he claimed to be? I then reflected on an age-old philosophy that came to mind. "When a man is young, he should plant a garden that he can sit down in when his digging days are done." Had the Grand Dragon planted a garden that he could rest in when he was out of prison and growing old? Could he rest peacefully, knowing he had conspired to have helpless men and women dragged from their homes and beaten in the dark of night by lawless vigilantes? Could a man who had no respect for human rights and the law find any kind of peace and serenity in the years to come? I concluded that there would be little peace in the garden for him when his digging days were done.

With Hamilton put away for a few years, seven of his henchmen had their appeals heard in federal court in Richmond, Virginia. They presented their case before a native of Charlotte, North Carolina, Chief Judge John J. Parker of the Fourth Circuit Court of Appeals.

The arguments the defense attorneys presented were stranger than fiction. I knew then that lawyers would stop at nothing to earn their fees and help defendants escape justice. They would not succeed.

The North Carolina Press Association honored the *Tribune* and the *News-Reporter* for the crusade. Here I am, seated left, next to Willard C. Cole at a Chapel Hill press conference.

AWARDED TO
Walter Horace Carter
for OUTSTANDING SERVICE
IN STIMULATING BETTER
CITIZENSHIP

CITATION

FOR COURAGE SHOWN IN THE
FACE OF GREAT PERSONAL DAN-
GER, TOGETHER WITH EDITORIAL
DILIGENCE, RESULTING IN THE
OVERTHROW OF A RESURGENT KU
KLUX KLAN IN NORTH CAROLINA

APRIL 3, 1954 by the
CIVITAN CLUB of
Albemarle, N. C.

CIVITAN INTERNATIONAL

C

BUILDERS
OF GOOD
CITIZENSHIP

Chapter Twenty-nine
New Defense—
"Church Whippings"

Seven of the most notorious of the Carolina Ku Klux Klansmen, all with prison sentences of from two to five years imposed in North Carolina state courts, faced Chief Judge John J. Parker in the U.S. Court of Appeals in Richmond, Virginia, on the morning of October 6, 1952. It was their last-ditch effort to avoid the chain gang.

All the defendants had been convicted in the kidnapping and assault of Dorothy Martin and her boyfriend, Ben Grainger of Fair Bluff.

Defense attorneys for the seven Klansmen unveiled a novel defense—one that was unheard of and unexpected. They called the floggings of Martin and Grainger "church whippings" and sought to justify the attacks by claiming they were a traditional form of punishment in early American Christian societies. The abduction, they contended, was not really kidnapping. It was just the churchmen's way of ensuring increased morality in the community.

At first, the three-man court of appeals seemed stunned with the defense arguments. Judge Parker interrupted the lawyers long enough to tell them that he had never heard of a "church whipping" in North Carolina or anywhere else.

But the defense attorneys stuck to their strategy.

"It is well known that since the early days of our republic in the era of Puritanical intolerance, so-called 'church whippings' have been carried out in many communities," they insisted. "The practice unquestionably prevailed before the Klan organization came into existence and continued through periods when the Klan was dormant.

"In rural communities, it will continue as long as religion in its narrowest sense forms a part of the community life. Notwithstanding the publicity attendant upon the recent Klan activities, this transgression on the part of the defendants in their instant case was no more than 'church whippings,'" the Klan attorneys pled.

Defense attorneys further contended that the original indictments did not charge the Klansmen with kidnapping or with the alleged crime of conspiracy to violate the statute.

Government prosecutors countered that there was substantial evidence to warrant convictions for kidnapping. They contended, too, that the men acted in conspiracy because their actions followed a prearranged plan.

The defense council tried to prove that there was no premeditated plan to take the man and woman across the state line for the floggings. They contended that the home of Mrs. Martin is only a mile from the South Carolina border and the Klansmen transported them to another state by accident. They did not realize they were violating a federal statute

Church whippings or kidnapping, the appeals court took the case under advisement and in a few days they ruled the seven Klansmen were guilty. They were to begin serving their prison sentences immediately. The judge obviously did not buy the claim of "church whippings."

"There is no merit in this contention," he said. "The federal courts frequently have punished offenders under the kidnap law for extorting a confession from a kidnap victim, for obtaining the services of a kidnapped person, for preventing the reporting of a crime, for obtaining transportation in the victim's car, for using the kidnapped person as a shield in a jail break, for placing the victim in a house of prostitution, and for the rape of a kidnapped person.

"Under the circumstances, the appellate court holds that seizure and interstate transportation of two victims for the purpose of flogging them constitutes a clear violation of the federal law against kidnapping."

The seven defendants were all from Columbus County: Early Brooks was sentenced to five years; Robert Hayes, Ross Enzor, Horace Strickland and Pittman Strickland all received three-year sentences; Carl Richardson got two years and Bobby Brooks was put on a twelve-month suspended sentence.

It was the last hurrah for the North Carolina Klan revival. The Ku Klux had sung its swan song in the Tar Heel State, but it still raised its head in South Carolina with a last-gasp public rally at Lake City in mid-October.

We were careful not to let our guard down and editorialized again with this two-column message on the front page:

THE KLAN MEETS AGAIN

The Ku Klux Klan, slapped down thoroughly in North Carolina, held a meeting and burned a cross near Lake City last Wednesday night. Thomas L. Hamilton, the Grand Dragon for the Carolinas was unable to attend. He is doing a stretch in the North Carolina prisons for floggings.

A robed but unmasked "Grand Titan" was present. He declined to give his name. He described Hamilton as a living monument to the Klan cause.

If Hamilton is a living monument, he is now living where all ruthless floggers and persons who take the law into their own hands should reside. The Grand Titan need not fear to reveal his name if he is a law-abiding citizen. But if he intends to wear Hamilton's shoes, he had better watch his step. Already he is treading on dangerous ground.

Sharing the platform on Wednesday night was a woman wearing a gold robe who said she represented the Klan auxiliary, known as the "Big Sisters."

The function of the Big Sisters has never been clear to us. Perhaps they administer by applying bandaids to the wounds inflicted by the Klansmen's whips. Obviously, an outfit such as Hamilton's Klan needs a full-time group of Big Sisters to roll bandages, repair whips and mend sheets.

The story of Hamilton's Klan, as unfolded in the North Carolina trials, was a disgusting tale of irresponsible sadism. The Hamilton Klan is not merely a symbol of bad racial relations, because white and Negroes alike have felt the cutting sting of Klansmen's whips. The Hamilton Klan is an affront to decent people everywhere and violates the principles of law and order on which all organized societies are founded.

In addition, the Klan does untold damage to the South by playing into the hands of the Northern liberals who want to place Southern racial relations under federal control.

Politics took front stage shortly after the Lake City Klan gathering. The Klan activity gave way to "Eisenhower Wins in

Landslide." But that didn't stop the South Carolina Klansmen from struggling to stay afloat while their leader was imprisoned.

The same issue of the *Tribune* carried an obituary of Troy Bennett, the former town councilman who had been convicted for Klan floggings and was spared a prison term only when his ailing heart gave out on him.

It was about this time that the first public recognition came for the *Tribune* and the *Whiteville News-Reporter* for their part in the long and difficult KKK crusade.

In Raleigh, William P. Bloom, chairman of the board of the Anti-Defamation League of B'nai B'rith, presented Willard Cole (of the *News-Reporter*) and me the first regional B'nai B'rith Awards for "Outstanding Community Service While Subjecting Themselves to Great Personal Danger."

I know I must have glowed from within all the way back to Tabor City that memorable evening. It's great to discover that others appreciate an effort that results in improving a society when there is unusual risk in the project. Such recognition often makes all the fear, anxiety and disappointment worth the costs. Lucile was elated over the prestigious award. That gold plaque still adorns the wall in my tiny Tabor City office.

On December 24, I paused a moment to look back over the year and think of all that had happened, good and bad. I wrote this editorial with the comatose Ku Klux Klan in the back of my mind:

CHRISTMAS AND A NEW YEAR

The week of December 25th comes faster every year. Yet that holiday season, to most of us, is the most pleasant time of the year. It's noteworthy that we celebrate this religious holiday and make it enjoyable. We are not humble or sacred enough, and, like all human beings, we are selfish. But Christmas makes us a little more charitable. It's a time when we hope God looks down upon his earthly creatures with a little more compassion and understanding than He does at other times of the year.

Following right on the heels of Christmas the new year begins. It's a time for all of us to think back over the past and promise to do more for mankind in the months ahead. It's a nuclear age now and there might not be many more New Years.

We at the *Tribune* have reason for being humble. We have been engulfed in the most dangerous and difficult campaign of our young lives. Maybe you have endured a year of trauma and turmoil too. At any rate, we look to the future with hope and confidence. Maybe God will give us a passing grade for 1952. We surely hope so.

The South Carolina Ku Klux Klan was still clinging to life. On the last night of the year, they scheduled another public rally at Goretown, a crossroads community on Highway 9 between Loris and North Myrtle Beach in Horry County.

I was delighted to find a sparse crowd of about three hundred. During Hamilton's heyday he had attracted five thousand or more. Maybe the death knell had been rung throughout the Carolinas. I went home reasonably happy. I would have to write about the KKK for the final time that last day of 1952.

B'nai B'rith presented Willard Cole and me the First Annual Southeastern United States Plaque for Public Service.

Certificate of Honor

An Award of the
Eastern North Carolina Press Association

•

This Certificate of Honor is Presented to

W. Horace Carter

Tabor City Tribune
Tabor City, N. C.

For:—

High courage, moral responsibility, unflinching integrity and devotion to the principles of real Americanism in conducting a vigorous editorial and news campaign against the unlawful acts of men masquerading as members of the Ku Klux Klan, who took into their own hands the punishment of those whom they deemed guilty of misconduct, setting aside the established laws of the State and instituting a reign of terror in Lower North Carolina.

The courage displayed in editorial writing and news reporting, undismayed and undeterred by threats of bodily harm, measured up to the highest standards of the newspaper profession.

Awarded this 28th day of March, 1952, by the Eastern North Carolina Press Association, in convention assembled at Wilmington, North Carolina.

SECRETARY   PRESIDENT

Chapter Thirty
Some Never Learn

Three robed strangers—as blind to the concept of brotherhood as the proverbial mice—made short, incoherent speeches at Goretown Tuesday night as the infamous Ku Klux Klan held its first public rally since the imprisonment of their Grand Dragon, Thomas Hamilton.

I reported this in the *Tribune* December 31, 1952. It was the last day of 1952, and in many ways it was the last gasp for survival by the dwindling band of vigilantes.

Three hooded speakers, introduced as the Great Titan, the Grand Kleagle and the Great Giant, never revealed their identities. They took turns lambasting the Jews, Negroes and communism, but seemed perturbed that not one ripple of applause was heard. The audience responded with eerie silence.

The Klan program began with the playing of the "Star Spangled Banner," which was followed by "The Old Rugged Cross." Twenty robed Klansmen marched around a fifteen-foot burning cross that was ignited a few minutes before the speeches began. Some in attendance never left their cars parked along Highway 9 adjacent to the tobacco field where a flatbed truck served as a rostrum. The misty night made it difficult for the torch bearer to light the oil-soaked sacks wrapped around the cross, a suggestion of the futility of the rally in general.

The blue-robed Great Titan read a prayer from a prepared script and followed that with the traditional Lord's prayer as the Klan continued in a religious motif, but their rhetoric and activities were everything but godly.

The Titan's tirade focused against the "enemies of the country" pointing out that these forces won a great victory in North Carolina with the conviction of his Klan brothers. Then he read a poem that emphasized another pilot taking the helm in time of trouble. The Klan would soon have another pilot at the helm, he said.

The Grand Kleagle was an elderly man who said he was a grandfather. His subject was the Jews. In his short talk, he was vociferous and made constant violent movements as he blamed the Jews for the world's troubles since biblical times. He did not get a response from the audience when he sat down.

The Great Giant was an obese man whose task was to talk the crowd into financial assistance for the floundering Klan. After appealing for their support, he passed around a hat. He got a sizable number of dollar bills, indicating that the Klan still had a number of sympathizers.

Circulars were distributed to potential members at the conclusion of the rally. About thirty or forty listeners took them. Most of the audience refused to accept the flyers and headed for their cars.

As at many of Hamilton's rallies, the speakers were generally poorly prepared, often losing their place in the written speeches and struggling with their composure.

I returned to Tabor City and wrote another anti-Klan editorial for the front page. It read:

SOME NEVER LEARN
Obviously some people never learn.

When the Ku Klux Klan was riding high in Columbus and Horry counties a few short months ago, law-abiding citizens eventually rose to the occasion, spoke their piece and voted their convictions from the jury and grand jury boxes. Those juries put many night riders in prison, including Grand Dragon Hamilton.

You would think that those adventurous souls who fantasize a phony glamour in wearing a bedsheet and watching a cross burn would have learned something from their predecessors who are now paying the price for their lawlessness. But there are still those who cling to the past and revolt against change. These are the troubled reactionaries.

Last night the Klan rallied at Goretown, the first public meeting since the collapse of the infamous gang that was convicted of night-riding floggings in Columbus County.

This meeting was called by the hooded mob's leaders on the eve of the change in law enforcement officers in Horry County. Present law enforcement officers have failed to get a single significant conviction of Klansmen in the county despite many dastardly beatings of men and women, blacks and whites, for more than two years. As a new sheriff and his deputies take over January 5, it is going to be interesting to see how the Klan operates. Will the KKK continue its lawless persecution of those it seeks to reform?

Sheriff John Henry has a task facing him. If the night riders go back into action, Henry will be under oath to do everything in his power to bring them to justice. Many, knowing the Klan helped elect Henry, believe that the hooded hoodlums can now do anything they want to without being arrested. They think they have it made.

We were convinced long ago that little justice could be found in the Horry County courts when Klansmen were involved. Many arrests were made, but always the cases were thrown out in the court for lack of evidence. Gathering evidence is a job for law enforcement and if local and state agencies can't produce that evidence after these crimes are committed, it is time to call for federal assistance.

John Henry has a duty to bring to the bar of justice those Klansmen who continue to flog helpless citizens. If he can't do this with his own officers, then he must ask for help from the outside to stop this menace to freedom in Horry County and throughout South Carolina.

Many situations in Horry County need investigating. There are powers-that-be in the courts and other high places who are fearful of any outside investigation, but if local officers cannot root out these evils, then every honest citizen should make his voice heard—bring pressure to bear on the officials for outside assistance. We must drive fear from the door of all Americans.

Sheriff Henry knows that he cannot expect any support from us if he fails to make a sincere effort to enforce the law against the Klansmen. He knows and we know that he got a lot of votes from Klansmen and ex-Klansmen in the recent election. Election support should have no bearing on on whom the law is enforced. Every honorable citizen wants criminals brought to justice. Failure to do so undermines the very essence of democratic government.

I had been gullible in Sheriff Henry's campaign and election. He had repeatedly told me in face-to-face conversations that he had never been a Klansman, wanted no help from the KKK and if elected, would do everything in his power to bring them to court for their lawlessness. He even went so far as to have us print five thousand multi-colored circulars stating emphatically that he was no friend to the Ku Klux Klan and would stop their activity in Horry County if he took office.

It was all a ruse to get our support. After we had delivered the circulars a week before the election, a friend came in the print shop and, upon seeing a scrapped Henry flyer on the floor, broke into a big smile.

"Did Henry order those flyers?" he asked.

"Yeah. He ordered them and has paid for them," I said, a little puzzled.

"That's one for the books," he replied. "I don't know for sure that John is a Klansman, but I do know he has the support of every one of the KKK's all over the county. They are the ones who will elect him and he knows it. He is pulling your leg with this printing job."

Ironically, he was dead right. Not one of the flyers was ever circulated. He must have burned them. But by spending those few bucks with us, he had hoodwinked me and the newspaper into believing and supporting him in the race. We learned soon enough, but I often imagined that Henry must have enjoyed a hearty laugh when he showed those flyers to his Klan buddies at the next klavern meeting.

But the sheriff would not get the last laugh. The FBI was close on the heels of a bevy of Klansmen who had escaped indictment in county and state courts. Sympathizers overlooked evidence and enforcement officers and prosecutors were often nonchalant in seeking indictments. Cases came to court ill-prepared. There was little interest in punishing the "church whippers" in Horry County. And they might have succeeded for years had not the F.B.I. stepped in.

As our "Some Never Learn" editorial had asked, federal investigators combed the swamps of Horry for evidence connecting Klansmen with a number of brutal attacks. Three weeks into the new year of 1953, they swooped down on nineteen night-riding Klansmen. They had been at work undercover for eleven months and two days. The editorial had prompted some phone calls to Washington, perhaps expediting the arrests. At any rate, Horry Klansmen faced the noose. Floggings would now stop. Local law enforcement could not protect the vigilantes in federal court.

It was a real pleasure to sit down and write about the F.B.I. crackdown in Horry County in the January 22, 1953 edition. I had waited so long for that moment! Often I wondered if it would ever come in that little corner of South Carolina where the *Tribune* circulated as much as it did across the border in Columbus County.

186

A few more crosses would burn.

With the Klan on the run, Tabor City looked for new industry.

Chapter Thirty-one
Completing The Job

Almost as sure as the proverbial death and taxes, when the Federal Bureau of Investigation focused on a case in the 1950's you could depend upon its being solved, regardless of the time and effort it required. So it was no great surprise on January 21, 1953, when the agents arrested nineteen night-riding Ku Klux Klansmen in Horry County and tossed them in jail for the brutal beating of George Kemper Smith at Nichols, South Carolina. Fruits of their lengthy investigation were harvested. It had taken time to gather solid evidence necessary to indict and hopefully convict the first South Carolina Klan criminals. All were charged with kidnapping and conspiracy to assault.

The little-publicized Smith assault occurred when a dozen or more Klansmen seized him in front of his home on the night of October 20, 1951. It was at the height of the Klan uprising. The kidnappers transported Smith across the state line near Fair Bluff to a desolate point known as "Lover's Lane." He had been lured out of his home by a stranger claiming car trouble, as had several of the other kidnapping victims. Masked Klansmen pounced on Smith after he stopped his pickup truck alongside the supposedly disabled car. One Klansman kept a pistol on Smith while others bent him over the truck fender and beat him with a heavy strap. F.B.I. agents described the attack as another "fender-strap method" that had been used on many of the victims in North Carolina.

Smith contended that the Klansmen never told him why he was beaten. He was released a short distance from home following the lashing.

The nineteen indictments were returned by a grand jury in Raleigh, just hours before the crackdown in Horry County. The F.B.I. identified all of the assailants as members of the once-notorious Fair Bluff Klavern that had been disbanded.

All those arrested were scheduled to appear in federal court in Wilmington, North Carolina, on May 18 and were released on $5,000 bond.

This crackdown in South Carolina brought more North Carolinians into the picture. Ten were among those previously tried and convicted for similar attacks across the line. Nine new faces were among the ones charged in the Smith case.

Special Agent William A. Murphy of the Charlotte F.B.I. office released the names of the Klansmen charged in that first South Carolina crackdown. They were:

James Early Brooks and Bobby Brooks, formerly of Fair Bluff, now of Raleigh.

Simon T. Enzor, Douglas Grainger, Ed Floyd Rogers, Jr., John A. Shaw, L. C. Worley and John Porter Shaw, all of Fair Bluff. Robert L. Hammond, of Cerro Gordo, North Carolina; John Nealey, Green Sea, South Carolina; Leo Harrelson, Mullins, South Carolina; and Charles Gilbert Enzor, Nichols, South Carolina.

Brooks was already in custody from a previous conviction. He was serving a prison term for the Woodrow Johnson attack and was under another four-year sentence in the Martin-Grainger kidnapping.

Horace Strickland, Pittman Foy Strickland, Eddie Carl Richardson and Ross Enzor were serving time at the federal penitentiary in Petersburg, Virginia, for their participation in the Martin-Grainger floggings.

The F.B.I. arrests in the Kemper Smith case brought the total number of Klansmen arrested in the Carolinas to 98. There had been 229 indictments in less than twelve months. It had left no doubt in the minds of the masses that taking part in Klan "church whippings" was unhealthy and a threat to one's precious freedom.

Klansmen quickly turned on each other when they faced prosecutors in the court. It reminded me of a simple little philosophy that my father had once passed on to me. He said, "If you are ever going to do anything bad, do it by yourself and then keep your mouth shut. Don't even let your best friend know about it, because in a crisis, or when he falls out with you he will use the incident against you." That was certainly true in the Klan episodes.

The turmoil had traumatized the coastal Carolinas for more than two years. It had created great fear in my household. I was elated that it was coming to an end. I no longer felt like my family and I were in the clutches of this sinister movement. It was like going home again.

I wrote a short editorial. This one called not for more arrests, but for legislative action. It read:

THE JOB NEEDS COMPLETING

The operations of the night riders have now been stamped out. It took a lot of effort by local, state and federal officers. Those mobsters responsible for terrorizing our communities are paying the price for their anarchy.

Getting the job done was long, difficult and painstaking. Often officers were faced with making arrests where inadequate laws existed. Except for the fact that the night riders carried some of their victims across state lines, making it a federal kidnapping offense, many of those mobsters might now be free and rampaging through our communities.

The North Carolina General Assembly should follow up by passing anti-mask laws that will prohibit persons from wearing robes, hoods and masks on public property. Many other states have such laws on the books now. Legislators should act during this session and thus make it much easier for law enforcement officers to keep the peace.

We also think it would be a good idea to make it illegal for any member of a city, county, or state police force to hold membership or be affiliated in any way with terrorist organizations like the Ku Klux Klan.

With these laws in force in the Carolinas, the citizenry could forever rest assured that there was little chance of floggings recurring.

Laws are made to protect and guide the people. An iron-clad anti-mask law coupled with prohibitions against law enforcement officers being affiliated with vigilante groups, would leave no doubt in the minds of the masses that to participate in mob violence in the dark of night while hiding identities behind hoods and masks is illegal and guarantees imprisonment for those convicted of such activities.

Within a month the anti-mask law was introduced into the General Assembly by Representative Addison Hewlett of New Hanover County and Senator Vivian Whitfield introduced it into the Senate. The bill covered all secret societies (political and military) and other secret societies circumventing the law. The law flatly prohibited cross burning on private property without the consent of the landlord. The law went further than many anti-Klan laws in other states. Since its inception, there has never been a vibrant Ku

Klux Klan movement in the Tar Heel State, although some small splinter groups have created problems.

The *Tribune* had obviously won this long crusade. It was time to move on to another challenge. I had worked to bring industry to Tabor City and had succeeded to some degree. A sewing plant was opening in a new community-owned building. I had promoted that project and enticed the New York firm to locate in Tabor City. I was teaching the men's Sunday School class in the Baptist Church, was active in the Rotary Club and had served as president of the Tabor City Merchants Association. I had also headed my share of Red Cross, cancer and other charitable drives, as well as serving as local Scoutmaster. I was an Eagle Scout myself, having earned the rank at age seventeen.

A town election was coming up in April. A friend or two suggested that I should run for mayor. Why not? The Klan crusade was nearing its end. Maybe I could be of some service. I threw my hat in the ring. It was a new challenge.

An Eagle Scout since age 17, I accepted the post of Scoutmaster in Tabor City.

Chapter Thirty-two
Legal Justice at Last

The final nineteen Ku Klux Klansmen came to trial in federal court in Wilmington on May 18. Judge Don Gilliam was presiding. These assailants had been arrested January 21 by the F.B.I. and charged with kidnapping and conspiracy to assault George Kemper Smith of Nichols, South Carolina. They were the first Klansmen to be arrested in South Carolina by the F.B.I.

No longer the brassy vigilantes who hid behind masks and robes with whips in hand, eighteen of the defendants pleaded *nolo contendere*. Only Robert Hammond pleaded not guilty. But Gilliam found him guilty, too, and pronounced sentences on all of the nineteen.

Three-year prison sentences were given to John A. Shaw of Fair Bluff and Leo Harrelson and Troy L. Gerald of Mullins.

Drawing one-year terms were Charles G. Enzor, Nichols; Simon T. Enzor and Ed Floyd, Fair Bluff; and John G. Nealey of Green Sea.

Receiving two-year suspended sentences and probation were James and Bobby Brooks, of Raleigh, sons of Early Brooks, who was already serving prison terms for earlier offenses. They were on probation from previous trials.

Garrell D. Grainger, L. C. Worley and John Porter Shaw, all of Fair Bluff; Robert L. Hammond, Cerro Gordo; and George English Cook, Mullins.

Five of the defendants were already serving time: Brooks, the former Fair Bluff policeman; Horace Strickland, the former Columbus County deputy sheriff; Pittman Strickland; Eddie Carl Richardson and Hezekiah R. Enzor. The concurrent terms would not extend beyond the time that they would be eligible for parole, varying from four to twelve months.

Testifying in the trial, Smith, the victim, said he begged not to be beaten, but was lashed fifteen or twenty times. He said at the trial that when he asked why he was being beaten, they said, "Because you ought to stay home more." He said his abductors wore white robes and hoods, like the one that District Attorney Cicero Yow showed him when he was on the witness stand.

Cameron Weeks, a defense attorney from Tarboro, struck at the victim's court record. Smith admitted that he had been caught driving drunk by Early Brooks, one of the defendants. He denied passing bad checks as the defense attorney implied. When asked if he hadn't taken a woman across the state line 100 times for immoral purposes, he denied the implication. Later he admitted that he had taken a woman into North Carolina on several trips.

It seemed that this attack, like many others, was a case of "church whipping" for alleged immoral conduct. At least that was the nomenclature defense lawyers used.

Only character witnesses took the stand on behalf of the Klansmen. Their lawyers in pleading said all the defendants regretted their Klan activities, adding that the Klan was "now officially dead in the Carolinas."

Judge Gilliam said he was inclined to believe that the Klan was dead, but warned that it had a strange way of coming to life. The jurist said if an organization like the KKK would aid officers in enforcing the law instead of "being their own accuser, judge and jury" the matter would be different.

This Klan trial was the last chapter in judgment in the war of terrorism that struck the border section of the Carolinas from 1950 through 1952.

Imprisoned Klansmen began applying for parole in July. All but four of the original fifteen convicted that fall were released. Grand Dragon Thomas L. Hamilton was still confined. He too would soon apply for parole. The State Parole Board decided that the facts in the case did not justify parole at that time. Hamilton would have to wear his prison garb at least a few more months. All other imprisoned Klansmen would be paroled by that time.

Late in October 1953, Hamilton publicly repented for his Klan sins. He released a letter to the press that called upon all of "my Klan friends everywhere to disband wherever you are. Come out in the open for the causes in which we believe. I will never again join or be active in any movement which is not open to any reputable citizen and whose membership is not available to the forces of law and order."

He went on to say, "I have no resentment toward Editors Carter and Cole who fought the Klan movement." The newspapers had helped to bring him to justice and tear his Klan empire apart. He pledged that his future included being a good citizen.

"I want to say to the people of Columbus county that I am truly sorry for the suffering and heartaches which the Klan brought to you. With the help of God, I shall strive to atone for my share in this sad experience. I harbor no ill will in my heart against any man," Hamilton wrote.

He ended his statement with these words: "I am through with the Ku Klux Klan and I believe that all of my former associates will best serve themselves and society as a whole by taking a similar stand. It has not been easy for me to come to a parting of the ways with many loyal followers who felt they had a duty to perform in the interest of society. I know they are dedicated to the principle of honesty and decency as I tried to be. I have prayed over the matter and I am sure that God would want me to stay aloof from any organization which presents an opportunity for a person to hide himself behind a mask and commit a crime. I now know that the possibilities for evil offset any good which might be accomplished in this matter.

"I will seek parole again soon. I hope no one will I doubt my humility and repentance. May I have the prayers and good wishes of all the people as I try to reestablish my home and educate my daughter." The once proud Grand Dragon at last admitted defeat. His repentance seemed sincere.

Solicitor Clifton Moore soon recommended parole for the ex-Ku Klux Klan leader. That was fine with me and my friend Willard Cole. We did not object to the parole. We had never wanted to crucify Hamilton. We simply wanted law and order restored in the community, which had been impossible while the runaway Klan movement swept over the land for so many months. Hamilton now seemed truly repentant and willing for the Klan insurrection to end.

At its next meeting the parole board released the former Grand Dragon. He returned to Leesville in time for Christmas 1953. He has not been heard from since.

I received an engraved invitation to appear at the Plaza Hotel in New York City to receive the Sidney Hillman Foundation Award. The presentation was scheduled for election day. Maybe I could win the mayor's race without my own and Lucile's votes. Besides, I badly needed the $500 cash that went with the plaque. I had not forgotten being part-time janitor at Endy High School where I was paid $15 a month. I had not forgotten working in a cotton mill for $10.87 for a forty-hour week. I would never forget working my way through the University of North Carolina in the News Bureau at thirty cents an hour. I had not forgotten trying to support a wife on war-time Navy pay which ranged from $96 to $153 a month. In 1953 a check for $500 was like manna from heaven.

I flew off to the Big Apple, received the check and the award, and made my short acceptance speech. I paraphrased some of the memorable comments made by my mentor, Dr. Frank P. Graham, as I thanked the Sidney Hillman Foundation for the honor.

> The American dream is to make this country safe for all races and religions, where opportunity does not escape the underprivileged and the minorities. Where men are brothers in the sight of God and in their own hearts. Where children can succeed in the schools and in their homes and later in an adult society. Where even the most humble will be accepted in a noble citizenry. Where human progress is made through religion, education and voluntary cooperation in the minds and hearts of the people. And where the struggle for success and fulfillment of historical Americanism is the best answer to fascism, communism and the vigilante movement that has harassed my home community for many months.
>
> The least of our brethren still can struggle and hope in America for freedom and know that the answer to error is not terror, respect for the past is not reactionary and the hope of the future is not revolution. Integrity remains without a price tag and the daily toil of everyday Americans is above pomp and power and it will not go unrewarded. America is a land where the majority doesn't mean tyranny and the minorities are without fear and hope is real in the minds of all people.
>
> I thank you for this Sidney Hillman Award and I will try to honor it and the noble man for whom it was named in the years ahead. Again, thank you very much.

I had barely returned to my room when the telephone rang. It was Edwin Wright in Tabor City.

"Hello, Mr. Mayor," he began. "You just won the election by about four to one. You better get back home and start running the town."

So many good things had happened to me. Would this be

good too? I would soon find out. The mayor had not only to meet with the town council at least once a month and make decisions almost daily for various departmental administrative chores, he was also the judge in Mayor's Court. That was held every Monday night and usually at least a dozen cases were heard. The mayor was paid one hundred dollars a year for his services. I had worked at many jobs for almost nothing. The mayor's would be no different.

THE SIDNEY HILLMAN FOUNDATION

To all persons to whom these Presents may come Greeting:
Be it known that

W. HORACE CARTER
Tabor City Tribune

WILLARD G. COLE
Whiteville News Reporter

JAY JENKINS
Raleigh News and Observer

Have been awarded

The Sidney Hillman Foundation Award for Writing in the Field of Daily Journalism for 1952:

Articles exposing the Ku Klux Klan
in Columbia County, N.C.

In witness thereof, we have caused this certificate to be signed by the President of The Sidney Hillman Foundation and our corporate seal to be hereto affixed in the City of New York on the Tenth day of June in the year of our Lord One Thousand Nine Hundred and Fifty-Three.

The Sidney Hillman Foundation

President

Cole and I received the Sidney Hillman Foundation Award in New York.

197

Columbia University
in the City of New York
[NEW YORK 27, N. Y.]

GRADUATE SCHOOL OF JOURNALISM
OFFICE OF THE DEAN

May 4, 1953

Mr. W. Horace Carter
TABOR CITY TRIBUNE
Tabor City, North Carolina

Dear Mr. Carter:

I take very great pleasure in confirming the fact that the Trustees of Columbia University have awarded the Pulitzer Public Service Prize to THE NEWS REPORTER and the TABOR CITY TRIBUNE for their successful campaign against the Ku Klux Klan.

In accordance with that award the University has ordered the engraving of two gold medals, one will be presented to the TABOR CITY TRIBUNE and the other to THE NEWS REPORTER, as tangible evidence of this selection. This medal will be sent to you as soon as it is received from the engraver.

With renewed congratulations, I am

Sincerely yours,

Carl W. Ackerman, Secretary
Advisory Board on the
Pulitzer Prizes

CWA:AD

198

TRIBUNE WINS PULITZER PRIZE

The Pulitzer Prize—the highest award made to newspapers in the United States—was won by The Tribune this week when the Trustees of the University of Columbia, New York City, announced their 1953 selection. [article text continues in small print]

The Tabor City Tribune

"TABOR CITY — THE TOWN WITH A CITY FUTURE"

VOL. VII, NUMBER 42   TABOR CITY, N. C. WEDNESDAY, MAY 6, 1953   5c A COPY; $2.00 A YEAR

SEWING SCHOOL HAS PARTY

Ladies who have attended the sewing school here sponsored by the Tabor Manufacturing Company recently had a picnic in the shade of the Enterline road. The school has been operating for several weeks and most of the local ladies pictured here will be employed by the shirt and pajama plant when the doors are opened for operation. [text continues]

Plant Opening Is Delayed

LEGION TO ELECT OFFICERS

Members of the Tabor City American Legion Post 245 were urged this week to attend a four o'clock meeting next Tuesday at which time an election of officers will be held. [text continues]

COOKING SCHOOL SLATED BY LOCAL FIRM

Carter Speaks In Norfolk, Va.

Local Pastor Revival Guest

Rev. C. V. Crutchfield, pastor of the local Pentecostal Holiness Church. [text continues]

Miss Caroline Jackson, daughter of Mr. and Mrs. A. L. Jackson, a rising senior at Meredith College was initiated into Sigma Pi Alpha, National French Language Society, at the National Congress in Raleigh on April 12. [text continues]

COUNTY WINS CATTLE HONORS

Columbus County won first place in the handsomeship contest and scored in the county group at three shows at the 2nd Annual Southeastern Fat Stock Show which was held in Wilmington April 28-May 2. [text continues]

Acme-Delco Lions Club To Present Show

Cancer Drive Extended Here

Woman's Club Meets Tuesday

The Tabor City Woman's Club will meet at the Clubhouse Tuesday, May 12, at 3:30 p. m. Mrs. C. H. Crutchfield, president, announced. [text continues]

Music, Band Teacher Sought For School

C. H. Fisher, Superintendent of the Tabor City Schools, met this week with the Civitan Club and the Rotary Club Monday night and outlined a plan for the hiring of a full time music, band and recreation director for the local schools. [text continues]

Cole To Speak At Guideway

Willard G. Cole, editor of The News Reporter of Whiteville. [text continues]

BERRY MARKET

199

From *Time* Magazine
May 11, 1953

Among the Pulitzer prizes, the top journalistic award is the one to the U.S. newspaper that has rendered the most "meritorious public service." Ever since 1917, when the awards were first made under the will of the late great Publisher Joseph Pulitzer, the "public service" prize has always gone to a daily, usually a big one. This week for the first time in the history of the prizes, the "public service" award for 1952 went to two country weeklies, published in North Carolina's Columbus County: the semi-weekly *Whiteville News Reporter* (circ. 5,007) and the *Tabor City Tribune* (circ. 1,500).

The two weeklies won their prize for stopping an invasion. The invaders: the Ku Klux Klan, which swarmed into Columbus County from neighboring counties in 1950 and began to terrorize whites and Negroes alike. *News Reporter* Editor Willard Cole, 46, and *Tribune* Editor Horace Carter, 32, locked arms for a long, tough battle. Branding the Klan "a (bunch of) gangsters," Cole and Carter, both native Tarheels and longtime friends, fought month after month with front-page editorials, dug up proof of K.K.K. floggings and atrocities and kept guns in their homes for their own protection.

After other papers joined their crusades, the uproar brought the FBI and state investigators to the county. As a result 16 Klansmen, including Imperial Wizard Thomas Hamilton, were sent to jail for terms up to six years (*Time,* Aug. 11), 46 others were fined a total of $15,850, and the Klan was smashed.

Chapter Thirty-three
Shocking News

It was just another Monday workday. The telephone rang. It was Jay Jenkins of the *Raleigh News and Observer.*

"Horace, you have just won the Pulitzer Prize," he said with such clarity that there was no mistaking his words. I can never forget them.

There was dead silence on the phone for several seconds. Then I replied:

"You don't mean it! For the Klan crusade I presume?"

"Yes, that's what it's for," Jay said enthusiastically.

"Which Pulitzer did I win?" I asked, getting worked up a little more with each word.

"The biggest one of them all. The Meritorious Public Service Award," Jay answered.

"I haven't heard anything about it, Jay, but thanks so much for calling. I hope this isn't some kind of joke," I said. "You would be sick to joke about the Pulitzer."

He laughed. "My boss, Jonathan Daniels, who nominated you for the Pulitzer has just been told about it by phone. You'll hear something soon I'm sure." Daniels was the well-known editor of the *News and Observer.* I had known he was nominating me for the award, but had no hope of actually winning. It was an honor just to be nominated.

I hung up the phone and slumped back in my chair. Could Jay be pulling my leg? Could this little weekly newspaper win the greatest journalism award in the world? It must be true. Jay couldn't be cruel enough to joke about it.

I had hardly caught my breath when a Western Union messenger came into the office with a telegram in his hand. I tore it open. It read: "I have the honor to advise that the University (Columbia) trustees have awarded Pulitzer Prizes to the *Tabor City*

Tribune and the *Whiteville News-Reporter* for public service. Grayson Kirk, President." It was ironic that the local Western Union franchise was held by the late Troy Bennett, one of the Klansmen convicted for participating in the attacks.

WESTERN UNION

W. P. MARSHALL, PRESIDENT

1291

The filing time shown in the date line on telegrams and day letters is STANDARD TIME at point of origin. Time of receipt is STANDARD TIME at p =5 45P

WL A013 PD=NCU NEWYORK NY MAY 4 425P=

=W HORACE CARTER=

=TABOR CITY TRIBUNE TABOR CITY NCAR=

I HAVE THE HONOR TO ADVISE THAT UNIVERSITY TRUSTEES HAVE
AWARDED PULITZER PRIZE TO THE TABOR CITY TRIBUNE AND
WHITEVILLE NEWS REPORTER FOR PUBLIC SERVICE=

GRAYSON KIRK PRES

I smiled an unbelieving smile. Though I was the first member of my family to enter journalism, I knew that this was the grandest of all writing awards. I had learned that during Journalism School at the University of North Carolina in Chapel Hill. It seemed impossible that a country boy who was not very scholarly could win such a prestigious prize. But I had the proof in my hand.

Never before had a weekly newspaper won a Pulitzer Prize. Furthermore, no daily newspaper in North Carolina had ever won it. Maybe we had done a pretty fair job of crusading, even with constant fear in our hearts and few dollars in the bank.

Mayor W. A. Williams came into the office that afternoon.

"I thought you might like to see a copy of the telegram that I just sent to Jonathan Daniels," he grinned, as he put the paper in my hands.

I read it aloud as tears came to my eyes. My voice trembled.

"The people of Tabor City join me in thanking you for your nomination of W. Horace Carter for the Pulitzer Prize. In our estimation it could not have happened to a better man. W. A. Williams, Mayor."

It was a great salve for all those harrowing months when I wondered if I had any friends and supporters in Tabor City.

Within twenty-four hours I was flooded with requests for pictures, biographical material and copies of some of the Klan crusade articles. Phone calls and telegrams poured in from all over the country.

One made a particular impression. It was from the University of North Carolina Department of Journalism. "Congratulations on Pulitzer Award. It marks a great day for North Carolina country journalism. Tom Lassiter and Walter Spearman."

Since 1951, the *Tribune* and I had won four major awards for the Klan fight. They included the B'nai B'rith Award, a Certificate of Merit from the Eastern North Carolina Press Association, a Citation of Merit from the North Carolina Press Association, and the North Carolina Junior Chamber of Commerce Distinguished Service Award as the state's "Young Man of the Year for 1952."

I appreciated all of that recognition. I was honored to have won any of them. But to win the Pulitzer, the dream of all newspapermen, was beyond comprehension.

J. A. Herlocker, the printshop foreman, dug up that big type again that I was saving for the second coming of Christ. He set a headline above the masthead on the front page for the Wednesday edition—"TRIBUNE WINS PULITZER." Would I ever be this happy again?

I wrote the story reporting the *Tribune's* good fortune:

> While I wrote every editorial and news story during the Ku Klux Klan campaign, I want to thank the other members of our newspaper family. I am proud to have had associates here in the printing department who always gave me great moral support and encouragement when the Klan tension was the highest. That had a great deal to do with our winning the Pulitzer. They always wanted me to keep up the fight even when it would have cost them their jobs if the Klan squeezed us out of business.
>
> Those persons who have been so supportive are: Mark Garner, my business partner of Myrtle Beach, South Carolina; Evelyn Leonard, social editor; Bill Oakley, J. A. Herlocker, C. W. Hucks and Wade W. Martin of the printing department. Then, of course, I want to thank my wife, who continued to solicit advertising for the newspaper during all of the crusade. Her confidence and support was always invaluable.
>
> I also want to thank the merchants of Tabor City and the nearby towns for their advertising support during

the boycott and campaign. Without that, all would have been in vain. We would have folded. And then I want to thank the loyal subscribers who continued to buy the paper even when harassed by Klansmen and sympathizers to boycott the *Tribune*.

One of the daily newspapers had this to say about our winning the Pulitzer:

"The late Joseph Pulitzer, crusading publisher, would certainly applaud the selection of the two small town editors if he had been a judge. Their campaign, often conducted at great personal risk, helped lift a reign of terror imposed on Columbus County by hooded night riders in 1951."

Hundreds of congratulatory letters and telegrams came into the office for weeks after the Pulitzer announcement. I still have many of those yellowed papers.

One suggested that I might be the only thirty-two-year-old ever to win the Pulitzer Prize for Meritorious Public Service. Until this day, I don't know if that is true.

The Town of Tabor City scheduled a banquet in my honor and presented me with an engraved wrist watch that named me "Tabor City Man of the Year." I thought of the Bible verse that says: "A prophet is not without honor save in his own country." To be so honored by my friends and neighbors was something I would never forget. And I don't think Lucile had ever been as happy as she was when she was asked to stand and be recognized for her patience and understanding in the face of hundreds of threats and constant harassment.

My head gradually returned to normal from its expanded size after the wrist watch presentation and being named Tabor City Man of the Year by the town's citizens. Maybe all this notoriety and publicity would make me a better mayor. I would soon find out. I had been elected without the time or opportunity to shake hands and kiss babies. Maybe I would find that time soon.

THE TRUSTEES OF COLUMBIA UNIVERSITY

IN THE CITY OF NEW YORK

TO ALL PERSONS TO WHOM THESE PRESENTS MAY COME GREETING

BE IT KNOWN THAT

TABOR CITY TRIBUNE AND THE NEWS REPORTER

HAVE BEEN AWARDED

THE PULITZER PRIZE IN JOURNALISM FOR PUBLIC SERVICE FOR THEIR
SUCCESSFUL CAMPAIGN AGAINST THE KU KLUX KLAN, WAGED ON THEIR
OWN DOORSTEP AT THE RISK OF ECONOMIC LOSS AND PERSONAL DANGER

IN ACCORDANCE WITH THE PROVISIONS OF THE STATUTES OF THE
UNIVERSITY GOVERNING SUCH AWARD

IN WITNESS WHEREOF WE HAVE CAUSED THIS CERTIFICATE TO BE
SIGNED BY THE PRESIDENT OF THE UNIVERSITY AND OUR CORPORATE
SEAL TO BE HERETO AFFIXED IN THE CITY OF NEW YORK ON THE
FOURTH   DAY OF   MAY   IN THE YEAR OF
OUR LORD ONE THOUSAND NINE HUNDRED AND FIFTY-THREE

PRESIDENT

205

This gold medallion symbolizes the Pulitzer Prize Meritorious Public Service Award presented to the *Tribune*.

206

I posed with my son Rusty in Chapel Hill at the presentation ceremony when I gave the Pulitzer Prize to the University of North Carolina Journalism Hall of Fame.

I chatted with University of North Carolina Chancellor Paul Hardin in Chapel Hill, February 4, 1991, when the Pulitzer Prize unveiling was held. (photo by Kathy Michel, *Daily Tar Heel)*

Chapter Thirty-four
Still Another Shock

A few months after the shocking news that I had won the Pulitzer Prize, another honor was bestowed that until this day I value dearly, almost as much as the Pulitzer. Again the overworked telephone brought the news of this unique distinction, of which I could only dream.

"Hello, this is the *Tribune,*" I answered on a Saturday morning when the office was closed and I was there alone. I never seemed to catch up. That's a situation that harasses a lot of small business owners.

"Horace, this is Roland Guidez in Chapel Hill. I am happy to inform you that the United States Junior Chamber of Commerce has just announced its 'Ten Most Outstanding Young Men in America for 1953.' You are one of the ten. It's great news for the Jaycees and I know it is great news for you personally," Guidez (known to all his friends as "Foo") brought me face to face with another tremendous honor that made me stammer.

"You must be kidding! I knew, of course, that you had nominated me, but to win such distinction is as unexpected as the Pulitzer. Thank you so much for calling. I'll never be able to thank you and the Jaycees for what this means to me. I'll run straight home and tell 'Cile," I said, and surely Guidez smiled at my excitement. I had been an active Jaycee for years. I knew how important the award was.

Later, that distinguished award was presented to me and the other nine in Seattle, Washington. I had the unique honor of being the first North Carolinian ever to receive the award, although the same year Right Reverend William Gordon, a fellow Tar Heel, was honored for his work in Alaska with the people of the Arctic.

In the span of three years, I had been named Tabor City Man of the Year, North Carolina Man of the Year and now "One of the Ten Most Outstanding Young Men in America," a national award. What else good could happen to a country boy who was as poor as the proverbial church mouse?

These clasped hands represent brotherhood, a goal of the United States Jaycees.

Fred Steffan, nationally prominent artist, drew this caricature of me and all of the ten young men honored in Seattle, Washington in 1953.

Look magazine Recognizes "Ten

Each year, the U.S. Junior Chamber of Commerce honors, from among all the successful young men of the nation, ten who have made the greatest use of their talents for the good of their communities and their country. *Look* joins in saluting this year's ten:

W. Horace Carter, 32, whose courageous editorial campaign in his Tabor City, N.C., *Tribune* broke the power of the local Ku Klux Klan.

Frank G. Clement, a World War II and Korea veteran who, at 32, was elected governor of Tennessee by the largest vote any candidate ever got.

Billie Sol Estes, 28, of Pecos, Texas, whose enterprise and business acumen made him a fortune and revolutionized farming in Pecos Valley.

The Rt. Rev. William Gordon, 35, the Episcopal Bishop of Alaska, who has dedicated his life to work among the people of his Arctic see.

Dr. Lloyd T. Koritz, 26, of Rochelle, Ill., who has risked his life many times in experiments with new techniques of artificial respiration.

Maynard M. Miller, 32, of Seattle, Wash., who has made major contributions to national defense by pioneer geological work in the Arctic.

Outstanding Young Men for 1953"

Sgt. Hiroshi Miyamura, 28, of Gallup, N.M., born in U.S. of Japanese parents, winner of Congressional Medal of Honor in Korean War.

Carl T. Rowan, 28, Pulitzer Prize reporter for Minneapolis *Tribune,* whose *How Far From Slavery?* is a significant study of race relations.

Dr. Albert Schatz, 33, of Fair Lawn, N.J., co-discoverer of streptomycin, now doing research on hormones, diseases of man and plants.

Douglas Stringfellow, 31, of Ogden, Utah, a World War II hero who was elected to Congress in the biggest GOP landslide in Utah's history.

— — —

North Carolina had two young men honored among the Top Ten in 1953. Presentation of the awards to these Junior Chamber of Commerce honorees was held in Seattle, Washington.

I made my first-ever cross-country airplane flight to the West Coast in a driving snowstorm to accept this award. It was as death-threatening as the KKK campaign had been.

Award of Merit
1954

Presented To

Horace Carter

The Tribune, Tabor City, N.C.

In recognition of his courage in battling the forces of intolerance and terrorism through a vigorous editorial campaign -- conducted in fearless disregard of his own safety in the face of threats of violence -- to banish hooded terrorists from his community, for his bravery in printing the truth in the noblest traditions of courageous journalism, for the high example which he has set for members of the National Editorial Association.

By the President of the

National Editorial Association

This was another national award received for the Klan Crusade. It was made in Baltimore, Maryland.

Chapter Thirty-five
What Others Said About Our Pulitzer

Letters, telegrams and phone calls poured in to the *Tribune* from all over the nation following the imprisonment of Thomas L. Hamilton and the dissolution of the Carolinas Klan.

Here are a few of the excerpts:

"Congratulations, best wishes and more power to you. Tabor City is pulling with you."—Citizens of Tabor City

"Many, many congratulations on your great honor. I always felt you deserved it, but honestly, I never thought the Pulitzer Prize people would do such a thorough job of dispensing honor where honor is due."—Furman Bisher, Sports Editor, *Atlanta Constitution*

"It has been the thought of many people during this era that pressure groups have represented selfish interests. It has been for accomplishment of eliminating one of these groups in our state that you have won world renown. Your action against the Ku Klux Klan has given courage to millions throughout the world."—Eugene Oschsenreiter, Jr., President of the North Carolina Junior Chamber of Commerce

"Congratulations on receiving the Pulitzer Prize for your magnificent fight against the Klan. I'm sure that no Pulitzer award ever has come to anyone who deserved it more . . . the entire press of the state takes pride in your accomplishment."—Reed Sarratt, Editorial Director, *Winston-Salem Journal-Sentinel*

"The 200,000 members of the United States Junior Chamber of Commerce have named you as one of the nation's 'Ten Most Outstanding Young Men in America in 1953.' We are proud of the contribution you are making to your profession and to the nation. It is an honor to be recognizing on a nationwide scale your individual contributions to the people of America and the entire world. Your outstanding contribution will give great inspiration to the coming generation." Dain J. Domich, President of the United States Junior Chamber of Commerce.

"I am pleased that you will be in Baltimore to accept the President's Award of the National Editorial Association. It's one for North Carolina, too."—J.D. Fitz, Assistant Publisher, *News-Herald*, Morganton, N.C.

"Please allow me to add my word of congratulations to the many you have received on winning the Pulitzer Prize. It was a richly deserved honor. You have brought great credit to yourself and to our state."—J.O. Tally, Jr.

"Congratulations upon being elected 'Man of the Year' and winning the Pulitzer Prize. I, along with everyone else, feel that you highly deserve and cannot be repaid for the granting of these honors."—A.C. Edwards, Jr., CPA, Charlotte, NC.

"The *Wilmington Star* is happy to congratulate W. Horace Carter and Willard C. Cole on winning the Pulitzer Prize Meritorious Service Award. These gentlemen won the highest honors in journalism for their completely successful fight against the Ku Klux Klan . . . they saved the Carolinas from the Klan and through their determination helped lay the vile organization so low that it is doubtful that it will ever rise again."—*Star-News*

"All of us here are mighty proud of your accomplishments and happy to see them crowned with the Pulitzer Prize. The story (of your winning) and your picture are on our bulletin board as an inspiration to our budding journalists."—Walter Spearman, School of Journalism, University of North Carolina

"This little note is simply to send you my heartiest congratulations on winning the Pulitzer Prize. Of course, the main thing is the great work you did in fighting the Ku Klux Klan and providing the dynamism for court action. It is encouraging in these times of fear and intolerance to see a small town newspaper do such effective work."—Frank P. Graham, United Nations, New York

"For the first time, the Pulitzer Prize for Public Service has gone to a weekly newspaper. . .the newspaper conducted a vigorous campaign against the revival of the Ku Klux Klan. It took a lot of courage in a rural Southern area where the Klan was rolling high, wide and handsome in racial night-riding activities. . . the Pulitzer honor is symbolic of the power and courage that is ever-increasing in the weekly, grass roots press of the nation."—Donald Ewing, Shreveport, Louisiana, *Times*

"Brave men must be ready and willing to raise their voices

in protest, regardless of the danger to themselves. The *Tabor City Tribune* is run by such a man, W. Horace Carter. It's an example for the rest of us."—*Charleston* (South Carolina) *News and Courier*

"Congratulations for winning the Pulitzer Prize. The University of North Carolina Library is interested in displaying issues of the *Tribune* for the period which covered the Klan. Can you supply us with the newspapers?"—I. T. Littleton, Chapel Hill, North Carolina

"The Detroit Public Library is featuring an exhibit on the Pulitzer Prize awards. Can you furnish us with copies of the *Tribune*?"—Catherine Haughey

"I suppose there are few things in the field of journalism more desirable than the Pulitzer prize. When it comes to one little you, who is so young, it must make you very proud. Congratulations."—Jerry Davidoff, New York

"You have done a great job and inspired me and many others with your courage. I want to pass along this verbal pat on the back for your fighting bigotry that turned into mob rule."—S. R. Heller, Norfolk, Va.

"Your selection as a Pulitzer Prize winner was richly deserved. I know that your efforts in the fight against the influx and growth of the Klan was at the very highest ideals."—Theodore Freedman, Anti-Defamation League of B'nai B'rith, Richmond, Va.

"My hearty congratulations upon your winning the Pulitzer Prize. You certainly deserved it and all law-abiding citizens of the state are proud of you. Please keep up the good work and all of us will continue to sing your praises."—Q. K. Nimocks, Superior Court Judge, 9th District

"Congratulations on your well-deserved Pulitzer award! Congratulations too on your fine piece of work for which the award is recognition. I am proud that North Carolina newspapers were the first non-dailies in the country to win the Pulitzer awards."—Weimar Jones, President, North Carolina Press Association

"Just a brief note to add my congratulations for your Pulitzer Prize award. I certainly think it was deserved and it made me very happy to read about it in the papers."—Coles Phinizy, Time, Inc., Atlanta, Georgia.

"I want to congratulate you upon winning the Pulitzer and for your work in fighting the Ku Klux Klan. I'm proud of you—and proud to have known you on the *Tar Heel* (student newspaper) in Chapel Hill."—Sid Bost, *Statesville Daily Record*

I know it will be hard for you to comprehend how much the

little people, especially in our area, appreciate you for what you have done. You have helped us to believe in the American ideal of fair play, justice and honor and I believe it as I have heard this said in our state. I thought it would be in order that we send this note of admission and thankfulness to you."—A.J.

"As a Southerner I am extremely proud to see this honor (winning the Pulitzer) come to our area. Congratulations."—S. M. Berry, National Association of Manufacturers, Atlanta, Georgia

"I am delighted that you are the recipient of the Pulitzer Prize. Congratulations."—J. H. Hanchrow, Anti-Defamation League, Richmond, Virginia

"We are happy that the Pulitzer Committee recognized your most important services in the public interest. Congratulations and best wishes."—O. W. Riegel, Lee Memorial Journalism Foundation, Lexington, Virginia

"Only yesterday one of our Sunday School teachers referred to you as a man of courage who stood up and fought for what he thought to be right, and he commended you for such. Being a friend and old Endy High School classmate, it surely made me feel good."—Mac Burleson, High Point, North Carolina

"You richly deserve the honor and prestige that is reflected through your receiving the Pulitzer Prize. My congratulations upon your success in eliminating a subversive element that existed in eastern North Carolina."—Albin Pikutis, Director, North Carolina Society for Crippled Children

"I can think of no one more deserving to win the Pulitzer prize than you. May you use this high honor to continue your efforts in promoting ideals which have made our country great."—W. P. Bloom, Anti-Defamation League, New York

"We note with great interest and great cheers that you have been awarded the Pulitzer Prize. It is certainly a fine recognition for a great achievement."—Alfred Dashiell, *The Readers Digest*, Pleasantville, New York

"The thrill of seeing your name listed among the winners of the Pulitzer Prize will always be a high spot in my life."—Harry Hollingsworth, *Durham Herald*, Durham, North Carolina

"Mae and I are so very happy with you! She said she was as proud as if our own son had won a Congressional Medal."—Roy and Mae Armstrong, Chapel Hill

"Congratulations for winning the highest honor in journalism, the Pulitzer Prize. You justly deserve it by your diligence and fidelity to duty. I wish for your continued success in the important field of news papering."—F. Ertel Carlyle, Congress of the United States, Washington, D.C.

"We are elated that you have received such wide acclaim for the services that you have rendered the people of North Carolina in fighting the Ku Klux Klan. As a former pupil of mine at Endy High School in Stanly County, we are so proud and extend our congratulations."—W. A. Murray

"It was with great pleasure that I read of your receiving the Pulitzer Prize for your excellent work fighting the Ku Klux Klan in Tabor City. In case my name does not ring a bell, we were in midshipman school together at Notre Dame in 1944. Congratulations."—W. H. Chester, Attorney at Law, Elkhart, Indiana

"I am sending a clipping from the *New York Times* about your winning the Pulitzer Prize. It certainly says some great things about you and your little newspaper."—J. Harold Stephens, New York

"The folks in Norfolk are still talking about your great courage. May your tribe increase."—Samuel Faverman, Norfolk, Virginia

"I am so proud of you. I'd like to think I deserve a little credit. But to be honest with myself, I must admit that in those school days at Endy I realized that you were going to succeed in whatever you chose to do. You were one of those rare students who come along in which you recognize added quality that is above and beyond. It's a great joy to me to know that maybe I influenced you a little and that you are succeeding beyond all of our fondest dreams. You used to be my star pupil and you still are."—Delletta Hartsell, Albemarle, North Carolina (my high school English and French teacher)

"Your battle against the Klan and winning the Pulitzer Prize has made all of us who knew you at Chapel Hill very proud to have known you."—Kat Hill, WSM-TV, Nashville, Tennessee

"The Pulitzer Prize is some compensation for rough going and hard knocks. I'm glad about it."—Phillips Russell, Chapel Hill

"We all miss you in Chapel Hill, but congratulate you upon the great honor you have brought to weekly newspapers and to North Carolina."—Edwin S. Lanier, Mayor, Chapel Hill

"I extend my heartiest congratulations upon your winning the Pulitzer Prize and all the other honors you have received. They are well deserved. It is something that you can be proud of all your life. You received the highest awards possible in your profession. No one is happier for you than I."—Clifton Moore, Solicitor 8th Judicial District

"Thank you for your courageous newspaper fight against the Ku Klux Klan. We need the spirit of truth written in these United States today as you have written it to dispel the malpractice that has made Jews scapegoats since the time of the Protestant Reformation in 1632 and 1645."—Belknap Battle, Raleigh, N.C.

"Congratulations on winning the Pulitzer award. Stanly County is proud as are all of us who know you."—Lucienne Whitlock Hinceman, Lancaster, South Carolina

"It was a splendid service that you rendered in this connection (Klan crusade) to North Carolina and indeed to the entire nation. Good wishes."—Christopher Crittenden, Director, State of North Carolina, Department of Archives and History, Raleigh

"I wish to add my congratulations for the work that you have done."—C. Edmund Fisher, Editor, *The Advance*, Amalgamated Clothing Workers of America, New York

"The Pulitzer Prizes, gold medals have gone to two weekly newspapers in North Carolina. Their editors decided to fight and expose the Ku Klux Klan. Floggings and terror from the Klan swept the area. These two country editors fought and won the battle. . . We suggest that if the fight against intolerance, bigotry, race prejudices, hatred and fear is to be won in this country, it must be won in the towns such as Whiteville and Tabor City."—Edward R. Murrow, CBS, New York

"Your fight against the Ku Klux Klan and your winning the Pulitzer Prize has made you a hero with me."—Charles Kuralt, CBS, New York

Chapter Thirty-six
Honored By U.S. Congress

With the Klan in shambles, its leadership imprisoned and the last knell of the dastardly floggings of the citizenry a chapter in history, national attention to the infamous Ku Klux Klan reorganization ricocheted even into the hallowed halls of the U.S. Congress.

The Honorable F. Ertel Carlyle of the North Carolina Seventh District, took the Floor of the House of Representatives on Monday, July 11, 1953. Under the heading of "Courageous Journalism," (Page A 4536—July 13, 1953) the Congressman made these remarks that were recorded for posterity:

> Mr. Speaker, two newspapers and two newspapermen in the congressional district which I have the honor to represent, the Seventh District of North Carolina, have recently received national and international recognition and I am sure that their noble deeds which have brought this recognition command the respect and admiration not only of this august body but of the entire country. I cannot permit this opportunity to pass without expressing my highest commendation and appreciation of these newspapers and these distinguished men because I know of their sterling worth and of their outstanding achievements. They have brought great honor to the State of North Carolina and to this nation and I am proud to number them among my good friends and valuable constituents.
>
> Of course, I am referring to the *News Reporter* in Whiteville, North Carolina, and the *Tabor City Tribune* of Tabor City, North Carolina and their editors, Willard G. Cole and W. Horace Carter, respectively. The editors are so completely identified with their papers that to speak of one is to speak of both.
>
> The Eastern North Carolina Press Association first recognized their courageous journalism as demonstrated

by their efforts to expose and unmask the Ku Klux Klan. They received the first certificate of honor ever given to members of the press of that area. This high honor was later followed by a certificate of honor from the North Carolina Press Association. Editors Cole and Carter, receiving only deserved recognition, were recently awarded the distinguished service plaque presented by the Anti-Defamation League of B'nai B'rith of ten Southern States. They were the first North Carolinians ever to be given such signal recognition.

Mr. Speaker, this honorable body is familiar with the recent designation of the *News Reporter*, Whiteville semi-weekly newspaper and the *Tabor City Tribune*, Tabor City, weekly newspaper, as winners of the Pulitzer Prize, highest honor within reach of the newspaper profession. As you know, these are the first non-daily newspapers ever to win the gold medal of disinterested and meritorious public service.

Another honor came to Editors Cole and Carter in June of this year when they were presented the Sidney Hillman Foundation Award for their mutual assistance, along with Mr. Jay Jenkins of the Raleigh *News & Observer* in the crusade against mob violence. It marks the first time that newspaper editors, either daily or non-daily, have ever won both the Pulitzer Prize and Sidney Hillman awards.

Mr. Speaker, I would like to call your attention also to the fact that Mr. Carter, a young man of thirty-two years of age, was selected as Man of the Year by the North Carolina Junior Chamber of Commerce and on June 9 of this year was elected mayor of Tabor City by a vote of more than five to one. Mr. Cole, who is forty-six, was not eligible for the Jaycee honor as Man of the Year.

These two great Americans from my district have won the hearts and have captured the imaginations of the entire country. They have set an example of courageous journalism which will be difficult for others to follow, but which proves the worth of our great tradition of a free press, always functioning in the public welfare.

I would be derelict in my duty at this time if I did not suggest that these forthright and diligent newspapermen, having merited the awards which have been bestowed upon them, are now clearly entitled to the thanks of the entire nation.

Chapter Thirty-seven
Crackdown on the Klan

Crime
Time magazine
February 25, 1952

From the South, the robed riders of the Klan came over the border of North Carolina on a hot July night in 1950. A column of thirty-odd cars carried the Ku Kluxers through tobacco, cotton, peanut and sweet potato fields, then drove slowly along the streets of Tabor City (pop. 2,028), a sleepy Tarheel town that likes to call itself the "Yam Capital of the World."

Except for a few blank shots and a wailing of sirens by the Klansmen, nothing much happened on that first ride. But the invaders soon came back again. They set up fiery crosses, and signed up recruits (at $4 a member). Then followed terror. In the space of a year, the robed riders struck more than a dozen times.

A night-riding mob of forty or fifty beat up a Negro housewife; it was rumored that they were really after her husband for philandering with a white woman. Other floggings were given to Negro and white victims variously charged with wife beating, failure to attend church, drunkenness, disrespect to parents, laziness. Warnings on Klan stationery were sent to many: one woman was told that there was only one man, specifically named, that she was to go out with. If she went out with anybody else, "steps would be taken." It got so, around Tabor City, that everyone polished up his shotgun, and the question "Have you been kluxed?" became understandable English language.

Not everybody took it lying down. Two newspaper editors, for one good instance, were strongly of the opinion that it was still a free country—or ought to be. Tabor City's *Tribune*, run by Editor Horace Carter, and the neighboring semi-weekly *Whiteville News Reporter* lashed out against the "infamous marauders." Their editorials began to attract support and outside attention. State and federal agents began investigation. Finally, last week, the FBI cracked down.

Ten Klansmen were hauled in on charges of kidnapping and flogging a white man and a white woman whom they had transported across the state line. The FBI said that the victims were forced to bend over a car fender, then were beaten with a machine belt nailed to a pick handle. Between blows, the victims were made to pray and listen to sermons and hymn singing from the Klansmen.

It was one of the Federal Government's sharpest attacks yet on the K.K.K. By choosing a clear-cut case of interstate abduction, the FBI can prosecute under the federal Lindbergh law, which provides a maximum penalty of death. Around Tabor City, at least, some of the robed riders were going to learn that the U.S. is not the fascist state they would like to make it.

Chapter Thirty-eight
Nothing to Lose

One night in the midst of the Klan crusade when my family was nervous and scared from a day filled with abusive telephone calls, hate letters and a scrawled threat in red wax on my car's windshield, my wife Lucile wiped tears from her eyes and spoke in halting sentences.

"Horace, why don't we move away from here? We will never be safe again. Even if these scoundrels who are beating up people are caught and sent to jail, what is to keep them from coming here and shooting you, burning down our house, or kidnapping one of the children just to get revenge for what you are doing to them?" It was obvious the crusade was making life miserable for her. It was nothing like the serenity of teaching school that she had loved.

"Honey, we may not win this fight. They have a lot of people in high places on their side, and the local law doesn't seem too interested in trying to break their back. I realize that the advertising and subscription boycotts have made it hard to pay our bills and keep food on the table. I think it is much harder on you than it is on me. But I can't quit now. They may put us out of business, and we may have to leave. If so, we will start somewhere else. We didn't have anything when we came here, and we don't have anything now. That makes it easier to leave than it would if we had really made a great success with our newspaper.

"You must realize that our lack of assets is one of the reasons we can stand up to these roughnecks. If we had a nice home, good printing equipment and money in the bank, we would want to protect it at all costs. But we are barely making ends meet. Remember what I told you once before, there are only two kinds of newspapers that are really free. The newspaper that is independently wealthy can crusade as much as it wants, and tell everyone who doesn't agree to go to hell. Then, there's the newspaper like ours that has nothing. We can likewise write what we feel and tell the critics to go jump in a lake. That's because we have nothing to lose. It's the newspapers in between that find it hard to campaign even for obviously great causes," I told her.

"But what if they kill you? What am I going to do then?" With that question she made a good case for dropping the crusade.

" 'Cile, I don't believe that will happen. I think we will win this battle. But whether we do or not, if we do survive, remember what some man of wisdom once wrote, 'man glows with victory, but he grows with defeat.' Win or lose, we will come out ahead for doing what you and I both know is the right thing to do."

She half-smiled through her tears and fear enveloped her face. She hugged the two children to her breast, and quietly whispered, "I'll do my best to understand and be as strong as I can."

She never again asked me to drop the campaign although the threats were unceasing, and grew more and more vile as the dangerous months slowly dragged on.

Almost forty years later, long after Lucile had died of breast cancer in 1982, I presented the *Tribune's* coveted Pulitzer Prize to the North Carolina Journalism Hall of Fame at the School of Journalism in Chapel Hill. I thought of her fear and devotion as I wrote the short speech that Dean Richard Cole had asked me to make. She had tearfully told me a week before her passing that she was proud of the many crusades I had fought for what I had perceived as right. I wanted my remarks at that presentation to reflect what she would have said had she lived to cherish this moment that was attended by our children, grandchildren and more than two hundred other members of my family and invited guests. She deserved to win the Pulitzer for supporting me even though constantly concerned for the safety of the children, our home and me.

I did my best as I made these remarks at the Pulitzer presentation:

> Once in a great while an unusual opportunity presents itself to journalists to stand up and be counted— we have a chance to cast a shadow that reflects our principles, our heart, indeed our very soul and character. We have a chance to mold attitudes and actions for what we perceive as good, right and proper for the people and the community that we serve. If we are truly convinced of the integrity of our position, and if it is fashioned upon ethical, godly, biblical standards, even the smallest of newspapers can cast a big shadow. That makes it important that we forever be sure of the stand

we take, and we must be willing to sacrifice time, serenity, economic security, and the physical safety of our own family. Every editorial crusade that's worth its salt will antagonize some portion of the readership or else its objective and reason for writing is trivial and ill-conceived. If you are not willing to make sacrifices and face the dangers, your crusade will fail. Facing disaster and making sacrifices for what you sincerely believe, often will rally the people in your corner, enhance your position and focus greater attention on the policy direction you advocate. It's then that the opposition feels the pressure. Your newspaper campaign becomes real, and your editorials are powerful. You feel some fear with every sentence, and you need courage.

Intimidation often stops noteworthy crusades. You are threatened with physical violence, your print shop will be burned, your handful of advertisers will be boycotted, your subscription list will evaporate. You may be facing a libel suit soon. These are the threats that both large and small newspapers face when they pursue an objective that they are convinced is American and in the best interest of the citizenry; albeit, some individuals may have to cease and desist from activities that steal rights and opportunities from the less fortunate. They become your enemies. Those who oppose your policy that endangers their vested interest, may threaten your very existence. The size of the shadow you then cast depends upon your courage and determination. The intensity of your crusade and dedication to your conviction measures the depth of your courage. You will feel fear, but where there is no fear, there is no courage.

When my telephone rang on a March morning in 1953 and Jay Jenkins, of the *Raleigh News & Observer*, said, "Horace, you have won the Pulitzer Prize," I was shocked.

"For what?" I promptly asked.

"For Meritorious Public Service for fighting the Ku Klux Klan. That's the biggest Pulitzer of them all," Jenkins said. That was startling information for the editor of a tiny weekly newspaper with only a few hundred subscribers that was less than a decade old and struggling every day to stay solvent. A dollar bill truly looked as big as a wagon wheel. Any of those torturous months could have been the last for the *Tribune*, especially since the KKK's announced boycott of our handful of advertisers pushed us deeper into a financial pit. Those economic realities were as much a deterrent to the Klan crusade as threatened physical abuse. At some points in time, they were the dominating anxiety and subsequent fear.

Crusaders begin with a dream of success and justice. Many times it seems tantalizingly close, but always it is just beyond your grasp. It seems you will never quite catch up with it. Again, that's when you must call upon your courage, your patience, your conviction that what you are doing is right. It will refurbish your stamina and confidence to fight on despite snail-like progress.

I did a lot of thinking that day after Jenkins called me with his heart-warming revelation. Maybe this was a reward for the fear my family lived with for nearly four years. Maybe it would encourage some lost advertisers and subscribers to return to the newspaper. Indeed those good things did happen to the *Tribune*—and quickly. Winning the Pulitzer has helped me every day of my life since Jenkins' call. The months of fear have been rewarded both tangibly and intangibly.

As I have often said since that traumatic era of fighting the Klan resurrection and the cruel floggings that ensued, I didn't deserve to win such a prestigious award. I did no more than any other editor would have done if such lawlessness erupted on his own doorsteps. The Pulitzer selection committee was simply looking for a weekly newspaper to award the prize to for the first time. No weekly had ever won this award. Why would a little weekly in a town of less than two thousand people that had as many bill collectors as it did subscribers be so honored? Then a reality came to mind that I think is of great importance to Americans in all walks of life. It's not the size of the dog in the fight, it's the size of the fight in the dog that counts. Indeed, with our meager resources we had fought like a much tougher dog, even though I was relatively inexperienced in editorial writing and had only reached my thirty-second birthday. I was on the right side and morally bound.

In America's past, a newspaper was one person or a husband and wife team. Editorials reflected the thinking and principles of an individual. The newspaper was a human being in that sense. His writing depicted his character. While it will be considered reactionary to say so, I believe that made for the finest journalism the country has ever known. That editor's opinion was often that of neighbors, friends and acquaintances with genuine compassion and interest in the populace. It was what the moral majority of those times felt and lived. The thinking was not regimented, and written from ivory towers. It was home based and simple.

Today, with 1,300 of the 1,600 daily newspapers in the United States owned and published by big chains, I think newspapers are no longer close to the neighborhood people that they serve. They seldom reflect the conscience of the local populace. Bigness does accomplish one important goal—it often keeps struggling newspapers solvent. Today many of the legendary weeklies of the nation have given up the ghost. Mom and Pop newspapers cannot survive in this modern world of television, high tech, taxes and assembly lines.

Too often today's newspapers and TV networks, even large ones, are intimidated. While every facet of the media should forever seek to protect the rights of all races, religions and sexes, we should not be afraid to print the truth about all people, even when it is not complimentary. Majorities and minorities are entitled to the same rights—access to the same news. But the wheel that squeaks gets the grease, and often minorities scream at the slightest suggestion of criticism. Much of the media then succumbs to the pressure and backs down. That's tragic.

Paul, writing to Timothy in the New Testament, pretty well summed up the attributes of a good journalist. He said, "God has not given us the spirit of fear, but of love, power and a sound mind." Those are inherent qualities of a good newspaperman.

I believe that we must live lives that are pleasing to God and acceptable to man, always aware that the greatest work of life is service to mankind. I measure success by the happiness we enjoy. It's the best yardstick. Happiness that is often untenable is more lasting when we put service above self, a trait found far less frequently today than a generation or two ago. It helps to make life worth living to want what we have rather than always having what we want.

For years I kept the gold medallion, symbolic of the *Tribune's* winning the Meritorious Public Service Pulitzer Prize in a safety deposit box. It served no purpose there other than to whet my ego when I occasionally ran across it. I decided to have it displayed at the School of Journalism so that it might encourage young aspiring journalists to fight for justice and principles and thus cast a big shadow wherever their careers led them. That's my hope now.

I remember an incident that happened when I was a student at the University of North Carolina and Skipper Coffin was Dean of the Journalism School. I was editor of the student newspaper, the *Tar Heel*. I had published one of my fiery editorials, possibly ill-conceived, charging some politicians and University administrators with pressuring Dr. Frank Graham to resign from the War Labor Board in Washington. They felt he should return to the University where he was president. Some of the powers-that-be wanted him to be a full-time president, World War II priorities notwithstanding.

My editorial insisted that Dr. Graham was man enough to be University president, and a member of the Labor Board at the same time. It irritated state senators, representatives and even the governor. I had to meet with the governor in Raleigh to explain my reasons for writing the editorial, but I was elated to get a complimentary letter from President Franklin D. Roosevelt.

One of the antagonized senators called me at the *Tar Heel* office. He sounded very angry.

"Meet me in the Journalism Department in half an hour," he demanded.

Already wishing I had never written the editorial, I rushed to Bynum Hall and the Journalism Department. Dean Skipper Coffin was sitting at his desk when I walked in.

"Horace, Senator John Umstead called me a minute or two ago. He said he was coming up here to bawl you out for writing that Graham editorial. I have a little bit of advice for you. I don't give a damn what he threatens you with. You stick with what you wrote. Don't apologize for a damn thing. Don't let him run over you and scare you to death."

I did stand my ground that day despite my youth, inexperience and the trauma of a one-on-one confrontation with a prominent state senator. That incident kind of shaped my life and my attitude about the editorial stands that I made in the years ahead. Upset readers over the years have threatened 131 libel suits against me and the *Tribune* for real or imaginary grievances. I always answered each threat in the same courteous way. "Stand in line." No one has ever gotten around to filing a libel suit.

In this relatively new nation, even a poor farm boy from humble parentage and with meager education can succeed against overwhelming odds when he opposes evils and stands up for principles in the face of obstacles. He can still cast a big shadow, and that is why, despite its shortcomings, this is the greatest country on earth.

I hope my beloved late wife would have liked what I said.

I was vest-popping proud to have the Pulitzer permanently displayed in the N.C. Journalism Hall of Fame in Chapel Hill. (Photo by Chuck Liddy, Durham *Herald-Sun*)

Chapter Thirty-nine
What Next?

When the dust finally settled, ninety-eight Ku Klux Klansmen had been convicted. They were either headed for prison, faced hefty fines or were on probation. Despite our inexperience, lack of resources and the small stature of our weekly newspaper, we had won this crusade.

Suddenly, I was besieged with honors. I had been elected mayor of Tabor City and named "Man of the Year." The North Carolina Junior Chamber of Commerce honored me as "The North Carolina Young Man of the Year." Right on the heels of that, I was honored by the United States Junior Chamber of Commerce in Seattle, Washington, as "One of the Ten Most Outstanding Young Men in America for 1953." I was in big company for the first time in my life. My name was a household word far outside the Carolinas and it was heady stuff.

And with the unbelievable phrase "Pulitzer Prize for Meritorious Public Service" now printed on the *Tribune's* masthead, a thirty-two-year-old farm boy had the world in his grasp.

Requests for personal appearances poured in. I tried to make as many of those speeches as I could and still maintain my little business. By the time 1953 was over I had spoken to 163 groups—including as many as seven appearances in a single day.

When I returned from a series of appearances that included interviews with Charles Kuralt on WBTV in Charlotte and Edward R. Murrow on a national CBS television show, as well as interviews with dozens of national newspapers, Paul Carrouth, the new pastor of St. Paul Methodist Church in Tabor City called.

"Horace, do you have time to drop by the church office and talk with me for a few minutes? I have something I'd like to say to you," he asked.

"Sure, Preacher, I'll get by there sometime before noon," I promised.

I walked into his office a little humbled. What would this

fine, intelligent man of God want to say to a tired weekly newspaper editor?

"Horace, did you ever think about where you go from here?" he asked, startling me with the question. "You are so young, have accomplished so much, have outstanding qualities and courage, and have benefitted from all of this great publicity. Don't you think you are being called to greater heights?" He asked the question in all sincerity. I was somewhat embarrassed.

"Well, Preacher, I had kicked around the idea of maybe running for Congress in this Seventh North Carolina District," I stammered. "At least, I might be able to better provide for my family."

"I think that would be great. Washington needs new life and courage like you have. Why don't you run next fall?" He was pushing me toward making a decision.

"I'll give it a lot of thought," I promised, a bit tentatively. I shook his hand, thanked him for his interest and returned to my office.

Days passed. Al Williams, the man I had succeeded as mayor, strolled into the office. He was an astute politician. His great personality and ability to always say the right thing in every circumstance made him a favorite of people throughout the area.

"Al, can I talk with you a minute?" I asked, beckoning him into my tiny office.

Williams was always ready to talk. He said, "Sure," as he sat down and I looked at him across my desk. We were fellow Rotarians, shared the same Sunday School class, and had been friends since the first day I drove into Tabor City in 1946.

"Al, I have been encouraged by a few friends and I'm considering running for Congress. What do you think about it?" I asked almost timidly, "You know Congressman Carlyle isn't going to run again."

"I think you would be an excellent congressman," he answered. "Let's talk to Raymond Mallard about it. He's the Democratic county chairman and knows everything about the political picture." Williams stood up, obviously anxious to visit with the political leader immediately.

Mallard, the only lawyer in Tabor City at that time, was later elected to the North Carolina Court of Appeals. He served as chief justice for several years and was prominent in all Democratic circles.

We entered Mallard's office and got the usual cordial welcome.

"What can I do for you two bigshots?" he asked with a slight smile.

"Raymond, Horace is considering running for congress. He asked me about it and I told him it would be a good idea to talk it over with you and get your advice. What do you think about it?" Williams got right to the point.

"That sounds like a winner to me," he replied. "You are really in the public eye because of this Klan campaign. You ought to do very well regardless of who runs against you." Mallard made me feel like I had real stature. Then suddenly his countenance changed. He looked me right in the eye and I knew he was having second thoughts.

"Wait a minute. You are registered as a Democrat, but didn't you write something in your column about voting for Eisenhower?" he asked. He was deadly serious.

"Yeah, I voted for Eisenhower and would do it again. I will always vote for the man and not the party in any election." I stood firmly behind my ballot.

Mallard was the kind of politician who would vote for a goat if it appeared on the Democratic ticket.

"Well, son, that was the kiss of death. We don't have but a hundred or so Republicans in this whole county. No one who has ever voted for a Republican can ever get elected here on the Democratic ticket. You got no chance. Might as well forget it," he said. His words obviously marked the end of the conference. I thanked him and returned to the office, more perplexed than before.

It was then that I completely dropped the idea of changing my address to Washington, D.C. I would be frustrated in Washington if I were elected. That was not my calling. I am first, last, and always a newspaperman. Even with this little weekly paper I had a chance to influence people toward the better things in life. Just maintaining character, integrity and a determination to make this a better community was rewarding enough for me. I knew I would never get rich in the weekly newspaper business. I would never make as much money as a congressman and I'd have to work much harder. But happiness and success are not measured by what you have. My yardstick has always been what you do. Real reward comes from wanting what you have, not having what you want. I had a fine wife and children. I could make this little newspaper successful. I could make a living.

I did just that for thirty-three years before turning it over to the second generation (my son, Rusty) and becoming just a columnist with the masthead title of editor-emeritus.

Judge Mallard became my weekly golf partner until his death. I remember saying to him, "Thanks, Raymond, for talking me out of running for congress. It's more fun to play golf with you and have time to hunt and fish with my friends and children. I would have lost it all if I had left the weekly newspaper business."

Tabor City suitably served as my capital for more than thirty years. It is a place that my words and efforts helped to shape as a community with unity and friendship. I will never turn my back on those roots.

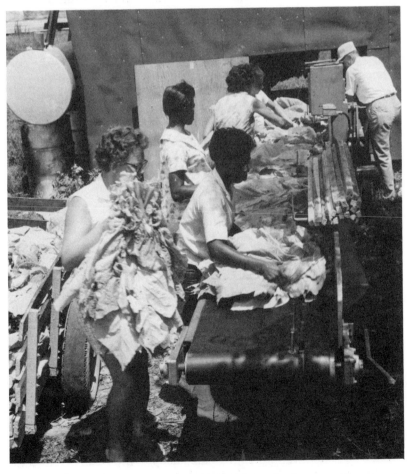

Columbus and Horry counties have always had many fine, hard-working farm people.

235

Epilogue

In 72 A.D., 960 Jewish zealots atop a mountain fortress called Masada, located on the Dead Sea in Israel, realized that their courageous two-year standoff of ten thousand invading Roman soldiers would end at daybreak. It was then that a high ramp constructed by slave labor over many months would reach the summit and the attackers would be able to cross the protective wall built by the zealots. Using their position wisely and diligently, the defenders of this twenty-acre plateau on the mountain top had embarrassed a division of crack Roman troops. Its general had been castigated by his superiors in his homeland for showing ineptness against such a tiny enemy force.

At last victory was in the grasp of the Romans. But when the invaders crashed over the wall at dawn, they found that all of the men, women and even the children were dead. They had committed mass suicide to escape enslavement that was their certain fate if captured alive by the Romans. They died for their political principles and the freedom that they cherished and so valiantly defended for two years.

The Masada story is a symbol for all who fight for principles today. It signifies the stand of the few against the many, the weak against the strong, the last fight for those who would give everything for political and religious justice and freedom. I realized that vividly when I visited this Israeli monument in October of 1990, while taking a much-needed break from writing this book.

I like to look at the *Tribune's* long fight against the Ku Klux Klan as our Masada. It didn't end with personal suicide, but the crusade could easily have been the demise of the newspaper. The principles of human rights and justice for all are worth fighting and dying for. Despite our lonely challenge to a strong, organized enemy by a humble, struggling newspaper that faced economic ruin, determination came out a winner. We believe the fight for right against the odds was worth the effort despite the virus of fear that gripped the community and often threatened our very lives.

Conclusion

Since the first recorded history when hieroglyphics and cuneiform vividly portrayed and documented man's inhumanity to man, suffering from the power of the majority, the rich, the strong and societal elite has been felt by the subjugated unfortunate women and racial minorities. They were doomed to servitude and performance of menial community tasks for centuries.

The United States has championed civil rights for minorities and women for more than a century, but extremely biased individuals in organizations like the Ku Klux Klan have rebelled against change and threatened the peace of the world with vigilante violence.

The change from slavery and second class citizenship to "equal rights" for blacks has now backlashed all over the nation. White workers of the country protest laws and decisions that give minorities and women an advantage. It's an understandable reaction and very human.

One of the congratulatory letters the Tribune received after winning the crusade against the KKK was from Thurgood Marshall, a black leader in the National Association for the Advancement of Colored People, an organization generally condemned and despised throughout the South.

Marshall later served admirably as a justice of the U.S. Supreme Court and he served civil rights and liberties well until his retirement at the age of 83 in 1991. Upon announcing his retirement, the press urged Marshall to make a statement as to whether he felt President Bush should appoint a black to replace him on the high court. His remarks are classic and they are a lesson for all to consider:

"There are black snakes that bite and white snakes that bite. President Bush should appoint the best qualified person for the post."

That simple reasoning is the answer to many of the problems between differing races and sexes. Those in government, as well as those in commerce and industry, should hold those jobs because they are the best qualified individuals available. That would not eliminate all bias and prejudice. That will be forever in the hearts of some people. But it would reduce conflict and turmoil that surfaces because of inequities on both the left and the right.

Convenient Order Form

I would like to have additional copies of this book,

Virus of FEAR

Please mail me _____copies to the address below:

Name:_____

Address:_____

_____

Enclosed please find check or money order in the amount of $19.95 that includes postage and handling for each book.

Please mail to:
W. Horace Carter
Atlantic Publishing Company
P.O. Box 67
Tabor City, NC 28463
Phone 919-653-3153

(Tear out & mail this sheet to publisher.)

Please ship me one copy of Atlantic Book checked below:

Hannon's Field Guide for Bass Fishing	$ 9.95
Creatures & Chronicles From Cross Creek	9.95
Land That I Love (Hard Bound)	15.50
Wild & Wonderful Santee-Cooper Country	9.95
Return to Cross Creek	9.95
Nature's Masterpiece at Homosassa	9.95
Catch Bass	8.30
Hannon's Big Bass Magic	13.50
A Man Called Raleigh	9.95
Damn the Allegators	10.95
Bird Hunters Handbook	11.50
Lures for Lunker Bass (Paperback)	12.95
Lures for Lunker Bass (Hardback)	16.95
Best Bass Pros, Vol. I	10.95
Deer & Fixings	11.00
Hunting Hogs, Boar & Javelina	10.95
Trophy Stripers	12.95
Forty Years in the Everglades	9.95
Fish & Fixings	12.95
Crappie Secrets	12.95
Best Bass Pros, Vol. 2	12.95